FOR KING AND COUNTRY

ALSO BY THOMAS A. LEWIS

The Guns of Cedar Creek
The Shenandoah in Flames: The Valley Campaign of 1864

FOR KING AND COUNTRY

GEORGE WASHINGTON
THE EARLY YEARS

Thomas A. Lewis

John Wiley & Sons, Inc.
New York * Chichester * Brisbane * Toronto * Singapore

This text is printed on acid-free paper.

Reprinted by arrangement with HarperCollins Publishers.

Published by John Wiley & Sons, Inc.

Designed by Alma Hochauser Orenstein

ISBN 0-471-10465-5

Printed in the United States of America.

10 9 8 7 6 5 4 3 2 1

To MYRON *and* MILDRED LEWIS,
who showed me how to persevere

Contents

PART III ACTION

Preface

A thousand suns have crossed the Blue Ridge Mountains outside my window while I have been writing this book. Hour by hour, the changing light has altered the mountains' aspect, now sketching in a previously unseen hollow, now flashing from a hidden rivulet. More than a dozen seasons have painted and repainted the ancient folds with broad, slow brushes of bright green, flamboyant crimson, and dead grey.

During this time, war has come to my country and crisis to my family, followed by peace and occasions of great joy. Empires of the earth have fallen and babies have been born, great eras of history and ordinary people have died. In each context, when my eyes have gone to the unchanging hills, I have seen them differently.

Our history is like those mountains. Abiding and immutable, it is yet different each time we turn to look at it, depending on the season of the world, on the quality of the light, and on the preoccupations of the observer.

And the light has surely changed in America. Ideas that once electrified us—from Manifest Destiny to man on the moon, from winning civil rights to winning the Cold War, from the Great Society to the Reagan Revolution—have lost their allure. The things we once thought we were in the world—policeman, landlord, banker, boss, the best and the brightest—are now the subjects of melancholy reflection, like an elder's remembrance of young ambitions. Who we are and what we think do not seem adequate anymore, and we do not know what to do about it. This triumph of doubt over dreams is a companion of maturity.

We crave a call to action and to optimism, a definition of ourselves that not only satisfies, but thrills. But ideas powerful enough to galvanize a people, to help a country throw off psychological depression, must be rooted in truths that can be expressed both in the present and the past tenses. Too few meet that test today. Factoids are the currency of our national discourse, small, bland statements that skip along the surface of ideas and sink from sight before the next evening newscast.

One of our national afflictions is cultural amnesia. Like a person who has lost all memory and thus cannot imagine what to do next, much of our society has disconnected itself from its hard-won knowledge of what it is, how it got here, and what matters. This involves a sin of both omission and commission: of not paying enough attention to history, and of learning the wrong things from it. These are mutually reinforcing sins. When we do not pay attention, it follows that we learn the wrong things, and when our learning proves useless, motivation dies.

Two of our society's primal icons, which we consistently both ignore and misunderstand, are George Washington—our prototypical man—and the Old West, the quintessential American place. We do not think of them as related, when in fact each was indispensable to the creation of the other (not paying attention). We think we know the moral character of the man, and of the legendary age, but we have ignored the terrible failings of their ethics (learning the wrong things).

Our notions of the historical West, most of them gathered from movies, suffuse our culture with an odd, artificial hue. It is a silly yet powerful folklore, made up of simplistic morality plays about lawmen and outlaws, mountain men and bears, cowboys and Indians. Our children play games based on this Golden Age that never was; our young people watch TV series celebrating it; we speak in its vernacular (hired gun, Mexican standoff, shoot-out, High Noon, desperado, straight shooter, on and on). We derive from it many of our standards of masculinity—courage, self-reliance, toughness, morality, and competence (although few appropriate measures of femininity).

These once-robust images look haggard and anemic in today's changing light. They exalt violence as a solution to problems, something violence never was. They reek of white racism, of male chauvinism; they glorify exploitation of people and the land. The frontier mentality is inadequate to the requirements of living on a finite planet crowded with multiracial, interdependent people where, to cite just one consideration, it is now apparent that violence destroys the user as well as the intended victim. To the extent that we cling to the inadequate totems of the Old West, we feel increasingly helpless, caught in a world of narrowing limitations and alien demands.

To become energized, we must unshackle our concepts of the possibilities. To grow and prosper in the new circumstances of the earth, we must reexamine the informing models of behavior we carry in our culture, we must understand them more deeply and appropriately, we must shuck off our cultural amnesia.

We can make a start with George Washington, because along with the legends of the West he stands tall in our psyche as a symbol of what we should be. But his truth, too, is usually expressed in the past tense. The symbol is impossibly remote from us, a granite spike into the sky of our nation's capital, a somber face glowering from Mount Rushmore. Like Thomas Connelly's Robert E. Lee, Washington remains a marble man, unrelated to us, encased in his deification, lost to mortality.

Let us break through the marble to the flesh. Let us accept the jarring idea that before his canonization, Washington was like us, that he failed, he lied, he connived for his own purposes, he lost his temper, was rejected by men and women of good judgment. These facts neither contradict nor diminish the high achievements of his life or the enduring quality of his character. They do, however, bring such a life as his within our reach. If he was the perfect person, fated and equipped by God for nobility, then knowing him has nothing to offer us as we toil under the burden of our own failures and shortcomings. But knowing that he, too, bore such a burden, and achieved despite it, raises our eyebrows in recognition and lifts our spirits in kinship.

To begin by accepting as the definitive man of the West George Washington, instead of a fur-clad Daniel Boone or a pistol-packing Wild Bill Hickock, will require checking a few assumptions.

First, let us locate the West. Whether you are traveling through time or through space, it begins at the first fold of mountains inland from the Atlantic: the Blue Ridge of Virginia, the Great Smokies of the Carolinas, Maryland's Catoctin, Pennsylvania's Poconos. Today, as in the eighteenth century, the people who live on one side of that ancient wrinkle of continental crust are fundamentally different from the people who live on the other. The difference has been blurred by our homogenized culture—knitted over with strands of identical fast-food restaurants, boutiques, and TV sitcoms—but like the San Andreas fault, its presence is detectable and its capacity for dramatic impact on our history is clear. In 1748, when George Washington first stepped across the Blue Ridge, the fault was active. It may be, however, that he never realized the significance of the ensuing struggle as he became one of the first Americans forced to reconcile mutually exclusive interests of East and West.

We have not thought much about this struggle. We are constantly reminded of other divisions of American life—ethnic, religious, and geographic. We know that the antagonisms between North and South led to our country's most agonizing war, and persist today in the sparring between the Sun Belt and the Rust Belt states. We know how our history has been shaped by epic contests between races (white vs. black, white vs. red), ethnic groups (French vs. English, Irish vs. German, now Asian vs. Hispanic), religious beliefs (The Church of England vs. everybody—Catholic, Quaker, Mennonite, Jew), economic principles (capitalism vs. socialism, planned economy vs. laissez-faire, new economic growth vs. quality of life), and of course political parties. But the ongoing, irreconcilable tension between East and West is as old and as profound as our sectional, religious, and economic differences.

The pattern that was being formed in 1748, that was an essential part of the struggle of 1861, and that persists today is defined by values as much as geography. An Easterner tends to value position—one's station in life, family connections and lineage, possessions and wealth. A true Westerner, on the other hand, loves action and change. To a Westerner, life is a verb rather than a noun, a dynamic striving in which potential is more important than achievement, character is a better resource than pedigree, and quality of life beats money every time. Many Easterners live in the West, and vice versa. But things happen in this country, constantly, because of these essential differences. Trying to navigate history without taking them into account is like trying to cross the Atlantic without correcting for the powerful influence of the invisible Gulf Stream.

These tensions deeply affected George Washington, in dimly perceived ways, during his formative years. What he made of the stresses and challenges set the pattern for succeeding generations. He did not intend to become a Westerner, of course. Quite the contrary—he ached to be an Eastern aristocrat of the English kind. Nor did he plan to be a light to succeeding generations, although he certainly intended to shine in his own. How he became what he became—Westerner instead of Easterner, American instead of Englishman, a world leader instead of a down-at-the-heels planter—is worth studying.

It is worth knowing how he succeeded, and in the light of a different century it is also important to know in what manner he failed. We have been content with knowing what he knew about the West—what he had to say about the settlers and the natives he encountered there. But now we need to reflect on what he never learned about his experiences there. Just as Sherlock Holmes found an important clue in the dog that did not bark in the night, we can learn as much from the silences as from the conventional noises.

As we shape our attitude toward the world we inhabit now, we need to understand that Washington, the father of our country and freedoms and society, is also an author and embodiment of two of the most grievous flaws in our American society: our collective contempt for other races, and our exploitation of land as a commodity of trade.

The mountains are changing again in their light, as Washington is in his. This is an attempt to capture the scene from here before it fades, to follow an ordinary young man—vain, burning with ambition, possessing few advantages—into extraordinary events, to see how greatness is not given whole, but refined from coarser stuff.

Our view will not be from the top of his monument, nor from the foot of Mount Rushmore, but from a height of six feet, two inches. We will not look back through the gauze of his later greatness, but forward from where he was, through the eyes of an uncertain, driven young man. We will consider what he knew, as reflected in what he wrote and read, and we will consider what he did not know. We seek to catch the boy in the act of becoming father to the man.

NOTES ON PRACTICAL MATTERS

This work relies heavily on the words of Washington and his contemporaries. Few of these exist in original form, but have come down to us in the form of copies transcribed by others. No attempt has been made here to replicate errors in spelling or difficulties caused by punctuation, when the culprit might well have been some clerk. In Washington's letters, for example, the word Conococheague appears as "Connongochieg," "Conogochege," "Conogchieg," and "Conogochieg." The priority has been to ease the work of the reader, and there has been no hesitation to remove from the eye's path superfluous misspellings, capital letters, semicolons, and even clauses when they obscure the obvious meaning and slow our progress to the point of the matter. Certain errors, on the other hand, are interesting, and have been preserved for the flavor they impart. Nothing has been eliminated from any quote that, if present, would change the meaning. Nor has anything been added gratuitously. Therefore, no ellipses (. . .) point the way to missing words or phrases (strings of dots on a page tend to slow reading and induce naps), and no (*sic*)s flag our superior knowledge of the rules of literature.

ACKNOWLEDGMENTS

I am indebted above all to W. W. Abbot, Dorothy Twohig, et al. for their monumental labors in compiling and editing the first complete edition of George Washington's correspondence. This book, whatever its merits, rests on the unshakable foundation of their scholarship.

I am grateful to Ben Ritter of the Handley Memorial Library in Winchester, Virginia, and Mary Morris of the Clarke County Historical Society, who helped nail down various arcana; and to Warren Hofstra of Shenandoah University, who convened, at the best possible time, a scholarly conference on "George Washington and the Virginia Backcountry."

The staff at the United States Army Military History Institute at Carlisle, Pennsylvania, and at one of my favorite refuges in the world, the Lloyd House annex of the Alexandria, Virginia, library, tend the lighthouses of history with patient and enduring professionalism, as do the dedicated volunteers of Mount Vernon and of the

Winchester–Frederick County Historical Society, curators of Washington's frontier headquarters.

Stuart Bell, former mayor of Winchester and the archetype of the Southern gentleman, graciously shared the fruits of a lifelong study of Washington, including the little-known warrants for the young officer's arrest.

I am grateful to all those in the National Park Service who contributed to the preservation and interpretation of the site of Fort Necessity, one of the most moving and effective historical parks anywhere.

And I acknowledge above all the essential and irreplaceable ingredient of this and all other works of my life—the love and support of Patricia, Andrew, Kim, and Jason Lewis.

Nor knowest thou what argument
Thy life to thy neighbor's creed has lent.
All are needed by each one;
Nothing is fair or good alone.

—RALPH WALDO EMERSON

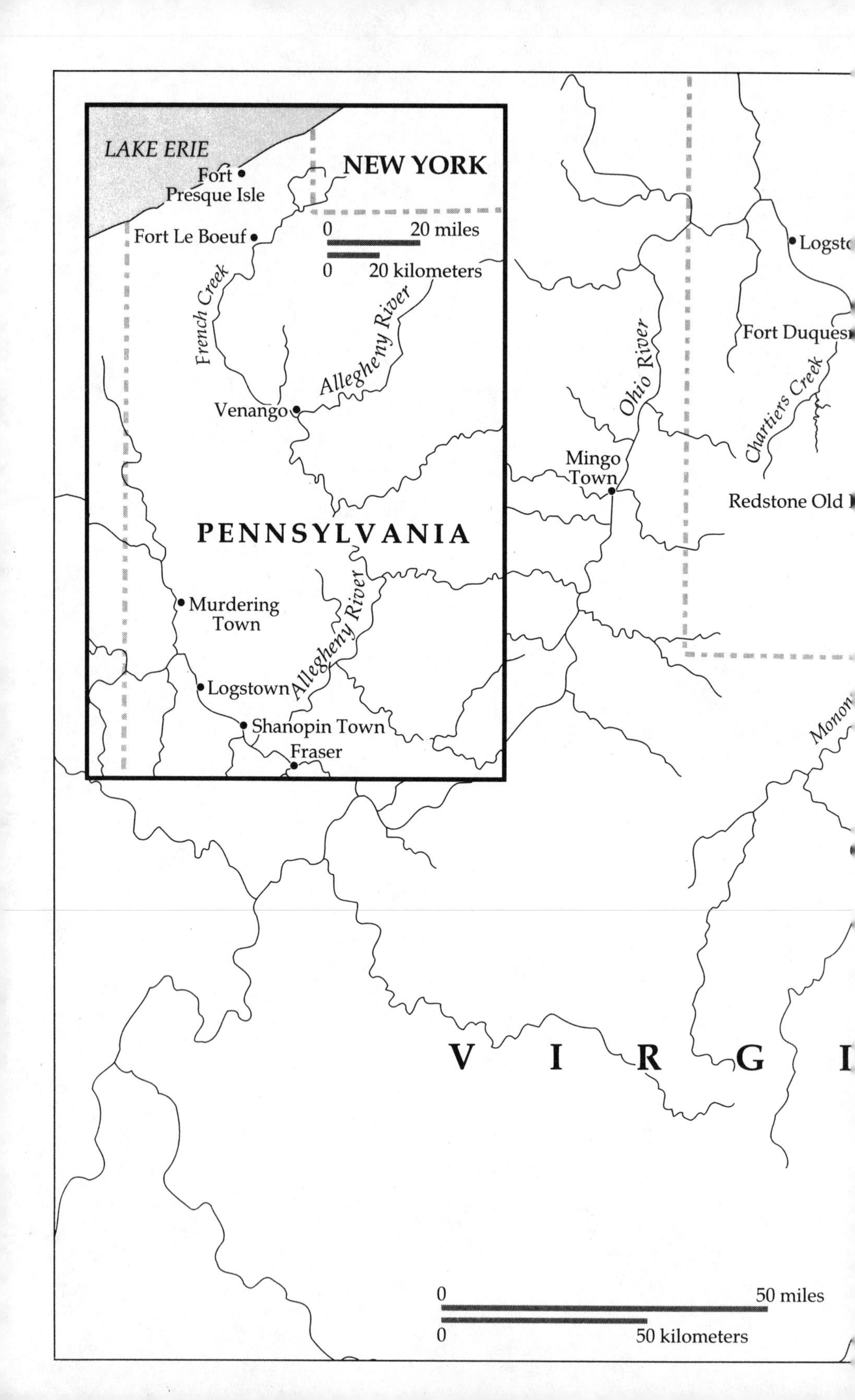
LAKE ERIE
Fort Presque Isle
NEW YORK
Fort Le Boeuf
0 20 miles
0 20 kilometers
French Creek
Allegheny River
Venango
PENNSYLVANIA
Murdering Town
Allegheny River
Logstown
Shanopin Town
Fraser
Ohio River
Mingo Town
Fort Duquesne
Chartiers Creek
V I R G I
0 50 miles
0 50 kilometers

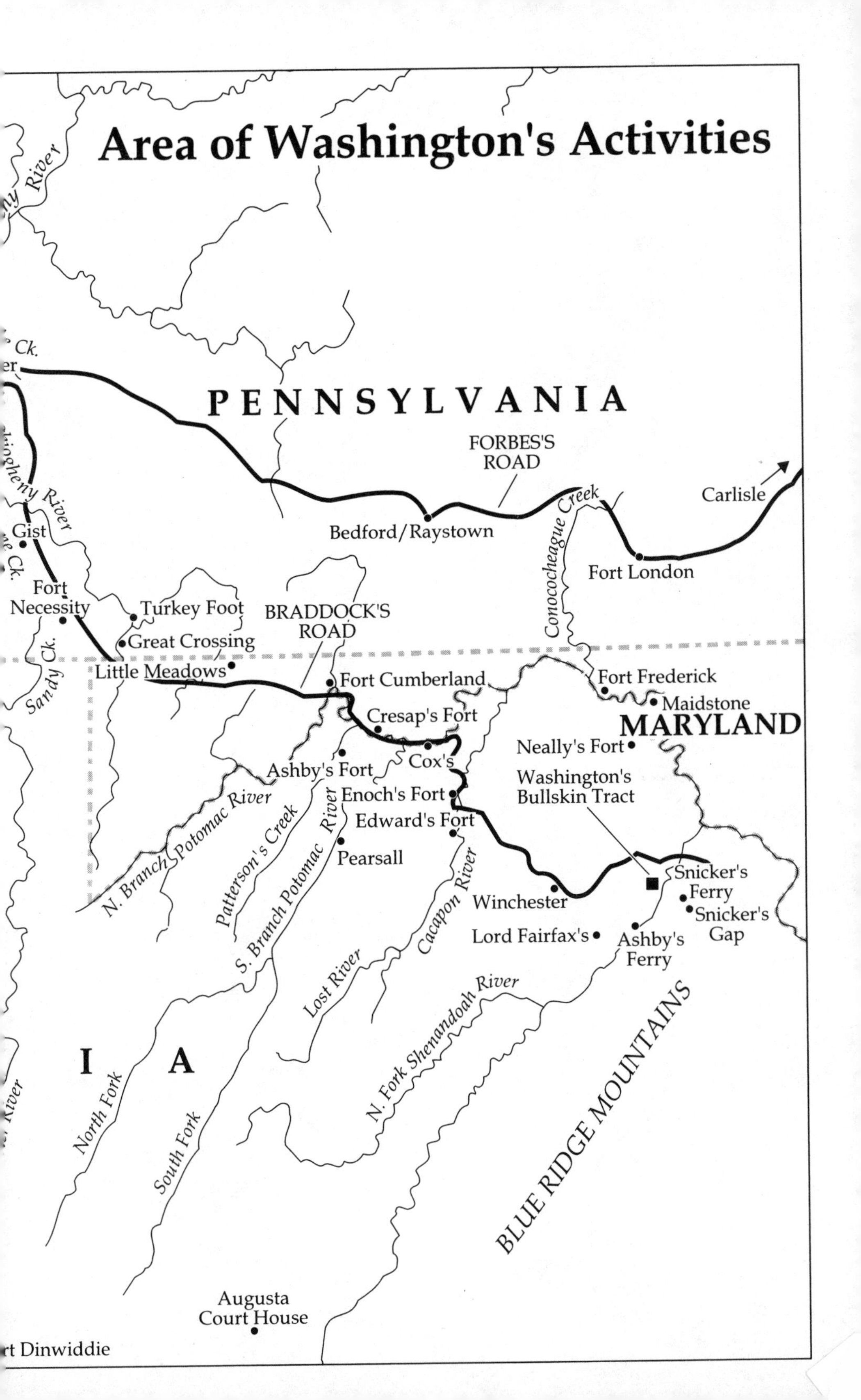

Area of Washington's Activities
PENNSYLVANIA
FORBES'S
ROAD
Carlisle
Bedford/Raystown
Conococheague Creek
Fort London
Gist
Fort
Necessity
Turkey Foot
Great Crossing
BRADDOCK'S
ROAD
Little Meadows
Sandy Ck.
Fort Cumberland
Fort Frederick
Maidstone
MARYLAND
Cresap's Fort
Nearlly's Fort
Cox's
Ashby's Fort
Washington's
Bullskin Tract
Enoch's Fort
Edward's Fort
N. Branch Potomac River
Patterson's Creek
S. Branch Potomac River
Pearsall
Cacapon River
Snicker's
Ferry
Snicker's
Gap
Winchester
Lord Fairfax's
Ashby's
Ferry
Lost River
Shenandoah River
N. Fork Shenandoah River
BLUE RIDGE MOUNTAINS
I A
North Fork
South Fork
Augusta
Court House

PART I

Knowledge

CHAPTER 1

The Adolescent

"Began My Journey in Company with George Fairfax, Esqr."

FRIDAY, MARCH 11, 1748

In the gathering, snow-flecked dark of a December evening in 1753, a ragged little band of men stumbled to a halt outside a log palisade on a swollen creek in northern Pennsylvania, fifteen miles from the shores of Lake Erie. Weary, cold, and haggard, some of them on gaunt horses, they had come as far as five hundred miles in nearly two months of hard traveling through the worst winter weather in memory. Close as they were to their destination now, and as inviting as the thought of shelter and fire and food must have been, caution was necessary; the fort was in the hands of an unknown number of armed foreign troops.

They were unlikely ambassadors, and they had no idea how fateful their encounter was to be. There were five fur traders, all but one of them rough, unlettered men intent on somehow wrestling a fortune from this wilderness. There were four Iroquois from the country around the forks of the Ohio River, one of them elderly and one very young. The party's leader was a young major of the Virginia militia who was singularly unqualified for this job. He had no military training or experience; his rank was largely honorary, bestowed by an organization of citizen-soldiers that was more social club than armed force. He did not know this country, for he had spent his entire life snuggled into the narrow strip of British civilization along the Atlantic coast. He knew little about the fur traders who had agreed to escort him here, virtually nothing about the French soldiers with whom he had been sent to negotiate, and less than that about the red men who accompanied him, whose country this was. But he knew the governor of Virginia, and here he was.

For the travelers, walking or riding in the bitter cold had been bad enough, but standing still was worse. They huddled into their buffalo robes and match coats while their young leader decided what to do next. The major's job was not to fight, but to deliver a letter from Governor Robert Dinwiddie of Virginia to the commander of the French forces marching southward along the Allegheny River toward its confluence with the Monongahela—the forks of the Ohio. In the name of his king, Dinwiddie had commanded that the invaders turn back. Whatever the French reaction, it would be the stuff of history.

The young man who carried the portentous letter had long intended to make a name, to project himself into history. But he had thought it would be on the quarterdeck of a ship of the line, or on horseback behind a crimson line of battle, with the roar of cannon in his ears and the heat of combat in his blood. Mostly he had expected his moment to come among more fitting companions. Instead, a chance to make his mark had come here, in the vast, snow-blanketed silence of the country beyond the Alleghenies, in the company of savage and half-savage men devoid of cultural grace or social standing. Most young men he knew, historic opportunity or not, would never expose themselves to such unpleasant surroundings. They did not feel the consuming, increasingly desperate ambition of the twenty-one-year-old George Washington.

The one whom Washington detailed to approach the fort was of all of them the least experienced in the wilderness. Jacob van Braam was a Dutch teacher of languages and fencing from the pleasant little port of Fredericksburg, Virginia, on his first trip beyond the mountains. (For Virginians, the Blue Ridge Mountains marked the edge of civilization and the Alleghenies, the edge of the world.) He was the only one present who understood any French, and so it was he who urged his horse forward to approach the dark palisade and announce their presence. Then there was nothing for the rest of them to do but wait for the reaction.

It was not long in coming. The translator returned in the company of several officers, who presented the compliments of Captain Jacques Le Gardeur, Sieur de Saint-Pierre, commander of His French Majesty's forces at Fort le Boeuf, and desired to know whether his visitors would do him the honor, considering the lateness of the hour, of accepting his hospitality. After they had eaten and slept, surely tomorrow would be soon enough to conduct their business?

It was all done with the smoothness and assurance of professional soldiers who had the upper hand, and knew it. There was nothing for the young major to do but summon what dignity he could, pretend he had a choice in the matter, and agree. They rode through the bone-chilling cold and the spitting snow, into the fort under the hard stares of the bundled sentries on the firestep. They eased their creaking bones from the saddles, turned to the welcome warmth of the cookfires, and accepted gratefully the hot soup always to be found in a French camp.

It did not take long for them to realize that the French force was less daunting than they might have supposed. There were only a few dozen soldiers to be seen, and they, too, were hundreds of miles from home, worn out, and short of supplies. They were an invading force, but if the truth were known, they were months behind schedule, riddled with illness, and fearful of the surrounding native population, to whom they had promised, but would not be able to deliver, enough food to last the winter. The commander who had got them this far had died in despair, and had just been replaced by a world-weary officer who had done his service to France and wanted most to go home and rest.

These facts the French made pains to keep to themselves, while Washington concealed any disappointment at not being able to conduct his business right away. Everyone found a place to sleep.

Thus did representatives of the empires of Great Britain and France prepare to lead their countries into history's first world war, fought on land in Europe, India, and America and on the high seas everywhere, its major prize being possession of the North American continent. Thus did George Washington take his first step onto the stage of history from the shadows of an ordinary life.

That, of course, is not how it seemed to him. The mission to French Creek was simply an opportunity, one that he had seen and grasped and that now he must bend to his will. He had begun applying his will to the world around him five years earlier, and he was beginning to get the idea. But the next few days would challenge him as he had never been challenged before. And thereafter would come an inexorable increase in both the frequency and the gravity of the problems he must face. The question of how much he had learned in five years had just become critical.

The year 1748 was the first of George Washington's ten years of adolescence, and when it began he was still adrift in formless childhood. His father had been an anchor, but his father had died five years before, when he was eleven. Their plantation on the Potomac River had been his refuge and his delight, but it was not to be his possession, for he was a third son, born to his father's second wife, in a society that still regarded the eldest son as the principal heir. The farm his father had bequeathed him, the small homeplace on Virginia's Rappahannock River near Fredericksburg, was his only legally; his formidable mother remained in residence and very much in control there. While he was ever mindful of his duties to his mother, as far as he was concerned they did not require his presence at Ferry Farm.

Physically, Washington was something of an odd specimen. He was a big youth, at six feet two inches looming a good six inches above the average man of his time. Imposing as this stature was, its bulk was not well proportioned; he was somewhat heavy in the hips and narrow in the shoulders. The wrists and ankles seemed inadequate to wield the enormous hands and feet. His red hair—not a flaming Irish red, but a subdued English auburn—was pulled back into its queue from a high forehead and a recessive hairline that gave his face the look of a blunt wedge, dominated by a nose of heroic proportions.

By 1748, the sixteen-year-old Washington was spending almost all of his time with his half-brother Lawrence, who as the eldest son had inherited the family's big plantation on the Potomac. Lawrence was not only a substantial planter (thanks to his inheritance), but had shown himself to be a man of action in his own right when in 1741 he had taken the king's commission and sailed away to fight the Spanish. Lawrence had a minor voice in the colony's politics and a share in one of its grandest business ventures, the Ohio Company. If he was not yet in the first rank of Virginia planters, he was closer to membership than their father had been.

To be of the first rank: Augustine Washington, the father, had grasped for that brass ring all of his life, accumulating land, managing the Principio Company's iron mine and works at Accokeek Creek, plotting with the gentlemen of the Ohio Company to develop the interior of the continent. Had Gus Washington lived twenty more years, he might well have made it to the inner circle of the old families, but he had fallen on the course at the age of forty-nine. Lawrence had a better chance.

But there was little hope for George. His little spot of land was hardly the foundation for an empire. The likelihood of his inheriting more was low. Yet clearly the life of a subsistence farmer was utterly unacceptable to him. A letter from his uncle to his mother in 1747, famous for its advice against sending young George to sea, contained other cautions as well: "He must not be hasty to be rich," James Ball wrote to his sister about her son, "but must go on gently and with patience as things will naturally go. This method, without aiming at being a fine gentleman before his time, will carry a man more comfortably and surely though the world, than going to sea."

Whether he was speaking in generalities or from particular knowledge, James Ball had it right; George would soon demonstrate that he was hasty to be rich, determined to be a fine gentleman, alert for the great chance. The need to elevate himself above the mass of humanity was to be paramount in his early life, and the first step up was provided by a collection of surveyor's instruments his father had left in a storage building at Ferry Farm. The fifteen-year-old learned to use them, and by the fall of 1747 had acquired a handy and lucrative trade. If he could not yet build his own land empire, he could provide an essential service to those who were building theirs, by laying out their lots and farms. For the rest of his life he would regard land as a jeweler inspects a gemstone, with minute attention to its flaws, facets, and value. And he got in the habit of recording meticulously the metes and bounds of property and of his own accounts and actions.

Early in 1748, during a winter stay at Lawrence's Mount Vernon, the young surveyor found himself within reach of a truly great chance. Four miles upstream, on the same bank of the Potomac, stood an even grander plantation house called Belvoir, home of William Fairfax. The illustrious Fairfax family was by far the most powerful on the Northern Neck—that part of Virginia between the Potomac and Rappahannock Rivers—simply because Thomas, Lord Fairfax, 6th Baron of Cameron, owned the Northern Neck in its entirety. It was fortunate enough for the residents of Mount Vernon that their neighbor William Fairfax was the Baron's cousin and his agent in disposing of and administering all that land. Lawrence had not been blind to the possibilities; he had married one of William's daughters. And now they found themselves living next to Lord Fairfax himself, who had just become the first member of the British peerage ever to take up residence in America.

Whatever the young George Washington might have dreamed for himself, the Fairfaxes possessed: land and power beyond measure, unassailable prestige throughout the civilized—which was to say, the English—world, and the glossy, easy elegance of behavior conveyed by possessing such assets from birth. It could not have occurred to their young admirer, at least not yet, that the Fairfaxes were not the first and highest representatives of a new order come to America, but the last vestiges of a degenerate and failed society that was about to disappear from the continent as completely and finally as the native civilization.

First, however, the Fairfaxes would play a major role in the development of their young neighbor, the man who more than any other individual would ensure that they and their kind passed forever from the American scene.

They were about to oversee a decade of young Washington's life remarkable both for what would happen and what would not. A rather ordinary young man, with few visible gifts, would be called by his country, tested by adventure and warfare, and would fire a volley that, in Horace Walpole's words, would "set the world on fire." He would establish his courage, his leadership, his integrity—all things his country would need in full measure. And he would find some of the things he needed most—the acclaim for which he thirsted, the place he most wanted to call home.

Yet this decade would be remarkable, too, for what it would not yield to George Washington. In addition to the highest virtues of an emerging nation, he would also come to embody two of its most glaring and persistent failings—its contempt for people of other races and its destructive exploitation of the land. His willful ignorance of the native tribes with which he would deal, as allies and enemies, throughout this period would reinforce his and his countrymen's blind contempt for all who differed from them. His lust for land—not land for growing things or grazing cattle, but land to buy cheap and sell dear, to buy in the gross and sell by the piece, to handle as a commodity—was something new in his time, but would become perfectly normal throughout American history, and along with racism would extract a high and bitter price from later generations required by no choice of their own to confront the damage already done.

With these two grievous exceptions, Washington would examine and reject many of the underlying assumptions of his society. This he would do not because he had an inquiring mind—quite the contrary—but because the fault lines of his society were so starkly etched, and were shuddering with such great quakes, that anyone who wished to keep his footing had to pay attention, and choose sides. Armed conflict was not the only symptom. He might spend one day in the drawing rooms of powerful aristocrats who owed their station and their allegiance to the King of England, the next night in the camp of men who had fought to bring down that king and replace him with a Catholic Stuart. He would command men whose comrades were slaughtered and countryside ravaged by the Duke of Cumberland, the Butcher of Culloden, now the captain-general of the army with which they were allied.

Not surprisingly, Washington would follow and then abandon many masters and ideals during his formative decade. None would have more collective influence on him than the Fairfaxes—one as mentor, another as patriarch, and a third as best friend. None would be more closely examined by him, more avidly emulated, or in the end more firmly rejected. But it would be a near thing.

In 1748, George Washington wanted to possess the kind of things Lord Fairfax had, to think the way Lord Fairfax thought, to be regarded as Lord Fairfax was regarded. Because he was for a time the compass for Washington's journey toward maturity, Fairfax's character bears examination here. And because the Virginia that Fairfax discovered was Washington's world seen through older and more cosmopolitan eyes, that world bears description here.

Thomas, Lord Fairfax, seventeen years old when his father died in 1710, had on that day become a peer of the realm, a gentleman by right of birth as his forefathers had been for five generations. The Fairfaxes had not always been noble; the first baron had bought the title on the cheap when King Charles I had been desperate for cash to finance his losing fight with Oliver Cromwell and the Parliament. Nor were the Fairfaxes, even when noble, able to remain consistently rich; the 5th Baron, Thomas's father, had been a spendthrift, had mortgaged his patrimony to the hilt, and had died in a seedy London rooming house while hiding from creditors.

But he had married well. Catherine Culpeper, herself the daughter of a baron, had enough of an endowment that with ceaseless struggle she was able to hold off her dead husband's creditors, preserve the family holdings (she would not sell Culpeper land, she declared, to lift Fairfax debts), and send young Thomas to Oxford. She wrote him there every month, letters filled with woe and cautionary advice: "Your father hath destroyed all that can be for you and me both; but I will do all that is in my power to get something again, and I hope you will deserve it of me this time." She urged him to "do well in the world to help comfort me after all the trouble I am forced to go through."

The young baron did as well as he could. He drank, he hunted, he giggled and danced (on one occasion, he recalled, for a span of "fairly thirteen hours, and pretty women for company made the time run pleasantly away"), bought guns, wigs, dogs, and horses, studied fencing and dancing, and somehow got most of the way through a college education. After three years, however, it became obvious that his more serious younger brother Harry could make better use of learning, and since there was not enough money for both to attend, the young baron cheerfully made way. His college provost observed drily in parting that Thomas had received "all the benefit of a college education, without the least inconvenience."

For a time the baron scarcely altered his routine of dancing, fox hunts, hare hunts, stag hunts, dining, and more dancing. He thought of a tour of the Continent, almost obligatory for young men of his station and stage of life. But there simply was no money, and it was time to take up a gentleman's career. A suitable post, one involving more honor than work, was easily arranged in the office of the treasurer of the king's household. While his mother struggled on with intractable debts, the young baron added to his repertoire of diversions coffeehouse conviviality, court intrigues, and literary pretensions (he became an associate of the famed poet and essayist Joseph Addison).

Reality threatened an unwelcome intrusion into this privileged life in 1719, when his careworn and exhausted mother at length succumbed. But as it turned out, there was no reason for the young baron to change his ways. Lady Fairfax, having taken his measure, had put his inheritance—the lordly Leeds Castle in Kent, Greenway Court in Southampton, properties on the Isle of Wight and in Virginia—into the hands of reliable trustees. Fairfax happily left the dreary details to them and returned to London society, where he remained, with occasional visits to his manors, for a dreamy decade. The idyll was briefly threatened two years later, in 1721, when Fairfax got on the wrong side of that consummate politician and vengeance-taker Robert Walpole and lost his job at court. The Fairfaxes being loyal Whigs, however, another position was easily obtained—as a cornet, or color-bearer, for the Royal Regiment of Horse Guards.

Meanwhile, England was changing. New fortunes were being assembled by people engaged in commerce with the far-flung colonies, in industries supplying that trade as well as the demands of an increasingly prosperous Britain, even in agriculture with the application of productive new methods. The newly rich took their place at the dining tables and in the drawing rooms alongside men with ancient titles and moldering manors. Maintaining one's place in society had always been expensive and had always involved debts, but as the engines of commerce accelerated, satisfying creditors began to require more than the word of a gentleman; now it took cash.

Fairfax's years of detached irresponsibility ended in 1728 with the expiration of his mother's trust. The Fairfax finances, which now became his sole responsibility, were in grim condition. Not enough money had come in to satisfy all the bequests made by Lady Fairfax, and there were no prospects for improvement based on the English estates. There was, however, the matter of the Virginia land.

In 1649, Lady Fairfax's grandfather, along with a Culpeper cousin, had been rewarded for loyal service to the failed cause of King Charles I. Charles had been executed in January of that year after two decades of strife and two civil wars, between Cavaliers (royalists, aristocrats, Catholics) and Roundheads (parliamentarians, populists, Protestants). Charles II, in exile and impoverished, rewarded the faithful Culpepers with a large grant of New World land. It was a vaguely defined gift, lying "within the heads" of the Rappahannock and Potomac Rivers. No one knew exactly where those rivers flowed or what precisely was meant by their "heads." But the king was after all in deep trouble at the time, England being in the iron grip of Cromwell's military republicans, and close questioning of the dimensions of the gift would have been gauche.

With the restoration of the monarchy a decade later, the grant took on reality, to the satisfaction of its beneficiaries and the indignation of Virginians—the king's generosity created a large, manorial proprietary in the middle of a colony that thought it had progressed beyond such feudal anachronisms. Those who already lived on the Northern Neck said they resented having to give their fealty to a middleman, a lord standing between them and their king. And they made much of the fact that other Virginians, once having paid their quit-rents as required by law, held their land as a matter of right. This was unusual under British imperial law, which granted possession of land within the king's dominion not as a right but by the grace of the sovereign. But Virginia had been founded by a commercial land company under whose charter a paid-up member had a right to a certain amount of land. Residents of the proprietary professed to find it distasteful to exchange this right for the traditional privilege.

But such arguments were more rationalizations of the colonists' ire than causes of it. The dispute was really about money and power. The governor of the colony and his council did not like the proprietary because within it they had no power to grant or withhold land. The House of Burgesses hated it because the quit-rents from its land went not to the treasury of Virginia but to the pockets of Lord Fairfax, who paid only a token rent to the colony. The residents of the Northern Neck loathed it because although the proprietary charged the same quit-rents as the colony—two shillings per hundred acres per year, payable in tobacco—it did not forgive quit-rents for the first seven years of residence, as did the colony. Moreover, the proprietary's collectors were a good deal more efficient and persistent than the colony's civil servants.

As colonial settlement spread westward, toward the nebulous boundaries of the Northern Neck, the settlers became ever more reluctant to pay Fairfax rents, and the colony grew ever more eager to establish its rights in order to contain the huge proprietary. The original grant had referred to the "heads" of the rivers, an ambiguous term that could mean either the head of navigation (the point where a river became too shallow for oceangoing vessels, also referred to as the falls), or the head spring, the source. King James II had cleared that up in 1688 when he had reissued the grant with a more specific reference to the first heads, or springs, meaning the source most distant from the river's mouth. The trouble was that no one knew where those head springs were.

Lacking such knowledge, at each major fork in the rivers concerned, someone had to guess which fork was the larger and thus, presumably, the longer. The assumption that width and length were related was not reliable; for many years it had seemed obvious to observers aboard ship that the Occoquan River, where it joined the Potomac downriver from the future site of Mount Vernon, was much the larger of the two rivers and therefore was the boundary between the Northern Neck and Lord Baltimore's Maryland proprietary. The discovery that the Occoquan dwindled to a creek a few miles above its deceptively wide mouth, while the narrower Potomac snaked away to the western mountains, was Maryland's loss and the Northern Neck's gain.

A similar problem arose at a cleft in those mountains called The Hole, later to be known as Harper's Ferry. There was found yet another fork, where the Shenandoah flowing in from the south met the Cohongoruton, or "River of Wild Geese," from the west to form the Potomac. In 1728, the year Lord Fairfax took over his affairs, Virginia's Governor Gooch took the position that The Hole was the source of the Potomac, the corner of the Northern Neck proprietary, and that therefore the Shenandoah Valley was his to grant, which he began to do.

There were similar problems with the southern extent. Settlers moving up the Rappahannock in search of land found that it forked a few miles above the falls into a northern and southern branch (the latter called the Rapidan). Did the half-million acres that lay between the forks of this river belong to Virginia, or the proprietary? No one knew, or could know, until a survey determined which branch had its origin farther west.

Decade after decade these controversies—between settler and proprietary, between proprietary and colony, between colony and Crown—simmered and matured, quietly distilling disagreement, inconvenience, confusion, and irritation into a more potent and volatile brew. As the eighteenth century progressed, the several layers of protection intervening between the 6th Lord Fairfax and his troubled legacy were removed; first his mother died, then his trustees departed, and finally his resident agent on the Northern Neck, Robert Carter, died in 1732.

Lord Fairfax had by then spent four years dealing with the problems and considering the possibilities of the Northern Neck, and he understood that he needed, in Carter's place, an agent whose loyalty and incorruptibility were similarly beyond question. He turned to his cousin William Fairfax, whom he had known since childhood. William was the second son of a second son and thus was caught in the common trap of being too low in status to inherit a living and too high to work for one. William had been given a genteel colonial position as a collector of customs; it was a small matter to have him transferred to the Northern Neck where he could, in addition, manage the Fairfax interests.

It was a happy choice all around, for William proved from the first to be both able and conscientious. He quickly discovered that the affairs of the proprietary were in a shambles, with quit-rents uncollected, grants unsurveyed, and the boundaries still undetermined. Speculators had reserved huge acreages that remained empty while they awaited a suitably profitable opportunity to resell them.

Moreover, he soon established that one of the most avaricious of these speculators had been none other than Robert Carter. During his tenure as agent, Carter had taken personal title to about three hundred thousand acres of land and had conveyed thousands of acres more to relatives, friends, and their children. As the owner of more Virginia land than any other individual excepting only Fairfax, Carter became known as "King" Carter. (The debt-ridden Fairfax must have been astonished to read, in London's *Gentleman's Magazine*, that Carter's estate included ten thousand pounds in cash.)

From 1732 onward, Fairfax was completely enmeshed in the tangled affairs of his Virginia land. The matter of the boundaries was of primary importance, and the baron knew how to resolve things; a few words to a few old friends, and the king's Privy Council ordered the governor of Virginia to appoint commissioners and surveyors to settle the matter once and for all. For good measure, the Lords Commissioner of Trade and Plantations sent along a letter, which was also an order, suggesting that the governor assist Fairfax "with your good offices whenever his Lordship shall have occasion for them." However, seeing to it that these orders were executed, and settling the many other confusions and disputes concerning the proprietary, obviously required personal attention. In 1735, His Lordship sailed to Virginia.

The society he found in the Tidewater was surprisingly congenial, and belied Virginia's reputation as a wilderness populated by commoners, criminals, and savages. The palatial manor houses of the established planters—the Carters, Lees, Harrisons, Byrds, and others—rivaled in grandeur and opulence the seats of England's landed gentry. In fact, since they were much newer than the typical English mansion, they were in some respects finer than the decrepit manors of the old country, having fewer leaks and drafts. Moreover, to his delight, Fairfax found that the pursuits of Virginia's aristocracy matched his own lifelong avocations: dancing till dawn, racing horses, shooting game, gambling, and drinking. In such glittering and convivial company it was easy to forget that the fathers and the grandfathers of these Virginia aristocrats had been refugees, fugitives, bankrupts, and outcasts of humble birth.

Another thing that Fairfax and the Virginia gentry had in common was long familiarity with debt. The plantations were self-sufficient in most staples, but their cash crop was tobacco, and few planters ever saw the cash. After a labor-intensive growing year, the hogsheads, or barrels, of cured leaf were shipped to England for sale at auction by the planter's London agent. Meanwhile, the agent had been procuring and shipping to the planter, on credit, necessities ranging from brandy to coaches, draperies to underwear, chandeliers to window glass. Sometimes the revenue from the year's crops covered the year's charges, often it did not. Debt billowed like a darkening thundercloud over the finest mansions of the New World, just as it did in the Old.

Fairfax would not have had much in common with the men of rough vigor who had staked out the enormous plantations, hewed out the expansive tobacco fields, and lashed together the family fortunes. He was entirely at home, however, with the third-generation heirs to that wealth, who found themselves so richly blessed at birth that it was easy to assume that they possessed virtues distinguishing them from ordinary people. It followed, as a corollary, that the imposition of their will on ordinary people was not only their right, but their duty. Bondage and slavery were all part of the natural order. The heirs had become precisely what their forefathers had fled.

Lord Fairfax was oblivious, as were most of his new friends, to the vivid signs of dry rot that were already blotching the finish on this replicate aristocracy. The decadence and greed that suffused the life of a King Carter, for example, were a given; it was the way the rich lived everywhere. Similarly, the oppression of the people whose labor provided the foundation for the fortunes—the slaves dragooned from Africa, the felons transported from England, the indentured servants enticed from Ireland—was normal. There was no other way to grow tobacco, tend gardens, clear land, saw logs, build stables, and feed animals, and there was no reason to seek another way.

What had begun to prey on the minds of a few astute managers, however, was the ever-increasing number, throughout the plantations, of "old fields"—large expanses of once-choice land that had been utterly exhausted by a succession of tobacco and corn crops taken without a thought for replenishment of the land. Scrub pine, the only thing that would grow on these ravaged expanses, was spreading among the stately mansions and manicured fields like a prickly green blight.

In England, where all the land had been claimed and fenced, such a problem might have demanded attention—had, in fact, given rise to such conservationist practices as manuring and summer fallow. But in America there seemed to be an infinity of land, sprawling away westward in endless rising folds, unoccupied except by savages and ruffians, simply waiting to augment the fortunes of the chosen and the strong. In the glow of opportunity reflected from these Western expanses, even disagreements such as those between Virginia and Lord Fairfax, on a scale of millions of acres, were of little consequence. And so the gentlemen moved toward a resolution of this minor matter with courtesy, refinement, and frequent recreation, as befit their stations.

Lord Fairfax was comfortable in Tidewater society, yet he was intrigued by the West. That, of course, was the disputed country. Virginia's Governor William Gooch was still arguing that the western boundary of the proprietorship should be drawn between the falls of the Potomac and Rappahannock Rivers, including nothing beyond the Tidewater. Failing that, he insisted that it should be no farther west than the Blue Ridge, running southwestward from the confluence of the Shenandoah and Potomac Rivers and excluding the Shenandoah Valley. Fairfax had heard glowing reports of the Valley; one of his major tasks before leaving London had been to defeat the efforts of a pair of promoters to start a settlement there independent of his interests. One of his first acts on reaching Virginia was to commission a surveyor to lay off fifty thousand choice Valley acres for his own use. And after a winter of socializing he headed west to see this storied country for himself.

The veneer of society wore away quickly as one moved away from the coast. The planters of the second rank, located upriver from the choicest coastal spreads, were still working for their living. They had smaller holdings with more disadvantages and had been at it a shorter time, and so tended to spend less time at cards and whiskey. Among these was Gus Washington, a distant relative of Fairfax whose acquaintance His Lordship soon made.

Between the last of the planters, on the fringes of the Tidewater, and the first rise of mountains to the west was the Piedmont country.

This was the country of the small farm, recently hacked from the all-encompassing woods by an indentured servant who had done his time, or a debtor on the run, or an immigrant who had been jostled away from the choice waterfront spots. Here were no gracious accommodations in great houses among refined people, but at best a spot on the floor of a rude ordinary, or inn, at the crossing of two of the rutted pigs' paths that here were called roads. Here was no refined society, but the company of worn people in homespun whose life was work and whose recreation was a stolen nighttime hour with their families or friends. Here there were no groaning tables spread with beef and fowl, breads and cakes, rum and beer, but wooden dishes carrying a slab of pork and a chunk of gritty cornbread or, where there were not yet mills to supply flour, simply boiled hominy.

The farther west one went, the harder life seemed, the more it was stripped of all leisure, decoration, and confidence. Not only one's livelihood but one's very existence could be snuffed out by a change in the weather, a passing animal, or a sudden illness. And when His Lordship pressed on over Ashby Gap in the Blue Ridge Mountains, he found he had passed another boundary, into a yet stranger land.

In the Shenandoah Valley, unlike the Piedmont, there were few castoffs and rejects from Tidewater society, gazing enviously eastward toward the lords of tobacco and the peers of England. To begin with, the Valley people were not English. The great majority came from one of two places: northern Ireland, whence the Presbyterian Scotch-Irish were fleeing by the hundreds of thousands, tired of being ground between the merciless Anglican overlords and the rebellious Catholic natives; and from Germany, where Austria and Prussia were contesting endlessly for preeminence and trampling heedlessly, again and again, the farms and towns of the ordinary people in places such as the Palatinate.

Like the original inhabitants of the Tidewater, the Valley people had come unimaginably far in search of freedom from arrogant aristocrats, inflexible bishops, and murderous generals. They had trooped down the gangplanks of Jamestown and Fredericksburg, Baltimore and Philadelphia, in endless procession, the Scotch-Irish and the Germans, turning and blinking in the bright light of the New World in quest of the chance they had heard was here—the chance to make something and hold onto it, to live without fear, to do as one pleased.

They found on their arrival that they could indeed do as they pleased, so long as they did not try to do it in the East. The Catholics of Maryland had their religious freedom and were not anxious to share it with Protestants. The Quakers of Pennsylvania did not want their common viewpoints diluted by interlopers, and saw to it that the newcomers were shunted west. The planters of Virginia were interested only in those willing to become temporary or permanent slaves, and of course made no place for others.

So the newcomers trudged west, into western Pennsylvania, southwestward along the flanks of Maryland's Catoctin into the valley of the Shenandoah. They built houses and barns of stone and log that stood as square and stolid as they did. They turned over the ground and grew what they needed for food and a little extra for trade. They did their own work, raised their own families, built their own towns and counties and churches and society. They contracted little debt among themselves, none with outsiders. Their imports were limited to what they had carried with them, their exports by the distance a man could drive a cow. They bent their neck to no man and gave no special allegiance to government, although they were prepared to do their obvious civic duties.

No people, no collection of characteristics, could have been designed to have less appeal to a man who all his life had judged others by the names and titles with which they were born; whose main struggle had been to find a way to pass away the endless days without boredom; who had not considered that either freedom or high station was something one could lose. No place could be thought of that would be more distasteful to an English baron accustomed to grand houses, great cities, formal gardens, and smooth roads.

Yet here is the great mystery, the one truly interesting thing about the life and character of Thomas, 6th Lord Fairfax: he loved this rude frontier, would fight for the next seventeen years to keep it part of his proprietary, and then would make it his home, becoming the first and the last of the British peerage to do so. His other eccentricities—he wore shabby clothes, was subject to dark moods, and seemed uncomfortable in the presence of women—paled to insignificance beside this astounding leap.

Greed did not account for it, although he was casting his gaze over an endless expanse of some three million acres whose ownership was contested. The colony, and indeed the Valley, was full of speculators whose avaricious practices Fairfax would never emulate. He would not, as was widely feared, try to uproot the settlers who in good faith had acquired their land from colonial officials or speculators whose right to convey the land he did not recognize. He remained ready to confirm all such titles, provided only that the surveys were proper and that they conformed to the common land-use regulation of the day: that their breadth be at least one-third their length. (This requirement was designed to prevent firstcomers from preempting all the bottom lands and water rights. One 865-acre parcel laid out to include seven miles of a creek, with a width of only half a mile, was unacceptable.) In any case, he could have set up his office in some fine Eastern house, or even in London, and directed his affairs from the bosom of society.

That is not what he did. He returned from his first visit to the Valley with an even stronger determination to maintain his interests there, and for that purpose returned to the seat of power in England to argue his case. The disputation—including the search for the contested head springs of the boundary rivers by fractious commissioners for Fairfax and the colony, arguments over how to interpret the new geographical information, appeals to men of influence in Williamsburg and London, legal arguments and counterclaims—consumed eight years. But on April 11, 1745, the Privy Council in London announced its decision: the western boundary of the proprietary would be a line between the first spring of the Conway River in Orange County, the source of the Rappahannock, and that of the Cohongoruton in the colony's northwestern mountains, origin of the Potomac. The Shenandoah Valley belonged to Fairfax.

Moreover, the previous year, representatives of the colonies of Virginia, Maryland, and Pennsylvania had induced the Iroquois League to sign a deed conveying to England all the land within Virginia, "as it is now or hereafter may be peopled and bounded." As usual, this document had different and unresolved meanings for the signatories; the Iroquois thought they were granting the English free access to the Shenandoah, while the English had in mind extending their grasp as far, a recent governor had said, as "the Great South Sea, including California."

The outbreak of yet another war between France and England (the War of Austrian Succession), along with the Jacobite rising in Scotland (on behalf of the Catholic pretender to the throne, "Bonnie" Prince Charles Stuart), for a time obscured the one undisputed meaning of the treaty—that the door to the Shenandoah was now open to white settlers. By the time it became apparent, Fairfax's ownership was established, and so was his intent to take up residence on the western frontier.

This highly unorthodox decision was to have a fateful effect on the careers of two young men: George Fairfax, William's eldest son, and George Washington, family friend and neighbor.

George Fairfax had come under the patronage of his illustrious relative the year the Baron had come to Virginia. George may have carried a trace of Negro blood in his veins from his mother, William's first wife, Sarah, who had come from the Caribbean. During George's boyhood, William had pleaded with his English relatives to help provide a proper education for "a poor West India boy, especially as he has the marks on his visage that will always testify his parentage." There was no response from the family.

Lord Fairfax proved to be not so fastidious in such matters. On his arrival in 1735, he had taken to the eleven-year-old boy and had arranged for him to travel to Leeds Castle to live with the baron's brother Robert and go to school. Ten years later, in April of 1745, Lord Fairfax brought George back to Virginia as the assistant agent for the Northern Neck, the designated successor to his aging fifty-five-year-old father.

In September of the following year, George Fairfax got his first taste of frontier life when he went with William to represent the family's interests during the survey of the newly established western boundary of the proprietary. The surveyors' job was to run a straight line for some seventy-five miles diagonally across the Blue Ridge and several ranges of the Alleghenies, some of the roughest terrain any of them had ever seen or imagined. George Fairfax accompanied the commissioners, who were not required, as the surveyors were, to challenge whatever precipices, swamps, and thickets happened to lie in their course. But no one had an easy time of it. They spent their days on laboring horses, besieged by insects, storms, deadfalls, flash floods, rock slides, and the fear of attack by some savage, human or animal. At night shelter was indifferent at best, and the only diversions were wild bouts of drinking that frequently led to brawls and always made the next morning's riding that much harder. It was, for George Fairfax, an entirely distasteful experience that he never wanted to repeat.

George Fairfax saw no reason to expose his person to unpleasantness or effort. Like his great-uncle the 5th Baron, George gazed out at the world from behind liquid, sensuous eyes and an imperious nose. But where the 5th Lord's petulant pout suggested abandonment to his urges, George Fairfax had a clamped, thin-lipped, downturned, judgmental mouth. Ten years of coddling at Leeds Castle had agreed with him, as did life at the magnificent Belvoir. He had enjoyed no special status among his schoolmates in England, but on the Northern Neck he was a minor god, heir not only to one of its major estates but to the power and wealth of the proprietary itself. As George Fairfax was to make clear by his subsequent decisions, it was his firm view that a man of such position and possessions had no business exposing his person to rain, hunger, or savages.

Yet that is precisely what he was required to do again, in the spring of 1748, by the taskmaster Baron, who wanted some proper surveys run on the enormous tract of land beyond the Shenandoah, in the valley of the South Branch of the Potomac, which had just been added officially to his proprietary. The work would be done by one of the surveyors from the original expedition. George Fairfax was to do what the commissioners had done on that occasion—go along and watch out for the Fairfax interests. And it seemed to his lordship a good idea to take along that bright young neighbor boy who was showing signs of becoming a surveyor.

George Washington was delighted to be asked. He was sixteen years old, the age at which young men begin to look beyond their families for role models. Lawrence Washington was losing some of his vigor and his hair by the time the twenty-four-year-old George Fairfax strode onto Belvoir with his English education, boundless possessions, and highborn ways. George Washington was awestruck. Here was a young man somewhat like himself who possessed broad experience, knew what he was going to do with his life, even knew how to behave around women. To be asked to go on a great adventure with the person you most admire is rare good fortune.

It is not surprising, then, that Washington's first personal journal begins with the words, in the entry for March 11, 1748, "Began My Journey in Company with George Fairfax, Esqr." Nor is it surprising that during their trip, and for a long while afterward, George Washington did his best to become George Fairfax. With such a guide and model, Washington saw the frontier for the first time through the eyes of a snob. Day after day of travel through wilderness and mountain ranges of stunning wildness and beauty drew the entry in young Washington's journal: "Nothing remarkable happened," although he did admire the "richness" of the land Lord Fairfax had earmarked for himself in the Shenandoah Valley.

Washington was an avid student of the methods of the surveying party, but the country and the people with which he came into contact drew only brief and disparaging comment. One of the longest entries details his shock at encountering a straw mattress lacking sheets and infested with lice. Offered supper in a frontier cabin in Frederick County, he was amused to see "no cloth upon the table nor a knife to eat with." It got worse, for soon there were no houses at all, and sleeping under canvas made one vulnerable to downpours, smoky fires, and tent-flattening winds. In camp not only was there no cloth on the table, there was no table: "Our spits was forked sticks, our plates was a large chip for dishes we had none."

His heaviest scorn, however, was reserved for the people who inhabited this unrefined land. On March 23, the surveyors encountered a party of about thirty natives, probably Delawares or Shawnees, where the South Branch of the Potomac joins the main river. "They were coming from war," Washington wrote, adding with a note of condescension, "with only one scalp." He thus concealed by belittlement—a favorite technique of the young and privileged—any human reaction, such as shock, that he might have felt on seeing such a grisly object for the first time in his life. Later, for amusement, the Virginians fed the natives some liquor, and sure enough soon had them "in the humor of dancing."

Washington could hardly contain his mirth as he described the scene, conveying the giggles that doubtless accompanied the retellings of the story in the drawing rooms of Belvoir and Mount Vernon. "They clear a large circle and make a great fire in the middle, then seat themselves around it. The Speaker makes a grand speech telling them in what manner they are to dance, after he has finished the best dancer jumps up as one awakened out of a sleep and runs and jumps about the ring in a most comical manner. He is followed by the rest then begins there musicians to play. The music is a pot half full of water with a deerskin stretched over it as tight as it can and a gourd with some shot in it to rattle and a piece of horse's tail tied to it to make it look fine." One can see the two Georges arching eyebrows at one another while the dark savages ran about "in a most comical manner."

And there was more to make one laugh. On April 4, a number of German families left their fields and cabins to come see what the surveyors were doing. They had ample reason to be uneasy about surveyors working in their neighborhood, given the long dispute over who owned this land in the first place and the many irregularities of the claims upon it. They "attended us through the woods as we went," wrote Washington, "showing their antic tricks. I really think they seem to be as ignorant a set of people as the Indians. They would never speak English but when spoken to they all speak Dutch." It was difficult to imagine people so ignorant that they did not speak English.

Apparently, however, there was nothing funny about the events of April 9. On that day the party ran out of food and had to scrounge around among the nearby settlers for enough supplies to make a meal. "We were obliged to go without," recorded Washington in disbelief, "until 4 or 5 o'clock in the evening." But they were not obliged to stand for such hardship. Without further ado, he recorded, "We took our leave of our company." The two Georges were going home, and they wasted no time about it; despite getting lost once, they were back in the arms of their families four days later.

Ambling their horses eastward away from inconvenience, they were two young fops, giggling through momentous times without a glimmering of thought for matters beyond the day's food and entertainment. One of them would continue thus to the end of his days, forever avoiding responsibility and difficulty, insulated from the consequences of folly by unearned wealth. The other, the younger, lacking such protection, would shortly be required to bestir himself.

But meanwhile, in this heedless, mocking year of their privileged lives, events heavy with significance were moving through deep-shadowed thickets, and dark harbingers wheeled in skies just beyond their horizon.

It was 1748, the year the French and the English signed the Treaty of Aix-la-Chapelle, proclaimed peace in their time, and immediately began preparations for the next war. Six days after the signing, a group of Virginia's finest gentlemen formally created a company for the purpose of claiming the Ohio country—the vast territory beyond the Allegheny Mountains, where the Allegheny and Monongahela Rivers formed the mighty Ohio and moved on toward the Mississippi. A few days later, the French governor-general of Canada moved to begin the restoration of his country's trading interests in that area.

It was the year the Iroquois met with the French in Quebec to tell them that despite the treaties and the deeds and all appearances, the Iroquois were not creatures of the English, but were free and independent and would remain so. It was the year that George Washington perfected his shaving technique and his billiards game, learned whist and dancing, studied fashion and personal style.

It was the year George Fairfax took a wife, with whom George Washington immediately fell in love. She was Sally Cary, daughter of an established planter of the lower James River, and if George Fairfax found her acceptable, George Washington thought her the acme of womanhood. She was eighteen, amiable and animated, and shared many facial features with her sixteen-year-old admirer; like him she had a broad forehead, wide eyes, and a generous nose set in a spacious oval that turned skimpy toward the mouth and chin. George Washington thought she was unutterably beautiful. He hungered for the sight of her, thirsted for a teasing exchange of words, and never afterward would he be able to think of her without choking up. It was a time of delirious celebration at Belvoir and Mount Vernon, and it must have seemed that the dancing and the laughter would go on forever. It was no time to dwell on Lawrence Washington's illness, which had forced his early return from the House of Burgesses; surely his nagging cough would pass and all would be right again.

Like heat lightning on a quiet night, the signs of trouble somewhere, coming sometime, flickered on through the summer of 1749, while George Washington helped lay out the metes and bounds of the city of Alexandria and got appointed official surveyor for Culpeper County. A little party of Frenchmen led by one Captain Pierre Joseph Céloron de Blainville moved through the vast country of what they called La Belle Rivière, stopping from time to time to bury with great ceremony a lead plate claiming the land for their Most Christian Majesty. The Iroquois, Delawares, Shawnees, and other natives who saw these rituals were every bit as amused by them as Washington had been by their dancing—and were as oblivious to their meaning. They did take seriously, however, the news that Governor Gooch of Virginia that July granted two hundred thousand acres of land west of the mountains to the Ohio Company. This news was spread eagerly among the tribes by the English traders from Pennsylvania, who used it as evidence of the venality of all English traders from Virginia, and worked up as much hostility toward the enterprise as they could.

This was also the year that Lord Fairfax acted on his decision to move west. To the undisguised horror of his protégé George Fairfax, the Baron happily took up residence in a rude log cabin on his Shenandoah Valley land. A larger and more comfortable manor house would come later, but it would never approach the elegance of the Tidewater mansions. His family worried about the Baron's surly and uncommunicative mood during this time, preferring perhaps to suspect that he was going insane than to accept his radical behavior. His state of mind may have had something to do with George Fairfax's refusal to be inconvenienced in his patron's service. The lad on whom the Baron had lavished so many favors simply would not leave the cosseted life of Belvoir. If Lord Fairfax was going to rough it, he would do so alone. Grumpily, the aging baron assumed most of the work of the proprietary himself and began to cast around for another agent. (His search would not end until 1752, when his English nephew Thomas Bryan Martin, then twenty-one years old, would move to the Valley and became his land agent.)

Despite the disappointment, and despite all expectations to the contrary, Lord Fairfax found his new life at the edge of the wilderness to be entirely agreeable. With his shabby clothes and his love of hunting and his amiable regard for the mounting tide of Germans,

Scotch-Irish, Quakers, and Englishmen looking for land and a new start and an even chance, he became not only well known and highly respected—which was, after all, his birthright—but well liked as well, which was his own achievement. He called his new home Greenway Court, for a little Culpeper manor in England that had pleasant associations for him as a getaway cottage.

He applied unfailing patience and consideration to the snarled affairs of the western landowners, including a monumental dispute with one Joist Hite, who claimed one hundred thousand acres of Fairfax land as his to sell under an arrangement struck with the Governor's Council. The disagreement became the longest-running lawsuit in American jurisprudence and was not settled until long after the deaths of all the principals. But while Fairfax challenged the speculators and firmly upheld his rights, he tried always to "quiet the minds of the people," as he put it, reassuring all concerned that whatever the outcome of the ownership question, they would not be displaced.

Neither William Fairfax, who was off on an extended visit to England, nor George Fairfax, who was busy being comfortable, had anything to do with these affairs. George Washington, on the other hand, was a frequent visitor at Greenway Court. His services as a surveyor were in heavy demand, and he needed the money. Surveying in the far country, where lines had to be sighted through woods and thickets, had to be done either in early spring before the trees leafed out, or in late fall after the leaves dropped. In November of 1749, Washington began a seasonal routine of spending some time each April and each November working on Fairfax land in Frederick County. No doubt he relished not only the work, but the close association with the powerful Fairfax. Yet his feelings were demonstrably mixed. Lord Fairfax was not living or behaving as a baron should. And his chosen neighbors were, as Washington saw it, "a parcel of barbarians, an uncouth set of people."

Yet as Lord Fairfax had affirmed by his actions, the future was to be here, among the barbarians. Clearly it was not going to be a future of great houses occupied by idle men whiling away the afternoons in rum-clouded ease, comparing the pedigrees of their horses and wives. A surveyor's work here was not in laying out vast manors for respectable gentlemen, but in marking out small farms for rude

Germans and unruly Scotch-Irish. Here a man gained acceptance, regard, and trust not for his name or title, but for his work, his steadiness, his ability and honesty. Lord Fairfax was accepted here not because he was a baron, but despite it. This was the West.

It must have been confusing to a young man trying to chart a course. If Lord Fairfax was to be his guiding star, and none brighter or loftier could be found, Washington would find himself living among savages and wearing seedy clothes. George Fairfax's example, on the other hand, far more attractive for its amenities, led to a life of leisure Washington could not afford. A great gulf was beginning to open between the two Georges; one of them had to work for his living. Washington's trade, the one thing he had got for himself by himself, was paying handsomely and offered good financial prospects, but led him inexorably back to the forest and the barbarians. Amid such pulls and strains, a young man needed the steady, friendly hand of an elder. It was fortunate that George had Lawrence, unfortunate indeed that Lawrence was dying.

CHAPTER 2

The Adjutant

"I Was Commissioned and Appointed by the Honorable Robert Dinwiddie, Esqr., Governor etc. of Virginia."

October 31, 1753

In the fall of 1750, George Washington had several reasons to be pleased with himself. At the age of 18, he had strengthened his association with the formidable Lord Fairfax, he was busy at his new trade, and he had saved a little money. With it, he fulfilled a primary ambition—to become a landowner in his own right. In October he bought two tracts along Bullskin Creek in the lower Shenandoah Valley, not far north of the holdings of Lord Fairfax, and in November added a third parcel for a total of 1,459 acres. But the lengthening shadow of Lawrence's illness darkened everything in George's life. The symptoms that had caused Lawrence irritation and then concern in 1749 became worrisome in 1750; he spent nearly a month at the warm springs of Berkeley, Virginia, in the hope that they would ease his cough. But neither then, nor during a return trip in March of 1751, did they have any effect on his decline, and now there was fear that another winter at Mount Vernon might be more than Lawrence could bear. He would go to Barbados.

George accompanied Lawrence on all these expeditions, without question or complaint setting aside his business affairs and fulfilling the role of eldest son. Lawrence had no sons. His wife had given birth four times over the years, each time to a daughter. Three had died within a few months, but the fourth, born in November of 1750, was still clinging to life a year later. But her health, and that of her mother, was too fragile for travel, and Lawrence would have had to make his somber quest alone had it not been for George. They set sail while September was still kind, and on November 3, 1751, landed in their tropical island paradise.

Their sojourn soon turned hellish. Lawrence got no better, despite the cheerfully ignorant assurances of an island doctor, and moreover he hated the unaccustomed idleness, the separation from his family and friends; hated the heat and the stagnancy of the strange, endless summer. "No place can please me without a change of seasons," he wrote William Fairfax. "We soon tire of the same prospect." George, for all his good intentions, was little help, because he was stricken with smallpox two weeks after their arrival and was soon in worse shape than Lawrence. By the time George recovered, after a month of suffering, Lawrence had decided to go to Bermuda, where at least the seasons changed. If that did not have a salutary effect—and hope was becoming more difficult to maintain—then he would return home to face the end. But the rest of his journey he would have to make alone. George had a future, and must return to it. On December 21 he sailed for Virginia.

George came ashore a changed young man. He had stepped far outside the life he had been making, and seemed to see it now with new eyes. Clearly he was about to lose another of his life's anchorages. The shelter of Lawrence's presence, house, and fortune, which had made possible the dabbling with a career, the round of parties and visits and flirtations, would soon be gone. George was about to mark his twentieth birthday, and suddenly the choices he faced were no longer idle speculations or diverting experiments, but of urgent importance. George Washington was abruptly immersed in a process that would never touch George Fairfax—he was growing up. Life had turned serious.

He had just spent a month at sea with an admired older brother whose greatest adventure, a dozen years before, had been to sail as a commissioned officer of the king in an expedition against Spain. It had been a comic-opera little war between England and Spain for the trade and colonies of the Caribbean, triggered when an English ship's captain named Robert Jenkins displayed to the House of Commons the ear he said had been sliced from his head by a Spanish coastal guard off South America. Retribution for the loss of Jenkins's ear, soon a *cause célèbre* throughout the English world, had been assigned to Admiral Edward Vernon, who for the next two years sailed around the Caribbean looking for Spaniards to punish. In 1741, with a force raised in the American colonies, he had set out to attack the Spanish trading center of Cartagena, on the Colombian coast not far from the isthmus of Panama. Lawrence Washington had been appointed captain of one of the four regiments of Virginia troops. It had not been much of an expedition—Admiral Vernon failed to take Cartagena, and Captain Washington did not even leave the ship—but it had been the ultimate adventure of Lawrence's life. He had named his estate Mount Vernon, and had used his brief military experience as grounds to seek, and eventually attain, the office of adjutant of the Virginia militia. Whatever thoughts and conversation had been stimulated by Lawrence's return to the Caribbean, whatever new perspective George gained on the familiar adventure story, military matters suddenly became prominent in his thinking. While on Barbados he had visited the island's armed forces and fortifications, and afterward wrote at length about their design and quality. Such considerations had not appeared previously in his journals, despite the ever-present threat of hostilities and conflict in the lands he had been surveying and buying.

He had become more thoughtful about other things as well. He analyzed the highly profitable economics of sugar cane, molasses, and rum, marveling that people with such advantages in trade should ever go in debt, which was common, or should tolerate interest rates of 8 percent, which he branded a "cancer." He noted that there was a great gulf between the wealthy planters and their poverty-stricken tenants; there were nowhere to be found any of those "who may be called middling people." Whether these reflections led him to look anew at the economic and social conditions of his Tidewater home—where there were similar gulfs between rich and poor, and a similar scarcity of "middling people"—he did not record. But it was a significant conceptual advance for a young man who until now had seen among those who were beneath his privileged station only "comical antics" and "barbarians." Now there were such things as "middling people." But it was his thinking about the military that took hold and stimulated action. On his return from Barbados he stopped off in Williamsburg to visit the new lieutenant governor of Virginia, Robert Dinwiddie. (Typically, appointment as governor of a colony was an honor bestowed on a personage who was not required to know where his colony was; residence and actual governance were the job of the lieutenant governor, whom the colonials addressed as "governor.") No doubt Washington's errand on this occasion was to deliver letters from such Barbados personages as Gedney Clarke, the Washingtons' host on the island, a relative by marriage of the Fairfaxes and a longtime associate and friend of Dinwiddie. Whatever the specific errand, it afforded a chance to spend some time with the new governor, to deliver news of influential friends, to establish a relationship with the supreme power in the colony—not as Lawrence's brother or Lord Fairfax's young friend, but as and for himself.

It would not be sufficient now for Washington simply to redouble his efforts as a surveyor and buy more land, although he did both in the spring of 1752. He needed more than that. Two things especially he craved: esteem and security. He had a good reputation, but it was clearly going to be a long road indeed, buying a piece of frontier land here and a patch there, to the heavyweight wealth that would bring the kind of deference afforded the Fairfaxes. All roads ahead look long to a twenty-year-old, but that one really was.

He did not feel at home at Ferry Farm, and now it looked as though he would not long be able to feel at home at Mount Vernon. His raw Shenandoah Valley land was an investment, not a place to live, and in any case he had no inclination to share Lord Fairfax's exile from society.

In his need for a home, and for someone who would not leave him, he reached out to Betsy Fauntleroy, whose father's plantation sprawled along the Rappahannock not far from Washington's homeplace near Fredericksburg. She was sixteen, and she had brown hair and eyes and a father solidly established in the first rank of the colony's planters. He asked her to marry him. But Betsy and her father could count, and evaluate real estate, and she rejected Washington's proposal in favor of one from another planter's son with a firmer grip on his legacy. By those lights, she made the right choice; Betsy Fauntleroy died rich.

Thus Washington faced his impending grief alone, with few resources and little support. Such situations strip away pretensions and reveal the bedrock of character. Washington's soon-to-be-familiar reaction to crisis was to review the situation until he spotted an opportunity, and then to attack in an unexpected direction.

In the spring of 1752, quite suddenly, he launched an ardent campaign to get an appointment from Dinwiddie as one of the adjutants of the Virginia militia. Lawrence had been the colony's adjutant for years, but would not be able to resume his duties anytime soon, if ever. (The letters from Bermuda were increasingly pessimistic: "If I grow worse, I shall hurry home to my grave; if better, I shall be induced to stay here longer to complete a cure.") Dinwiddie had a plan, of which he made no secret, that when the adjutancy should become vacant he would divide its duties among at least three men.

George was determined to be one of those three. He wished, of course, to have responsibility for his home neighborhood, the Northern Neck, which undoubtedly would be one of the districts. But he either concluded from his own assessment, or was told by Dinwiddie on making a personal appeal, that another man had an almost unassailable claim to the office. He was William Fitzhugh, whose military and social credentials, as a veteran of the Cartagena expedition and a well-connected planter, were impeccable. In January, however, the widower Fitzhugh had married a lady with even larger landholdings than his, in Calvert County, Maryland, and had moved there. Fitzhugh expressed interest in being the absentee adjutant of the Northern Neck militia, but readily admitted that his residence in Maryland might not be acceptable. Washington lunged for the apparent opening.

On June 10, apparently not pausing to review his syntax, Washington dispatched a fervent letter to Dinwiddie: "If I could have the honor of obtaining that [adjutancy] in case Colonel Fitzhugh does not, or either of the other two; should take the greatest pleasure in punctually obeying from time to time your Honor's commands, and by a strict observance of duty, render myself worthy of your trust reposed in me; I am sensible my best endeavors will not be wanting, and doubt not, but a constant application to fit myself for the office, could I presume your honor had not in view a more deserving person." The thrust of this muddled appeal was that if appointed to the job, Washington promised to learn how to do it.

A few days later, Lawrence returned to Mount Vernon, but there was no joy in the reunion with his family. Quite the contrary; hope was gone, and Lawrence was intent on hurrying to his grave. He did what he could to put his various business and family affairs in order, wrote out a long and complicated will, and on July 26, he died. As expected, George had lost both his brother and his second home. (According to Lawrence's will, his wife Ann was to have Mount Vernon for her lifetime, after which it would pass to their daughter Sarah. If both should die without descendants, then the property was to go to George, with the proviso that if he died without descendants, the estate would pass on to his brother Augustine. Thus, even if George eventually inherited the property, until and unless he had children, he would be a tenant, never the owner.)

As one of the executors of Lawrence's estate, George was surprised to find that the anchor on which he had relied had not been as sturdy as he had thought. He found his half-brother's affairs to be in a state of "utmost confusion." There were many debts, poorly recorded. The young man who had not yet faced financial difficulty, who kept his small affairs carefully recorded and balanced in his account books, who had pursed his lips at the idea of Barbados planters going into debt, was shocked. It would take more than three years to sort everything out.

The matter of the adjutancy, however, had to be dealt with at the next session of the Governor's Council.

In the century and a half of their existence, the colonies of British America had seldom enjoyed the protection or assistance of His Majesty's armed forces. Instead, the tradition had arisen that when there was real trouble, usually from marauding savages, the men of the afflicted community would band together and take care of it under the command of their most prominent citizen, whom they acknowledged as their colonel (but designated, with cheerful British disregard for consistency, their county lieutenant). As civilization had moved westward, so had the troubles, and with tranquility in the East had come complacency. Muskets that once had been kept oiled and ready began to collect cobwebs and rust on their pegs over the fireplace. The periodic gatherings once dictated by fear and necessity became inconveniences. In the absence of an external threat, willingness to submit to discipline evaporated. Military skills—in marching, camping, logistics, deploying for a fight—atrophied.

The colonial government resisted this relaxation. The assembly passed ordinances requiring able-bodied men to keep their muskets oiled and at least some powder and ball handy. County lieutenants were appointed from Williamsburg and supervised by an adjutant to make sure they called the men of the county together now and again to remind them how to hit a target with a musket ball and get from a marching column into a line of battle. Attendance at these musters was made mandatory. But as the years passed with fewer and fewer incidents in the settled parts of the colonies, the militias there were permitted a genteel disintegration. The colonel of militia was still one of the most honored men of the county. The ordinances were obeyed, but the gatherings became less and less military, more and more social.

Governor Dinwiddie, aware of the increasing likelihood of conflict in the West, was concerned about the rustiness of the militia. That was why he had resolved to name more adjutants, better motivated to fulfill their duties "in instructing the officers and soldiers in the use and exercise of their arms," as he put it, "in bringing the militia to a more regular discipline, and fitting it for service, besides polishing and improving the meaner people." In the event, he created four districts, not three, and named the new adjutants. George Muse, who had acted as Lawrence's assistant adjutant and had accompanied the Cartagena expedition, got the Middle Neck, the country lying between the Rappahannock and York Rivers. Thomas Bentley was named for the western frontier. The Northern Neck, as Washington had feared, went to the expatriate William Fitzhugh. But the backwater Southern District, along the fringe of the colony south of the James River, was to have as its adjutant George Washington, who lived farther from his district than Fitzhugh was removed from the Northern Neck.

It was far from a complete victory, but was a win nonetheless.

On his own, Washington had made and used an association with the governor; had maneuvered carefully among a number of influential people; had made and pressed his case; and had won an appointment. Less than a year after setting his sights on a military career, while possessing neither knowledge nor experience, he had been commissioned a major of militia with responsibility for a large section of Virginia and a salary of £100 per year. It was a good beginning, made without Lawrence and without obvious help from the Fairfaxes. It was only a beginning, however; it was not exactly what he wanted, and it most certainly was not all he wanted.

A traditional source of security and prestige for a well-bred British subject who was not an eldest son was a king's commission as a military officer. Aside from the honor, such a commission conveyed something else very much on Washington's mind—security. An officer who was disabled, retired, or whose unit was disbanded received half pay for life. These commissions could be obtained by military merit, but usually were bought, for more cash than Washington was likely to have available in his lifetime. The going rate for the rank of captain was £1,200 sterling, for that of major, £2,000.

There was another, less orthodox route to the prize. In times of emergency, when the Crown found itself short of military forces, it sometimes dispensed commissions to colonial officers of outstanding merit. It was an expensive practice, and was resorted to only reluctantly—colonial soldiers were held in universal contempt by British officers, for lack of professionalism or lack of breeding, or both. But commissioning them was deemed necessary in certain cases, such as the expedition to Cartagena in 1741; Lawrence Washington and his fellow officers had received king's commissions, and after their brief sojourn had been pensioned for the rest of their lives. The example could not have escaped George's attention.

The rank of major in a moribund colonial militia was not much of a prize, especially when it involved service far from home, in strange counties, at great inconvenience and loss of income. But it could be a threshold to far greater things if one made the most of it. This George Washington was determined to do. The governor directed that a general muster of the militia be held in September 1753. Washington took the oath of office and donned his uniform in February and, after celebrating his twenty-first birthday, went to work. His task was to make sure that the county lieutenants were prepared to drill their companies. This implied, of course, that the adjutant knew what the colonels were supposed to know, and presumably Washington spent a time in intense study of military tactics. Presumably he also visited the lieutenants of the counties under his supervision, or imitated other adjutants and paid someone else to do so. If he did either, this habitual keeper of accounts and writer of journals wrote not a word about it. He left no record of his activities between February and October of 1753.

If during this time Washington gave any thought to what the militia was likely to be called on to do, if he looked up from the concerns of a novice adjutant, surveyor, socialite, and land speculator to survey the political skies of his world, he saw them darkening fast.

England and France, after five years of uneasy truce, were increasingly anxious to return to their interminable war. They had not yet finally determined who would dominate the tangled Old World, with its fractious nationalities and religions constantly at war in the name of some addled monarch or wrathful god. Nor was it clear who would rule the world's vast seas, the better to grasp the refined wealth of the ancient East, the rougher riches of the American and African continents, and whatever else might come to hand beyond. Spain had been for two centuries a contender for all these prizes, but had weakened. It was obvious now to white Europeans that the world would be inherited either by French Catholics or English Protestants.

Nowhere was their confrontation more direct, or for higher stakes, than in America, where the thin ribbon of English settlement along the Atlantic coast was bracketed north and south by the French colonies of Quebec and Louisiana. Westward lay a vast uncharted repository of inestimable wealth in furs and land, waiting for the strong to claim it. While the French enclaves were stretching tentacles toward each other along the Ohio and Mississippi River systems, the English corridor was beginning to bulge westward, especially from the colonies of Pennsylvania and Virginia, toward and over the Alleghenies into the Ohio River country beyond. The French interest was in the fur trade, but the English were fascinated by a commodity that offered far greater and quicker profits to the dealer—land.

Such large themes and grand prizes were hardly the stuff of everyday life and thought in British America. The rich, established planters were inclined to avoid or ignore change as a threat to their fortunes. The great majority of the colonists were poor, and spent their waking hours in toil, preoccupied by survival, hoping to scrape together enough of the necessities of life to sustain them in their old age, which came fast and had no pity. Thus most people left geopolitics to His Most Christian Majesty, Louis XV of France, the equally Christian Protector of the Faith, George II of England, and their respective officers, agents, and courtiers.

But personal ambition was another matter. Although it was the constant preoccupation of the royalties, monopolies, aristocracies, and oligarchies to seal off the strata of society and require all people to be content with who they were and what they had, the overlords could never quite stamp out the mysterious and improbable idea that ordinary people should be able to improve their situations. The notion was always bubbling up here and there, percolating through the supposedly impermeable strata of society.

Ambition combed the populations of eighteenth-century Europe, removing the burrs and the wild hairs, the dreamers and the rebels, with a strong east-to-west stroke that settled the rest back into their places in the structures of inertia. It drew the strongest (or most desperate) to the American colonies. Soon, when the firstcomers had replicated the aristocracies and monopolies they had fled, one could no longer move upward from poverty except against the massive resistance of entrenched superiors. Then ambition drew dissatisfied underlings away to the western frontier, where, among strangers, a good year of fur trading or a good claim of some river-bottom land could make a man as aristocratic as any.

Of course, it was not the case that the governments of Britain and France were interested in the American West because they wanted to provide their least privileged and most unruly citizens with a better life. To the contrary, the official interest was in adding to the fortunes of already wealthy merchants through expanded trade, and to the coffers of the kings through new opportunities for taxation. Whatever their motivation, in the year 1753 a number of unruly individuals and two kings had focussed their attention on the American heartland.

In February, in the same week Washington was sworn in as district adjutant, the French launched a major expedition toward the Ohio country. The first objective was to build a fort at Presque Isle, a spot on the shore of Lake Erie where a hooked finger of a peninsula formed a sheltered harbor. This was accomplished before the winter was over, and spring saw the men hard at work on the next phase: smoothing a path for the fifteen-mile portage necessary to reach French Creek, part of the Ohio watershed. From there the plan was to extend French control, in the form of a series of forts connected by a secure line of communications, into and through the Ohio country.

By June, word had reached Williamsburg—and had been fretfully relayed by Governor Dinwiddie to the other colonies and to London—that a French force of eight hundred men was moving south toward the Ohio. Before long they completed their second fort at the terminus of the French Creek portage, in westernmost Pennsylvania about thirty-five miles above that stream's confluence with the Allegheny River. They called their redoubt Fort le Boeuf, or Fort Buffalo.

Of all the colonial governors, only Dinwiddie seems to have been exercised by these considerable encroachments. The governors of New York and the rest of New England expressed little interest in his feverish dispatches—their western boundaries were already established. Maryland, too, had no room for westward expansion. Pennsylvania's charter held its boundary to within three hundred miles of the Delaware River; it stood on the threshold of the Ohio country, would in fact lay claim to the forks of the Ohio, but could go no further. Its traders developed a major interest in the wealth to be had there, but its Quaker-dominated colonial government would not countenance any course leading toward possible hostilities. The Carolinas were too far from the action to be much concerned. Only the Virginians who had ambitious plans for the Ohio country were aroused by the implications of the French movements.

But Dinwiddie did get a reaction when he complained in June to his superiors in London: "I hope you will think it necessary to prevent the French taking possession of the lands on the Ohio." His answer arrived four months and a few days later, on October 21—an immediate response, given the mechanics of trans-Atlantic communication in 1753—when a sloop of war sailed into Yorktown with specific instructions, from King George himself, to counter the French threat. It soon became widely known in and around Williamsburg that the first step would be to deliver to the French expedition a stern warning, while the colony prepared to back the warning with military action if necessary. Dinwiddie summoned his council to meet on October 27, and the House of Burgesses to convene on November 1.

On October 26, George Washington rode into Williamsburg, nostrils flaring to the scent of opportunity. It was common knowledge that an emissary to the French would be required. Surely an administrative officer of the militia, a district adjutant, would be an appropriate nominee. And of the adjutants available, Washington must have reasoned, surely the one who was youngest and most vigorous, who had some experience in the western wilderness, and who was eager to go, would be the obvious choice.

In fact, the obvious choice for the job was Captain William Trent. Trent had become Dinwiddie's favorite emissary to the denizens of the far country, even though he was a Pennsylvanian with close ties to the likes of Thomas Penn and Benjamin Franklin. For eight years he had been a partner of one of Pennsylvania's two foremost fur traders, George Croghan, and on occasion had traveled with the other, Conrad Weiser. But as a contemporary observed, "ambition seized him violently" from time to time, as when, in 1746, Trent deserted his partner Croghan to become "a man of figure in the conquest and settlement of Canada." When that did not work out, he threw in with Croghan again, only to desert him again in 1752 to take up the cause of Virginia in the Ohio country.

If Trent had made his move in order to become in Virginia what Conrad Weiser was to Pennsylvania or William Johnson to New York—the preeminent trader to whom the government looked for guidance in its diplomatic and financial dealings with the tribes—he was soon well on his way. In June of 1752, he went to the Iroquois administrative center of Logstown on the Ohio River (twenty miles downstream, or northwest, from the confluence of the Allegheny and Monongahela Rivers) as a Virginia commissioner to take part in a major conference. When it developed that the Twightwee people on the Miami River were being besieged by the French and needed reassurance of English friendship, Trent was sent on the long journey to comfort this major tribe.

By 1753, Trent had demonstrated proficiency in speaking on some occasions for his colony (Governor Dinwiddie had named him unofficial representative of Virginia in the Ohio country), on others for his company (he had been appointed a factor for the Ohio Company), and, with the advent of the French, on still others for the British Crown. It was not always possible to know which voice he was using at any particular time. In the summer of 1753, Trent had played all his roles effectively. He had returned to Logstown, where he learned that the French were moving south in force toward the Allegheny and the Ohio. After dispatching a complete report, Trent had succeeded where others had failed in persuading the Ohio tribes to attend a conference in Winchester in September to discuss the tangled question of England's (or more accurately, in this case, Virginia's) rights in the Ohio country.

Thus for more than a year Governor Dinwiddie had been relying on Trent as his chief emissary to the western tribes. "As you are thoroughly acquainted in the woods I must refer this affair to you," Dinwiddie said in one letter of instruction. "You know how to frame a speech to the Indians in their style, better than I can." Obviously, then, Trent would be Dinwiddie's first choice for conducting any mission involving the Ohio country. But in fact there were two such projects that required expediting in the fall of 1753. One was patriotic—the embassy to the French. The other was commercial—the construction of a trading post and fort at the forks of the Ohio.

It was becoming clear to all involved that this location was the key to the intensifying struggle between the French and the English in America. It was the place where the Allegheny River, running southwest from the vicinity of Lake Erie in French Canada, met the Monongahela River flowing northwest from Virginia. From their confluence the Ohio curved northwest, then recurved to the southwest, visiting the principal trading towns of the Ohio Iroquois, the Delawares, and the Shawnees as it flowed toward the Mississippi River. The rivers were the roads—for French and English fur traders transporting the wealth of the backcountry, for war parties seeking or fleeing their enemies, for hunters and explorers and fugitives—and in the great northwestern territories, all roads met at the forks of the Ohio. George Croghan had begun trading near the forks in 1741, and ever since had been trying in vain to get Pennsylvania to build a fort there. The Delawares and the Iroquois living there had not only given their permission, but with the menacing approach of the French had urged that the fort be built. But Pennsylvania's pacifist Quakers would spend not a penny for a military installation, and despite the competitive opportunity thus offered, the Burgesses of Virginia had been equally reluctant to bear the expense of such a far-flung enterprise.

The Ohio Company, on the other hand, had seen the potential for profit in the place. A high-volume fur trade centered on the forks was the first phase of the Company's plan for the maximum exploitation of its land grant. In 1751 the Company had ordered a road laid out to the forks, and the next year had begun clearing it. It was essential to the Company's future to occupy and hold the forks.

Robert Dinwiddie had been a shareholder in the Ohio Company before he was named governor of Virginia. The task of establishing the company's post at the forks would go to his best man—William Trent, who had already looked over the ground where it was to be built. The diplomatic mission to the French forces could be handled by someone else.

That someone presented himself to the governor as an enthusiastic volunteer on October 26. Dinwiddie heard young Washington out, and the next day met with his council, revealing to them the details of the blunt instructions from their sovereign: "If you shall find that any number of persons, whether Indians or Europeans, shall presume to erect any fort or forts within the limits of our province of Virginia, you are to require of them peaceably to depart, and not to persist in such unlawful proceedings. And if, notwithstanding your admonitions, they do still endeavor to carry on any such unlawful and unjustifiable designs, we do hereby strictly charge and command you to drive them off with force of arms."

This was a ringing call to arms and, for Robert Dinwiddie and George Washington, to opportunity. It mattered little that the "limits of our province of Virginia" were unknown; that whether the French moves thus far had been "unlawful" was open to legitimate debate; or that the French designs were certainly no less justifiable than, for instance, those of the Ohio Company. What mattered to

Dinwiddie, it seems, was that here was a chance to advance not only the cause of the British Empire but the borders of Virginia; this operation would be conducted by Virginia authority far to the north of the colony's obvious sphere of influence, and could serve to outflank Pennsylvania's westward extension. It would plant the shield of the Crown between the Ohio Company and the French. And it would place Virginia, hence Dinwiddie, at the center of tense and fateful negotiations between the world's two primary powers. The possibilities were infinite.

Similarly, Washington could not have failed to grasp the portent of the emerging conflict or the opportunities they presented him in his recently adopted career. If he could succeed in placing himself at Dinwiddie's side in the forefront of these rapidly evolving events, his route to the rank and acclaim he coveted would surely be shortened. It is not necessary to assume that either Washington or Dinwiddie was driven only, or even primarily, by personal ambition. In their public statements and writings, and doubtless in their own minds, they were loyal patriots of the British Crown reacting to unbearable provocation by a traditional enemy.

According to the minutes of the October 27 council meeting, "the Governor acquainted the Board that George Washington Esqr., Adjutant General for the Southern District, had offered himself to go properly commissioned to the commandant of the French forces, to learn by what authority he presumes to make encroachments on His Majesty's lands in the Ohio." The offer was accepted and the appointment made. A committee of the council drafted a letter to the French commander and a letter of instructions to Washington for Dinwiddie's signature.

On Wednesday morning, October 31, Washington began his journey.

PART II

Ignorance

CHAPTER 3

The Traders

"I Engaged Mr. Gist to Pilot Us Out, and Also Hired Four Others as Servitors."

NOVEMBER 14, 1753

The two-week journey from Williamsburg through Fredericksburg (where he engaged Jacob van Braam) and Winchester to Wills Creek was for most of the way familiar to George Washington. On cresting the Blue Ridge Mountains, he saw to the west a succession of forested mountain ridges interspersed with rivers and creeks flowing northeastward to join the main stem of the Potomac, the major tributaries occurring at approximately ten-mile intervals. There was the Cacapon River, then the South Branch of the Potomac, Patterson Creek, and finally the North Branch of the Potomac. Beyond the North Branch one crossed a continental divide, the east front of the Allegheny Mountains, and found thereafter that the rivers ran northwestward toward the Ohio rather than northeastward toward the Potomac. Where the North Branch made its bend southward to become the main stem of the Potomac, it was joined by a stream coming in from the north called Wills Creek.

There, on a knoll beside the confluence, overlooking a narrow valley and a dramatic riven gap in the mountains to the west, was a much-used trading camp. It was just thirty miles west of Berkeley, whose warm springs Washington had visited often with his ailing brother a few years before, but when he arrived there on November 14, 1753, he was in unknown territory, among alien people. He was also among people, and in a place, that would play pivotal roles in his life for the next five years.

The men he found settling in for the winter at Wills Creek were westering men, and Washington probably had not seen their like before. That they had little in common with Eastern plantation society goes without saying, but they were also far different from the Valley pioneers whose patches of ground the young surveyor had staked out and whose rustic, foreign habits he had ridiculed. This time he recorded no comments about comical antics, although the appearance of these Englishmen must have shocked him. They were bearlike, shaggy men, steeped in wood smoke and sweat, whose familiarity with loneliness and danger had put an unbridgeable distance between them and ordinary mortals.

As in any time and culture, that distance was signified by unorthodox clothing. While their basic dress of shirt and trousers (or shirt with breeches and hose) was not unlike that of an Eastern farmer or laborer, the finishing touches represented a triumph of Western pragmatism over Eastern fashion. The most striking was the hunting shirt, a garment adapted from the natives. Usually made of coarse linen—buckskin was terribly uncomfortable when wet—this capacious overshirt hung almost to the knees, and was simply folded over for an approximate fit at the midsection. The shoulders were caped with an extra layer of fabric to help deflect rain, and the edges of the cape were fringed to draw off water and promote faster drying. The belt, always fastened behind, carried most of the items long experience had shown to be essential for survival—knife, tomahawk, mittens in winter, perhaps the bullet bag. Such things as chunks of bread, strings of jerked meat, and cloth for cleaning the musket were thrust inside the fold of the hunting shirt above the belt. With a powder horn and a possibles bag (containing the paraphernalia required to reload and maintain the musket) slung over the shoulder, a mountain man was always ready to travel.

These were the outriders and skirmishers of the implacable English advance into the heartland. Their primary occupation was fur trading, which involved ranging the wilderness with pack trains and flotillas laden with such things as knives, pots, muskets, and trinkets, which they exchanged for pelts collected by native hunters. Among their contemporaries and historians to come, these mountain men enjoyed a romantic image as long-hunters, free rangers of the farthest wilderness, canny fur traders and diplomats. Their casual courage while confronting (with only their wits and their Pennsylvania rifles to call on for help) the darkest nightmares of the age—trackless wilderness, savage tribes, and raging animals—would stir the souls of men for generations to come.

As they were forced to probe farther and farther afield to satisfy Europe's insatiable demand for beaver hats, they scouted the country, made the first estimates of its wealth, met the inhabitants, and reported what they learned to the colonial authorities. Thus when governors or gentlemen of commerce needed to make an arrangement with the natives—as they frequently did now that land was replacing fur as the commodity of choice—they hired a trader as agent; those in New York sought out William Johnson, while Pennsylvanians went to Conrad Weiser or George Croghan, just as Dinwiddie had been relying on William Trent and Christopher Gist. The presumption was that the traders' long experience with the tribes had made them familiar with native languages, culture, and mentality. As a close look at Christopher Gist demonstrates, that presumption was usually wrong.

Washington and Gist were to be comrades for five adventurous years, during which they would face mortal danger together more than once, and during which Washington would turn to Gist more than any other individual for advice about dealing with the tribes. The story is inherently interesting, but all the more so when one considers what Washington did not learn from Gist, and the friendship that did not flourish between them.

Christopher Gist was more than twice Washington's age, having been born forty-five years or so before their 1753 meeting. Dark of hair and complexion, Gist, like Washington, stood half a head above his contemporaries at about six feet two inches, and weighed a solid two hundred pounds. Washington hired Gist to be his "pilot" for the farther journey, and engaged four more traders encountered at

Wills Creek to be what he called "servitors." Apparently he saw them as just another lot of barbarians who must be made to do their duty.

In fact, as Washington would soon learn, Gist had enjoyed a better education, a wealthier family background, and higher social status in the East than had any Washington. The Gist family had figured prominently in the history and commerce of Baltimore. Gist's father, Richard, was one of the commissioners who originally surveyed the town, and the family had accumulated a major fortune in the business of wholesaling furs. Disaster, in the form of a major warehouse fire, had struck not once, but twice. After the second fire in 1732, the younger Gist, hounded by agents of the British Fur Company for a king's ransom of £10,000 sterling in repayment for the destroyed pelts, had moved to the Yadkin River in northwest North Carolina. He had lived and traded there until moving to Wills Creek in 1750, and since then had been ranging the far country (to be known one day as Ohio, Kentucky, and Tennessee). But it was not wanderlust that had taken him there, nor did he evidence any of the romantic traits later attributed to mountain men, such as love of the wilderness or admiration for the natives or dislike for the ways of society. And he most certainly had no intention of spending the rest of his days ambling through the woods. He had come north from Carolina to become the principal explorer, surveyor, and agent of the Ohio Company. He was working for the richest and most powerful men in Virginia, and he was intent on becoming one of them.

Far from being some simple backwoodsman, Gist was a remarkable synthesis of America's Eastern and Western societies, undoubtedly the first and one of the very few such that Washington would meet. Gist could (and did) don the silks and ruffles of an Eastern planter and take his ease among glittering company in the drawing room of a Philadelphia merchant or Tidewater baron. On the other hand, he could slip on his hunting shirt and stride without the slightest hesitation into any camp of red or white savages in the Great Northwest, for he was known on the frontier as a man who would travel farther, bear more hardships, work harder, and if necessary fight nastier than any normal man. If Washington found this complex personality at all interesting or unexpected, he did not record a word of reaction.

Washington may have thought he "hired" Gist as a "pilot," but it was neither the young major's uniform, money, mission, nor imperious manner that induced this veteran ranger to join the expedition. It was, as Gist recorded in the first sentence of his journal of the expedition, "a letter from the council in Virginia"—the governor's executive council, of whom many were shareholders in the Ohio Company. It was the Company and its goals that commanded Christopher Gist's loyalties and ambitions.

The Company was intent on establishing a business relationship with the native populations of the Ohio country. What the investors had in mind was not the customary haphazard trade conducted by footloose wanderers, but an organized enterprise with established commercial centers and a network of roads. The roads were essential. No river network linked the settled areas of Virginia with that vast area. Instead, river after river crossed the path of the Ohio-bound, offering dangerous barriers in spring, fall, and other times of high water. The thickly forested slopes of the intervening mountains denied passage to all but single files of people, on horses or on foot. Trading on the scale envisioned by the Ohio Company would require a constant shuttling of wagon trains between the forks of the Ohio and the port of Alexandria, and that would require the clearing and bridging of about two hundred miles of roadway. The first half of that distance, from Alexandria to Wills Creek, was passable; the second half was a considerable challenge.

A road had been hacked out from the first Company center, at Wills Creek, to the second—where Redstone Creek met the Monongahela some sixty-five miles to the northwest—and toward the site of the third and most important, at the forks of the Ohio thirty miles beyond Redstone. Gist was staying as close as he could to all this activity; he had built a new home, which he insisted on calling his plantation, not far from the Redstone store, on a tributary of the same creek, and was about to move there permanently. Washington had found him at his old Wills Creek cabin only by chance.

There were fortunes to be made in establishing and developing this trading network, yet in the Company's design it was only the first phase. The trading posts would become forts, then towns, then centers of settlement whose first citizens would enjoy incomes of a size and permanence beyond imagining. In his journals, Christopher Gist rhapsodized about what he had seen in the far country, but it was not its beauty that moved him most. "This place," he wrote of one stretch, "is fine, rich level land, well timbered with large walnut, ash, sugar trees, cherry trees, etc. It is well watered with a great number of little streams or rivulets, and full of beautiful natural meadows covered with wild rye, blue grass and clover; and abounds with turkeys, deer, elk and most sorts of game particularly buffaloes, 30 or 40 of which are frequently seen feeding in one meadow." Such splendor might have moved another man, but Gist found it lacking a crucial element: "In short it wants nothing but cultivation to make it a most delightful country."

That image of a future cultivated, delightful country that Gist carried in his mind did not include any vestige of the people already living there. He was little interested in the Shawnee, Delaware, Iroquois, and Miami families he encountered, except as a problem requiring a final solution. On his first, rambling circuit of the far country beginning in September of 1750, he had visited the principal villages and many of the leading figures of the country's inhabitants. He had been to the western Iroquois center of Logstown (where, he noted, "I found scarce anybody but a parcel of reprobate Indian traders, the chiefs of the Indians being out a hunting"); to Shanopin's Town some ten miles downriver, or northwest, where he met the foremost Delawares, Tamaqui (known to the English as King Beaver) and his brother Shingas; to Muskingum, where lived the Wyandots, who had split with their fellow Hurons and ended their alliance with the French; to the Shawnee town far down the Ohio near its confluence with the Great Kanawha, where he completely misread the attitude of that tribe and reported them to be "great friends of the English"; and to the far western town of Pickawillany, home of the Twightwees, foremost of the four tribes known collectively as the Miamis. (On his return to his South Carolina home, Gist's accounts of his travels deeply interested one of his son's playmates, a neighbor lad named Daniel Boone.)

Yet during all this time, in all these places, Gist learned remarkably little about the native people with whom he was dealing. He learned almost nothing about their languages, their societies, their beliefs, or their ways. His description of what he called the "antics" of the Wyandots while performing their sacred Feather Dance was just a shade more respectful than Washington's account of native ceremony.

Gist never learned that the most important organizations within the tribes he was visiting were the clans, family groups denoted by bird or animal symbols. On inspecting a deserted camp he once came across, and seeing the image of the foremost clan of the Miami tribes, Gist completely missed its significance. "Their captain's name or title was the Crane," he opined in his journal, "as I knew by his picture or arms painted on a tree."

Gist carried with him a secret assignment from Thomas Lee, the president of Virginia's executive council, to try to win from the western Iroquois tribes expressions of loyalty being withheld by the Great Council at Onandaga. But Gist never seemed to get beyond counting the tribes' fighting men and appraising their land, although he did quickly learn to be circumspect about surveying. "It was dangerous," he noted, "to let a compass be seen among these Indians." They called a compass a "land stealer." He knew the Delawares were in some kind of a relationship with the Iroquois League, but did not inquire into the matter. "They are not properly a part of the Six Nations," he wrote dismissively, "but are scattered about." It was as though he did not want to make the effort to learn about people who were not going to be part of his future.

Confronted by intriguing events, Gist noted them and let them go by. In December of 1750, he was in the Wyandot village of Muskingum, where George Croghan had a trading post and had called a conference of all the English traders in the area to discuss the increasing danger posed by the French and their allied tribes. Gist decided to read aloud from the Bible on Christmas Day, as a service to his fellow Englishmen already gathered there and perhaps as an inspiration to their heathen hosts. The idea caused a good deal of dissension among the whites, who were concerned about whose denomination of Christianity might be favored by Gist's reading of the Scripture, and many of them stayed away for fear of being defiled by an erroneous emphasis. Croghan's interpreter, Andrew Montour, who served Gist in the same capacity, invited "several of the well disposed Indians," who came readily to listen.

And they were apparently moved by the Holy Gospel. They thanked Gist for bringing them the Word; they invited him to live among them and instruct them in the principles of Christianity; they gave him a name in their language; they asked him to conduct marriage ceremonies for their couples and baptize their children; they professed their loyalty to God and England; and one individual assured Gist that "he and his family always observed the Sabbath Day." It was, of course, meaningless talk, simply their way of making an English missionary, which they took Gist to be, feel welcome in their town. They were not lying, they were observing their etiquette, and they succeeded; Gist's lengthy account of these proceedings in his journal fairly glowed with satisfaction. But to the contradictory events of the next day he gave short and sullen shrift.

A troublesome female captive of the Wyandots, who had recently escaped and been recaptured, was taken the next morning to the outskirts of the village for a little sport. She was released, and when she began to run in terror some braves gleefully chased her around for a while, then caught her, clubbed her to the ground, lanced her through the heart, scalped her and played a game of keep-away with the dripping hank of hair, then hacked off her head. The fun over, the braves moved on to another distraction, leaving the mutilated corpse lying in full view of the village. At nightfall, some of the appalled whites, having gingerly asked permission to do so, crept out and buried the remains. That is all Gist bothered to record about the event. If he saw any contradiction between the unctuousness of Tuesday and the savagery of Wednesday, he did not remark upon it. And if he knew the intriguing details of the executed woman's story, he did not bother to mention them.

Some time before, a Wyandot named Eagle Feather had been hacked to death in his sleep, obviously by one of the two women who lived with him—either his longtime wife, Mary Harris, or a newly acquired captive known only as Newcomer. Both women were white. Mary Harris had been snatched from her New England home at the age of ten, forty years before. Whether the sudden appearance of a younger woman in Mary's household had anything to do with the events that followed cannot be known, but a few mornings later, Eagle Feather was found dead and Newcomer was gone. Newcomer had murdered her husband, wailed Mary Harris, and had fled in the night. A party of braves went out, tracked Newcomer down, and brought her in. The accusation was not true, she protested; Mary Harris had killed her husband in a fit of jealous rage and would have done the same to Newcomer had she not run for her life. It was all too complex to sort out, and Mary Harris had been with them a long time; the Wyandots took Newcomer out and dispatched her.

When he left Muskingum on January 15, Gist passed through the little village where the widow Mary Harris lived—on a stream called, in her honor, White Woman's Creek—and talked with her. "She still remembers they used to be very religious in New England," he recorded, "and wonders how the white men can be so wicked as she has seen them in these woods."

It may be that Gist, who was keeping his journals as a record for his Ohio Company employers, thought it best to keep his more interesting and complex thoughts to himself. He made scant mention, for example, of his relationship with George Croghan, who did not want to see the Ohio Company succeed in the northwest. Where Gist was a Marylander in the employ of Virginia, Croghan was a thoroughgoing Pennsylvanian. He had emigrated from Dublin to Philadelphia in 1741, and had settled five miles west of Harris's Ferry (the future Harrisburg), where he had plunged into the fur trade. A decade later he enjoyed a reputation in his commonwealth second only to that of Conrad Weiser.

For much of the time on this 1750 expedition, Gist and Croghan travelled together, Croghan lending his interpreter to help Gist communicate with the tribes and Gist on one occasion helping Croghan draft an unauthorized treaty between the English and Miami peoples. On his return, Croghan found himself in deep trouble with Governor James Hamilton of Pennsylvania both for exceeding his authority and for consorting with an agent of the Ohio Company. Gist, who wisely did not put his name on the treaty (and whose journal entry for the day it was signed consisted of the words, "Nothing remarkable happened in the town"), seems to have escaped censure.

But Gist's ignorance of the tribes was not just a matter of diffidence or discretion; it was both deliberate and dangerous. During three years of exploring the Ohio country, he had sought to win first the acceptance, then the friendship and loyalty of the tribes for the English trade and cause. He had lost no opportunity to profess, in his own language and ways, undying friendship for the people he intended to help displace. As intelligent as Gist was, he apparently neither wrote nor thought about this schism in his thinking, this profound ethical contradiction. Even when he was forced to respond to it, as he was in a tense situation during his explorations of 1752, he did so dishonestly.

His instructions for this second tour of the Ohio country had been specific: to site a road from Wills Creek to the Monongahela (at the Redstone Creek site); and to "find good land" on the south side of the Ohio River along the vast, 250-mile crescent between the forks and the confluence with the Great Kanawha River, "convenient for our building store houses and other houses for the better carrying on a trade and correspondence down the river." For four months Gist and his son Nathaniel had pored over the country. He told any natives he encountered that he was there merely to invite them to a conference in Logstown, "at the full moon in May next," during which lavish presents would be distributed from "the King of Great Britain" and "the President of Virginia, Colonel Lee."

Obviously his proprietary actions spoke louder than his conciliatory words. He and his son were on their way home in March when "an Indian who spoke good English" caught up with them with a question from two of the leading sachems of the Delawares, Oppamylucah and Tamaqui (whom Gist called Beaver). The messenger was polite, but insisted that he required an answer, and it was obvious that a great deal, including the fate of Gist and his son, rode on the outcome of this encounter.

The great men of the Delawares, said the representative, wanted Gist to answer a simple question. Since "the French claimed all the land on one side the River Ohio and the English on the other side," the sachems "desired to know where the Indian's land lay."

It was, of course, the central question. Oppamylucah had put the same question to Gist some weeks before, when the trader was on his way west, and on that occasion Gist had been unable to think of anything to say. "I had made him no answer," Gist recalled. "I was at a loss to answer him, as I now also was." But this time, clearly, something had to be said, and it had better be reassuring. After some white-knuckled thought, Gist made the attempt. "My friend," he began hopefully, "we are all one king's people and the different color of our skins makes no difference in the king's subjects. You are his people as well as we, if you will take land and pay the king's rights you will have the same privileges as the white people have. And to hunt you have liberty everywhere, so [long as] you don't kill the white peoples' cattle and hogs."

The messenger ordered Gist and his son to stay where they were, and took the inspired lie back to his sachems. After two days of thought they told Gist the answer was acceptable, and he could go on his way.

With considerable relief, Gist returned to Wills Creek and the struggle that fully engaged his thoughts, knowledge, and abilities—the contest with his fellow traders, agents, and surveyors for supremacy in the northwest. In this contest the mysterious savages were merely pawns to be kept out of the way; the real opponents were people whose language, customs, and motivation Gist understood very well. Some were Virginians; not far to the south, the Greenbrier Company was pressing westward and northward from Augusta County under the leadership of the Scotch-Irishman John Lewis, with the support of a coalition of prominent men in Williamsburg—including the Speaker of the House of Burgesses, John Robinson—that was scarcely less influential than the members of the Ohio Company.

The most vigorous contestants, however, were Pennsylvanians, whose efforts in the Ohio country were led by Gist's erstwhile mentor, George Croghan. While appearing to help Gist as escort and provider of translators, Croghan had been warning his friends among the tribes that Gist and the Virginians intended to build a fort in order to take control of the entire area, and that their roads would let the enemy Catawbas more easily come in and raid.

Marylanders, too, had their aspirations in the West, but were preoccupied with the effort to establish their northern border at 40 degrees of latitude, a boundary that would have included Philadelphia. That dispute had raged in open warfare until 1739, when by order of the king's council a provisional boundary had been established at 39 degrees 30 minutes, some twenty miles south of the 40th (later to be fixed more precisely by the surveyors Mason and Dixon). The controversy still simmered, however, and may have accounted for Maryland's failure to pursue its western interests with the vigor of Virginia and Pennsylvania. Such crosscurrents distracted the traders, confused their communications with their commercial and political employers, and unravelled all attempts to forge a unified

English policy toward either the native tribes or the French.

On his return in 1752, Gist's next move in the intercolonial competition was to try to gain appointment as a commissioner to an important conference that Virginia wanted to hold with the Logstown tribes in June. But his gambit was declined, and he was forced to watch the ascendancy of William Trent in the favors of the new governor, Robert Dinwiddie, and the Company. Gist was assigned to do a relatively menial job in partnership with a man who had been one of the most robust advocates of Maryland's expansion.

Thomas Cresap, forty-seven years old in 1752, was a feisty Yorkshireman carpenter, surveyor, and farmer who took his own views and freedom seriously enough to seem, as a contemporary sadly noted, "born unto trouble." He also took seriously Maryland's claim to the 40th degree of latitude and had settled near there, on the Susquehanna River, thus becoming the most northerly, as well as the most vociferous, of the Maryland insurgents into Pennsylvania. When a Pennsylvania sheriff came with twenty-three armed men to evict him on November 24, 1736, Cresap held them off until they burned his house down around him. They took him away in irons and imprisoned him in Philadelphia for two years, an act that precipitated the worst of the border warfare between the states and led to the fixing of the boundary by the king's council.

Thereafter, Cresap decided to become the most westerly of Maryland's residents instead of the most northerly, and entered the fur trade from a post on Antietam Creek. This enterprise was a total failure, so he tried again, setting up this time at the confluence of the South Branch and main Potomac, fifteen miles downstream, or east, of Wills Creek. From 1743 on, he prospered there, and in 1748 was one of the organizers of the Ohio Company. The Company had directed him in 1751 to build the first thirty-five miles or so of its main road to the northwest, from Wills Creek to the forks of the Youghiogheny. In the spring of 1752 he and Gist were commissioned to extend the road to the confluence of the Youghiogheny and the Monongahela, some ten miles upstream from the forks of the Ohio. They went to work on it while, not far to the southeast, George Washington surveyed Fairfax land in Frederick County and reflected on his recent trip to Barbados.

As June approached, Gist and all connected with the Company

turned their thoughts if not their feet toward Logstown, for a climactic conference with the tribes of the Ohio that was to be the culmination of all the explorations, manipulations, and preparations that had been necessary to form the Company, arrange its land grant and acquire the first shipment of trade goods. Things were ready to go. The only technicality in the way of full-blown operations was that the tribes still thought the land was theirs. The purpose of the Logstown Conference beginning on June 1 was to disabuse them of that notion. The device would be to ask the tribes to confirm the eight-year-old Treaty of Lancaster. Since the Iroquois League had already signed this treaty, and since its terms gave the Virginians all they wanted, there should have been no problem.

The problem was, of course, that there were at least two irreconcilable interpretations of what the Lancaster Treaty meant. Even when they were trying to deal forthrightly with one another, which was seldom, the two races confronted an unbridgeable communications gap. The Iroquois conducted all their business orally, using ceremonial belts of colored beads called wampum to authenticate official communications and to help remind the tribal historians of the details. To them, what was said at a conference was everything. To the English, conversation was merely a preliminary; all that really mattered was the written document specifying the conclusions reached. The sachems found the English reverence for signatures and seals a bit silly, and went away remembering all that had been said. The English, meanwhile, chuckling over what the sachems had allowed them to put down in writing, went away clutching their legal document.

Thus, after meeting for three weeks at Lancaster in 1744, the Iroquois tribes had left believing they had succeeded in defending from the encroaching whites their rights in the Allegheny Mountains. They had insisted on and had been guaranteed the right to travel freely the traditional Warrior's Road to the country of their favorite enemies, the Catawbas. The leader of the Great Council of the Iroquois, Canasatego, had been adamant in his demand that any white settlers encroaching on the Warrior's Road—particularly the Virginians moving into the Shenandoah—must either move back east or share their produce with the Iroquois using the road. In other words, English settlement must stop at the Warriors' Road or, with proper guarantees and consideration, at the headwaters of the rivers flowing westward into the Ohio. The deal was done and the Iroquois accepted a settlement worth £500 for ceding land that the whites had already claimed and occupied.

The representatives of Pennsylvania, Maryland, and Virginia had been much relieved by the outcome at Lancaster. The tribes had been on the verge of open warfare over English encroachments, and this was a favorable settlement of existing disputes. Moreover, relations with the Iroquois had been thus improved just at the outset of King George's War with the French (which was part of the War of Austrian Succession, which followed the War of Jenkins's Ear, etc.), making it unlikely that the tribes would go over to the enemy. But the Virginians were not content with all this. When they wrote their document, they recorded that in return for their £500 in gold and goods, the Iroquois were executing a deed "recognizing the King's right to all the lands that are, or shall be, by his Majesty's appointment in the colony of Virginia." According to this writing, the sachems had signed away, at the very least (for Virginia's franchise was continental in scope), the Ohio country. But that is not what had been said.

The Logstown conference, designed to confirm the Lancaster outcome eight years later, was an untidy affair from the beginning. The plan was to summon the sachems to Virginia, dazzle them with £1000 worth of gifts, and then "explain" the situation, since, in the words of the commissioners' instructions, "some doubts have arisen about the treaty of Lancaster, and surmises have been spread as if the Six Nations thought themselves imposed upon by it." First, the Virginians lost control of the meeting place. George Croghan, who because of his gracious assistance to Gist knew the Company's intentions in detail, had moved to spike them with a deft maneuver after Gist had left the Ohio country in 1751.

On May 28, Croghan and Montour had convened a council of their own at Logstown that had much the same agenda as the one planned by the Virginians. They presented a large gift from Pennsylvania, and discussed the question of an establishment on the forks of the Ohio. This was a tangled question in Pennsylvania; the proprietors and Governor Hamilton wanted to build something impressive but cheap, military but not very, a building, they said, "that tho' very small it may look fort like." The Quakers in the assembly, however, would have nothing to do with anything that even looked fort-like, and the governor apparently knew full well he could never get approval for it. To avoid a fight he could not win, Hamilton told Croghan not to make "any public mention of building a fort."

Yet Croghan returned from Logstown bearing an explicit request from Tamaqui of the Delawares to Hamilton of Pennsylvania that "our brother will build a strong house on the Ohio River soon." Such militant Englishmen as Croghan and Hamilton took such a request to be for a military installation, for protection against the French. But the meaning was not at all clear. The Delawares and others often asked for trading posts to be built near them, and it may well be that this was what Tamaqui meant by "strong house." But Croghan called it a fort, and Hamilton saw no choice but to sigh, make the request to the Assembly, and see it overwhelmingly rejected. It was the firm view of the Assembly that Croghan and Hamilton were overstating the danger posed by the French and misinterpreting the desire of the Delawares for "a strong house."

Croghan's gambit may have further strained his relations with Governor Hamilton, but he had spoiled the plans of his Virginia counterparts. Perhaps the Ohio tribes were interested in getting Pennsylvania and Virginia into a direct bidding war for their trade; at any rate their response to the Ohio Company invitation to Virginia was highly unsettling: "Our brothers of Pennsylvania have kindled a council fire here, and we expect you will send our Father's speeches to us here, for we long to hear what our great Father the King of Great Britain has to say to us his poor children."

In addition to being outmaneuvered by the Pennsylvanians, the Company men soon learned that their opponents within Virginia had scored a victory. Governor Dinwiddie had figured in Virginia politics for a decade, had been a member of the Ohio Company for a year, and had been appointed governor the previous July, but had not reached Williamsburg to take office until November of 1751. His inexperience in office may account for the fact that in early 1752 he failed to control the selection of the Logstown commissioners, with the result that the conference was conducted by Burgesses who were not Company men. The three commissioners were Joshua Fry, a mathematics professor and mapmaker from Albemarle County;

Lunsford Lomax, a member of the House of Burgesses from Caroline County; and, worst of all from the Company's point of view, the Scotch-Irishman James Patton of Augusta County, an avid land speculator and sometime partner of John Lewis in designs that directly competed with those of the Company. Gist, Cresap, and Trent were reduced to attending the conference as mere agents of the Company without official standing. Croghan, meanwhile, announced himself on scant authority (he was bearing a perfunctory message of goodwill from Governor Hamilton) as a commissioner from Pennsylvania, and managed to get himself treated as such throughout.

Whether Company men or not, the Virginia commissioners understood that their mission at Logstown was to gain the approval of the tribes for the settlement of the Ohio country. And what is more, Governor Dinwiddie instructed them, they were to do so without agreeing to the expensive proposition of building a fort at the forks. But the officials found it extremely difficult to get down to business when the principal chiefs did not appear on time, and the Shawnees took the opportunity to raise a controversy.

The Shawnees professed to be angry that the commissioners had no answer to a months-old request from the Twightwees for support against the French. The commissioners regarded this matter as a minor irritant, since in their view the Shawnees were mere subjects of the Iroquois. But in the absence of Iroquois authority and the presence of the vociferous Shawnees, the case had to be dealt with. The affair turned out to be another time bomb lovingly fused and placed in Virginia's lap by George Croghan.

Back in February, the Twightwees had appealed to Pennsylvania for support in their increasingly violent confrontations with the French and France's tribal allies, who deeply resented the Twightwees' ties with the English. The besieged Twightwees and their aggressive allies, the Shawnees, were ready to conduct open warfare with the French interlopers, but first wanted unequivocal assurances of the availability of arms, ammunition, supplies, trade goods, and if necessary, reinforcements.

Croghan had a vested interest in their request, and indeed may have encouraged it. Since 1744 he had operated a large and thriving trading post at Pickawillany, in the far-off Miami country, and had no doubt had a great deal to do with the tribe's formal alliance with the English, arranged in 1748. The principal chief, Unemakemi, who had been called La Demoiselle, became better known thereafter as Old Britain. To the French, the loss of the allegiance of this tribe, in its highly strategic position between the Ohio country to the south and the rich fur territory of the Great Lakes country to the north and west, was intolerable. When blandishments had failed to recover the situation, the French had resorted to threats, one of which Gist had seen delivered while he had been at Pickawillany.

Croghan had relayed the Twightwees' plea for help to Governor Hamilton of Pennsylvania. While sympathetic, Hamilton knew that the Quaker-dominated assembly would never approve such confrontational tactics, and he deflected it. "The circumstances and real inclinations of the other Indian nations among whom you live," Hamilton wrote, "with regard to these bad men the subjects of the King of France, are not so well known to me to enable me to give you proper advice." But the Virginians were going to convene a council soon, and they might as well have something to do. "The counsellors and commissioners for Virginia will be better enabled on the spot to judge of what shall be proper for you and the other Indian Nations to do, and will, I doubt not, give you good and faithful advice." Then Croghan looked on, no doubt with some amusement, as the bewildered commissioners at Logstown tried to figure out what the Shawnees were angry about and what the Twightwees wanted. The Virginians at length patched things up by announcing that William Trent would take presents and assurances to the Twightwees after the conference (which, as it turned out, was much too late).

Confronted by a fog of unfamiliar considerations, a sea of indistinguishable red faces and a babble of indecipherable tongues, the commissioners plodded on, grimly applying English logic to the savages. Next they took up the problem of the Delawares, who had to be dealt with since they were living on the land the Ohio Company intended to develop. They, too, were supposed to be a subject people of the Six Nations, but showed distressing signs of independence. Moreover, one never knew who was speaking for them; sometimes it was Tamaqui, sometimes his brother Shingas, other times Oppamylucah. In the English view, people were either masters or subjects, and they could not countenance this business of dealing with one person at one conference and later another. They demanded that the Iroquois name a Delaware leader with whom they could negotiate. To make their meaning perfectly clear, they said he should be the king of the Delawares, a term that had no meaning whatsoever to the tribes.

The fog surrounding the commissioners soon thickened. They could not even be sure they were in contact with the Iroquois League. As their conference opened on June 1, a chief whom they assumed came from the Great Council at Onandaga stood and ceremoniously welcomed them "in the name of the Six United Nations." But later that day the Virginians discovered to their considerable consternation that their invitation to the Council had never been forwarded to Onandaga, but was being handled locally. There seemed little point in proceeding, but neither was there any way to stop.

The fog seemed to lift a little on June 4, with the arrival of the best-known Iroquois diplomat of the northwest, the Seneca sachem Tanacharison. Here at last was a recognized authority of the Six Nations, and the commissioners craved such an individual, with whom they could deal comfortably and repeatedly. His exact role, however, remained a mystery to the English. He represented the Onandaga Council, but frequently disagreed with it; he seemed to have authority over some of the tribes of the Ohio country, but not all of them; and he did not impose his will sternly and openly, as for example a royal governor would, but slyly, with a great deal of maneuvering and manipulating and building of consensus. To signify their befuddlement over what he was, the English dubbed him the Half-King.

Tanacharison's arrival was deliberately dramatic. As he came into view floating down the Ohio in his canoe, with the English colors flying in the bow, he was greeted with enthusiastic volleys of musketry. He swept ashore, fixed the English flag to his house, and went into a series of private meetings with his fellow Iroquois that lasted for five days. James Patton, who kept the minutes of the proceedings for the commissioners, was impressed by Tanacharison, writing, "he seems to be a person of great dignity in his behavior." Later, Patton carefully crossed out the words of admiration.

Finally, on June 9, Tanacharison was ready to conduct a preliminary meeting with the commissioners. By that time he knew exactly what they were after and had prepared his response. It was as smooth as glass. He thanked the Virginians for letting him know what the Onandaga Council had done at Lancaster all those years ago, since the Council, he said, had never admitted to the Ohio tribes selling any territory beyond the Warrior's Road. By keeping this important piece of information to itself, he said, the Council had caused many disorders that might have been prevented. But Tanacharison was sure, he added, that the Council "would confirm whatever they had done."

As the commissioners listened to the translation, distracted by the flickering fires and the crowded copper bodies with their garish decorations, it must have taken a while for them to grasp the import of what Tanacharison had said. He had not challenged the Virginians' interpretation of the Lancaster Treaty, but had expressed only warmth and gratitude to his visitors while blaming all difficulties on a distant, anonymous Council. But wait. The whole purpose of this conference had been to get final, immediate approval from the Six Nations for the Ohio settlement. Now it appeared that the principal representative of the Onandaga Council did not know what the Council had done, or intended to do, and that it would take weeks, perhaps months, for him to find out.

The next day, pressing on despite everything, the Virginians presented their gift and made the formal public statement of their case, with heavy emphasis on the written record. "You made a deed," at Lancaster, they told the sachems, "recognizing the King's right to all the land in Virginia as far as it was then peopled or should thereafter be peopled or bounded by the King our father for which you received the consideration agreed upon." The Lancaster commissioners had promised, in writing, "under their hands and seals," to make additional payment when settlement spread farther back, and had done so, sending a lavish gift out with Conrad Weiser in 1748.

Having thus proved that they had bought the land, the commissioners proposed to buy it again. "Now the King your father, to show the love he bears to justice as well as his affection for you his children, has sent a large present of goods to be divided among you and your allies which is here ready to be delivered to you and we desire you may confirm the treaty of Lancaster." And they stipulated what that confirmation would mean: "a settlement of British subjects on the southeast side of the Ohio."

But the tribes should rest easy, because even after selling the land the second time they would not lose it. "The King our father by purchasing your lands had never any intention of taking them from you but that we might live together as one people and keep them from the French, who would be bad neighbors. From such a settlement greater advantages will arise to you than you can at present conceive."

Tanacharison began his response with a note for the record: Weiser had indeed brought a gift in 1748, but had said it was a gift from Pennsylvania. "He never made mention," said Tanacharison blandly, "of the King our Father." In the matter of the settlement, he said, he would need more time to respond. "We assure you of our willingness to agree to what our council does or has done but we have not the full power in our hands here on the Ohio, we must acquaint our council at Onandaga of the affair and whatever they bid us do we will do." Meanwhile, the Virginians should feel free to build "a stronghouse at the mouth of Monongahela," but not to begin a settlement there. As to the Virginians' argument that a settlement was needed to provide food for the people in the "stronghouse," they should rest easy, Tanacharison said, "we will take care that there shall be no scarcity of that kind until we can give a full answer."

The only thing Tanacharison was prepared to grant the Virginians was their request that the Delawares be given a king. No such rank existed among them, but it would make the English happy to know who should sign Delaware documents. The principal confusion had been between the brothers Tamaqui and Shingas, each of whom spoke for his tribe on different occasions. Tanacharison chose Shingas to be the king. But since he was not at Logstown, Tamaqui stood in for him at the ceremony, during which he was outfitted with what Patton described as "a rich jacket and a suit of English colors, which had been delivered to the Half King by the commissioners for that purpose."

However gratified they might have been by this charade, the commissioners found themselves in a situation that appeared to be irretrievable. For their gift, their trouble, and their conference the

Ohio Company had gotten permission to build a fort it did not want to build, had been denied permission to settle on the Ohio, and had even seen the Lancaster treaty called into question. They had been sure they would prevail, and had, in the words of Patton's journal, "drawn an instrument of writing confirming the deed at Lancaster and containing a promise that the Indians would not molest our settlements of the southeast side of the Ohio." Not willing to give up, or to waste a perfectly good instrument of writing, the commissioners sent Andrew Montour—the translator who usually worked for George Croghan—"to converse with his brethren the other sachems in private."

No one ever reported what Montour said or did, but when he was through the paper was signed. That was all the commissioners needed. The paper said that they had won, that the door to the Ohio country was open.

But according to the commissioners' instructions there was one more piece of business, and they wisely left it to the last. Noting that a "large house" had been made available eight years earlier at the College of William and Mary for the education of the children of the tribes, but that disappointingly few had been sent to attend, they repeated the offer of free schooling. "The advantages of an English education," one of their number intoned, "are greater than can be imagined by those who are unacquainted with it. By it we know that part of the world from whence we came; how nations for some thousands of years back have arose, grown powerful, or decayed; how they have removed from one place to another; what battles have been fought; what great men have lived and how they have acted either in council or in war. But the greatest of all is, that by it we are acquainted with the will of the great God, the creator of the world and father of us all, who inhabits the skies, by which the better people among us regulate their lives and hope after death to live with Him forever."

Apparently Tanacharison, experienced diplomat or not, was for a moment speechless. It was only "after a short pause," Patton recorded, that he replied: "Brethren, we heard of the offer which was made us at Lancaster, and we thank you for that which you make us now, but we can give you no answer until we consult the Onandaga Council about it."

On June 16, the participants began to disperse from Logstown. The commissioners headed for Williamsburg to report to Governor Dinwiddie. William Trent and Andrew Montour travelled west to the Miami River with gifts and assurances for the Twightwees. Gist, now the Company's official surveyor, was given a choice assignment—to recruit the first settlers for the Ohio country and prepare to lead them there. He soon reported that he had fifty families ready to go.

In the view of the Company, its principal problem was solved and its plans for the invasion of the Ohio could and must go forward quickly. Ambitious plans were laid for a trading post (not a fort) at the forks, to be followed by another at the mouth of the Great Kanawha, nearly two hundred miles downriver, and, "at convenient distances" in between, "proper stores and houses for the reception of persons removing to settle there and security of their goods while they were building."

There were a few nagging details to be resolved. Legal conveyance of the land to the settlers required an order from the governor and council. Prudence required that the Logstown Treaty with the Ohio tribes, which confirmed the Lancaster treaty with the Iroquois Council at Onandaga, be confirmed in turn by the Onandaga Council. All this must be accomplished and the settlements established before the French could get there in force. But these formalities and practical considerations seemed minor in comparison with the victory that had been won; Virginia had become the primary colonial power in the Ohio country, relegating Pennsylvania to secondary status, and the Ohio Company was firmly established as the agency of that power. And Christopher Gist appeared to be positioned as the leader of the westward movement. He and everyone connected with the Ohio Company were poised on the verge of total and magnificent success.

They were on the crest, but somehow could not seem to get matters onto the downward slope. The application to the governor and council for formal permission to take possession of their first two hundred thousand acres of land, presented in November of 1752 (while the council was, among other things, dividing the adjutancy into four districts and appointing George Washington to one of them), was not approved. Neither was it disapproved, but lacking action the Company could not begin to sell the land.

The problem appeared to be uncertainty that the Company had yet bought the land. Governor Dinwiddie was intent on organizing yet another council with the Iroquois, this one with representatives of the Onandaga Council, at Winchester in the spring of 1753. It may have been that Dinwiddie did not feel confident enough to take final action, even with the conveyance signed by the Ohio tribes, until he had formal approval from Onandaga.

The Company took what action it could in the interim. It ordered Gist "to proceed in the settlement and survey as fast as possible," and appointed Trent its factor to carry on trade. Gist happily continued the building of his new plantation, as he called it, east of Redstone Creek, midway between the Monongahela and the Youghiogheny Rivers. This location, while not on the lands targeted for development by the Company, was on the road between Wills Creek and the forks of the Ohio, and would be an extremely valuable way station and staging area. Gist soon had settled there twenty families, including that of his son-in-law William Cromwell, and was ready to manage, assist, provision—and of course profit from—the northwestward migration. He and Cresap were hard at work laying out the first proposed settlement on the Ohio, a trading post and village sited at the mouth of Chartiers Creek a few miles below the forks.

But during this further delay the Company's aspirations came under attack from every quarter. Having bested the Pennsylvanians, at least for the moment, the Company men now found themselves in fierce competition with fellow Virginians who also scented fortunes in the Ohio Country. The most intolerable of these challenges came from one of the land companies that had been breathing down the Ohio Company's neck from the start. Headed by John Blair, a member of the Governor's council, this company had been granted by the council back in 1745 a parcel of one hundred thousand acres lying west of the Fairfax grant and along the Potomac and Youghiogheny Rivers. In the early spring of 1753 the surveying partners in the Blair company, William Russell and Andrew Lewis (of the Augusta County, Greenbrier Company Lewises) began to lay out their lots.

The first line they surveyed arrowed through Gist's plantation, between the land of Gist and his son-in-law. Worse, it severed the road between Wills Creek and the forks. But when challenged, the only compromise Russell and Lewis would make was to veer off a little from Gist's residence, insisting that most of the settlers there were on Blair company land. Meanwhile, another member of the governor's council, Richard Corbin, had entered a counterclaim for three parcels of Ohio Company land, 190,000 acres in all, using as his reference the map commissioned and submitted by the Ohio Company to support its own claims. The Ohio Company hotly protested all these incursions to the council in Williamsburg, which, finding that it was rather seriously divided against itself, delayed consideration of the protests for a full year.

While being thus stymied by their own government and assailed by their fellow Virginians, the Company men learned, late in the fall of 1752, that the French threat to their ambitions had suddenly turned dangerous. On the very day that Trent had left Logstown bearing gifts and reassurances to the Twightwees on the Miami River, the French had struck out viciously at the recalcitrant tribe. On the morning of June 21, a French agent named Charles Langlade had led a massive surprise attack on the town of Pickawillany by hundreds of Ottawas and Chippewas. They overwhelmed the town's defenders and captured many of its residents. They killed one of the seven English traders present and made five captive; they made an example of Old Britain by boiling and eating him; and they destroyed three thousand pounds of trade goods. Most of these had been charged to Croghan's accounts, and since without them he could not trade for the furs with which to pay his bills, he was ruined.

It was a fate that loomed for every English trader, be he Virginian or Pennsylvanian, Ohio Company or Greenbrier Company, Anglican or Quaker or Presbyterian, if the French continued to push southward from the Great Lakes into the Ohio country. And in the fall and winter of 1752, they pushed. In the spring of 1753, William Trent was writing the governors of both Virginia and Pennsylvania angry letters "acquainting you of the French and Indians killing and taking our people prisoners." By this time Dinwiddie was making heavy use of Trent to keep in touch with the Ohio tribes and of Andrew Montour to communicate with Onandaga, where the Iroquois Council showed no interest at all in Dinwiddie's plans for another council at Winchester in the summer. But Onandaga was having no truck with the French either; Montour reported that the Council there had responded to a French overture by saying that the Ohio lands "belong to the Indians, and neither the French nor the English should have anything to do with them." Dinwiddie took heart at this rebuff of the French, disregarding the fact that it was an equally stern rebuff of the English.

Dinwiddie would not give up on the conference, but in what may have been a face-saving change of course he now began to refer to it as merely an occasion to deliver goods to the Ohio tribes. He took the reports of the French offenses more seriously than did his council, which expressed the collective opinion that "we don't think the irregularities complained of against the Indians to be so threatening as [the traders] apprehend them."

But as summer approached, it became apparent that something far more serious was afoot than random harassment of the traders. The French were reported to be moving south in force, not just a few officers with some native warriors but organized troops, intent not on raiding but on building forts. They were coming down the Allegheny to stay. This was confirmed beyond doubt on May 6, when Governor George Clinton of New York notified his fellow colonial governors that French units in strength had passed Fort Oswego on Lake Ontario, bound for the Ohio country.

Governor Dinwiddie was thoroughly alarmed, and kept William Trent in constant motion through the summer to gather intelligence and try to retain the loyalty of the Ohio tribes. He had competition even in this enterprise from within his own colony; William Fairfax, acting for the executive council in what he called "the governor's name," dispatched the trader William Russell, of the Blair land company, to Logstown to find the French, warn them off, and report on the state of the natives. At the same time another trader named Barnaby Curran was there on behalf of Trent and the Ohio Company setting up an August conference. Dinwiddie later mocked Russell for getting no closer than 150 miles from the French, sneering, "I believe he was afraid to go to them."

At the August conference with the Logstown Iroquois, Trent persuaded them to travel east to Winchester to meet the governor of Virginia. Afterward, Trent sent Dinwiddie his assessment of French intentions based on his interrogation of the Ohio warriors. The French, he wrote, had dispatched 1500 soldiers to build three forts on the Ohio within the next three months. "They declare publicly they will have all the land as far as Allegheny Hill and will build towns and forts where they please."

No wonder Gist and his fellow traders (and would-be real estate agents) were willing to forget their rivalries for the moment and escort the young Virginia major to the nearest French outpost to warn the intruders off. An appeal to their patriotic duty to Virginia and their king would not have moved one of them a single step into the forest. But the fate of the Ohio Company and their future fortunes hung in the balance. Neither they nor Washington knew just where the nearest French fort was, but they knew its direction, and that they had a long way to go. The party set off from Wills Creek on November 15, the day after Washington arrived there.

CHAPTER 4

The Tribes

"We Set Out about Nine O'Clock with the Half King, Jeskakake, White Thunder and the Hunter."

NOVEMBER 25, 1753

On Friday, November 23, 1753, after a week of travelling through heavy rains and snow, young Major Washington saw for the first time the lodestone of the Ohio country, the key to the continent, the focal point of a worldwide struggle, the flash point of a world war—the forks of the Ohio. As it happened, he was required to wait there until one of his "servitors" arrived with a canoe with which to carry their baggage across the swollen Allegheny River. Thus he had nothing to do for a while but wander over the site and fix it in his mind. Later, he recorded his musings in his journal: "I spent some time in viewing the rivers, and the land in the fork, which I think extremely well situated for a fort, as it has the absolute command of both rivers. The land at the point is 20 or 25 feet above the common surface of the water, and a considerable bottom of flat, well-timbered land all around it, very convenient for building. The rivers are each a quarter of a mile or more across and run here very nigh at right angles; Allegheny bearing northeast and Monongahela southeast. The former of these two is a very rapid, swift-running water, the other deep and still, with scarce any perceptible fall."

That night the party crossed the fast-moving Allegheny and the next day made their way downriver along the north bank of the Ohio to the site opposite the mouth of Chartiers Creek where Gist had laid out a prospective settlement. Washington reported that he did not like what he saw. He thought it a "greatly inferior" location for a fort: "The hill whereon it must stand, being a quarter of a mile in length, and then descending gradually on the land side, will render it difficult and very expensive making a sufficient fortification there. The whole flat upon the hill must be taken in, or the side next the descent made extremely high, or else the hill cut away: otherwise the enemy will raise batteries within that distance, without being exposed to a single shot from the fort."

This was stagecraft. Washington had none of the expertise in military engineering to which he was pretending, as his mistakes in the coming year would amply demonstrate; his entire prior education on the subject appears to have been a conversation or two with Lawrence about the defenses of Barbados. Moreover, as he must have known, the Chartiers Creek site was selected not for a fortification from which to withstand armies and artillery, but for a store and village. The Ohio Company was trying to avoid the cost of a military installation. Of course the Forks, not the site of the store, was the military key to the area, and anyone who was thinking in military terms saw that immediately. Back in August, William Trent and Andrew Montour, worried by the approach of the French, had looked over the area and had chosen the Forks as the site for any fort to be built there. Washington's claim to superior judgment on the subject was mere pretention. His observations were also, of course, correct.

There was already a village of twenty families or so in the immediate vicinity of Gist's townsite at Chartiers Creek. It was Shanopin's Town, presided over by Shingas—he who had become, by the grace of the Virginia commissioners, King of the Delawares. Washington now invited him to yet another conference at Logstown and they travelled there together, arriving at sundown on Sunday, November 25.

By sundown Monday, Washington had met three of the key tribal leaders of the Ohio country—Shingas of the Delawares, the Oneida Monacatoocha (also known as Scaroyady), and Tanacharison of the Seneca (who, as was his wont, came on the scene with a flourish after all the other players were settled in). That evening, Washington rose in the longhouse (the elongated log structure that was the distinctively Iroquois council hall), delivered his first formal address to the leaders, and began a relationship that for the next several years would be intense, continual, mystifying, frustrating, and fateful.

Yet in the mind of Washington, in the records of events set down by him and others at the time, and in almost all of the histories written afterward, the people with whom he was now dealing would never be afforded anything approaching the respect due one human being from another. The red people were, in the haughty view of Washington and his associates, uncivilized, uneducated, unclean, immoral—and uninteresting. The young major regarded Tanacharison, and all his kind, as comical figures "having nothing human except the shape."

Such assumptions of racial superiority frequently stained the history of white Europeans, quenching curiosity, forestalling inquiry, and obstructing the transfer of information from those branded as savages to those calling themselves civilized. Whites could accept simple, practical lessons—the uses and advantages of the hunting shirt, moccasin, or tomahawk, of potatoes, corn, or tobacco—as accidental discoveries by the heathen that white men could put to better use. But anything subtle or complex, such as a different social organization or concept of government, the haughty Europeans dismissed out of hand as primitive. The idea that there was anything to be learned from the history and culture of these peoples was regarded as preposterous, if indeed the idea ever occurred to anyone. As in other places and times, the wages of ignorance were death.

The fallacies began with the very names of things. The name applied to the race—Indians—was and remains a testament to ignorance, and to the typical European insistence that what they had found must be what they had been seeking, whether or not there was any resemblance. Benighted Columbus, who happened to stumble across the American continents while looking for another one, who failed to understand what he had found or where it was or whom he had met there, branded an entire race of humans with the label not of a great discovery, but of a tormented mistake.

But one who wishes to be careful, to grant people the dignity of being called by the names of their choosing, faces daunting difficulty.

Typically, Europeans did not ask a tribe for its name, but asked a nearby tribe what the neighbors were called. Relations between adjacent tribes were frequently hostile, and it followed that so were the names given in answer to the question. The word Mohawk means "man-eater." The Delawares were named for an English lord whom they never saw. The word Iroquois is not found in the Iroquoian languages, but belongs to the other major Eastern language group, the Algonquian, and is a pejorative meaning "rattlesnake people." In later years a major Plains tribe came to be known as Sioux, which translates roughly as "sons-of-bitches." All these tribes referred to themselves, in their own languages, as "The People." No more egocentric than any other race or tribe, they usually added an adjective meaning the real, or original, or chosen people. Thus the Delawares were to themselves *Lenni Lenape*, the Iroquois were *Ongwe Honwe*, the Sioux *Lakota*, and so on.

Few Europeans knew or cared that the Iroquois were not in fact a tribe, but a league of tribes that had devised an advanced form of government with which the whites had been in uncomprehending contact since arriving on the continent. After a century of interaction, the whites knew virtually nothing about the Iroquois confederacy—even though both France and England regarded it as the key to the looming struggle for the continent. The league of the six major tribes living within and westward of the colonies of New York and Pennsylvania had been in existence for at least two centuries, perhaps longer, when the first whites came ashore. The facts of its origins are lost in legend, but were attributed to the vision and energy of two prophets named Deganawidah and Hiawatha (with whom Longfellow's later epic poem had nothing to do).

The purpose of the Iroquois League was to end the constant fratricidal wars among the five tribes who formed it—the Mohawks in eastern New York, and to the west the Oneidas, the Onandagas, the Cayugas, and the Senecas. Later the Tuscaroras were admitted to the League, which then came to be known as the Six Nations. The central symbol of the League was the Tree of Peace, a great white pine whose living roots extended to the four extremities of the world, and whose crown was watched over by a fierce eagle alert for threats. The vision was not of a passive peace, but of one imposed and maintained by armed power. The remarkable aspect of this Iroquois doctrine was that power was only the means to the end, and the end was peace. As one Iroquois described the dream, "the land shall be beautiful, the river shall have no more waves, one may go everywhere without fear." It was the potency of this idea, as well as the ferocity of its advocates, that accounted for the astonishing longevity of this confederacy of supposed savages.

Tanacharison was a member of the League's westernmost tribe, the Seneca, and probably was one of the eight sachems who represented his tribe in the Great Council. The number of tribal representatives varied, from perhaps three to eight, but each tribe had equal voting power. The League was a federal confederacy.

European ignorance of the Iroquois League, and the consequences of that ignorance, were appalling. In Tanacharison, Washington had encountered a man who embodied the strengths, the weaknesses, and the crisis of his people, who stood at the center of the affairs whirling about the forks of the Ohio and who held enormous influence over their outcome. He represented a far grander political alliance than Washington had yet encountered, was playing a far more subtle and intelligent game than Washington ever suspected, and was bearing a burden as heavy as that of any diplomat in history. But all the arrogant young major saw was a vain, unreliable, childish, and frustrating aborigine. Washington's later legacy to his countrymen would be forever tainted by his monumental failure to comprehend the reality.

If Washington, or Gist or Fairfax or any of them, had wanted to know this man Tanacharison, it would have been easy. He stood willing to answer questions never asked, eager to offer gifts never accepted, ready to negotiate anything but the dignity and freedom of his people in order to create some kind of partnership with the newcomers. His efforts were barely noticed.

If one had wanted to know him, one would first have inquired as to his clan. The English understood about tribes, and knew that Tanacharison was a Seneca, but few ever asked to know the most important single fact about his identity—his clan membership. An Iroquois infant became at birth a member of the mother's clan—a network of relatives denoted by an animal or bird. There was a Turkey clan, a Bear clan, and so on. Clan membership defined one's role and possibilities in life; youngsters were taught to behave as a member of their clan should behave, to rely on clan elders for help and advice, to regard only certain other clans as appropriate sources of a marriage partner. The clans extended across tribal lines; members of the Wolf clan of the Senecas, for example, would be welcome in the longhouses of the Wolf clan of the Mohawks (and forbidden to marry their daughters), although they would need interpreters in order to speak to each other.

All this formative information about one's clan identity came from the mother or, in the case of a male child, from the mother's brothers. The father's relationship with his children was mainly biological; his responsibilities for providing education, guidance, and leadership lay with his sisters' children, who, unlike his own offspring, were members of his clan. Even when comprehended, such a network of associations is exceedingly difficult for someone steeped in patriarchy to follow or keep in mind. And since even comprehension required effort, it was virtually nonexistent in colonial America.

Although the clans were everywhere evident, and were dominant in tribal affairs (determining, for example, the tribe's representation on the Onandaga Çouncil), they remained virtually invisible to white men, even one who spent as much time among them as did Christopher Gist. "This Beaver," he recorded, "is the Sachamore or Chief of the Delawares. It is customary among the Indian chiefs to take upon them the name of any beast or bird they fancy, the picture of which they always sign instead of their name or arms." These pictures that Gist found scratched with charcoal or vermilion on rocks or peeled trees near tribal campsites were in fact an open book of fascinating information for anyone who learned to read it. They often recorded the adventures of the camping party, its identity and purpose, and current gossip. Nor was that all the information to be gathered, only the most obvious. A learned observer could identify the tribe by its cookfire: Shawnees used a kettle beam placed on two forked sticks, Ottawas suspended their kettle from a diagonal sapling braced at one end, Chippewas used two crossed sticks, and so on.

White ignorance of these matters was not merely academic, it affected relations between the two races at almost every turn. One of the most obvious and dramatic effects has remained virtually unnoticed to the present day. When white men, French and English alike, had something important to say to the tribes, they persisted in talking about the wishes, commands, and generosity of a great white father. The image was selected for its powerful connotations for Europeans. One's father commanded respect, loyalty, fear, and obedience, according to natural and immutable laws—unless, of course, one lived in a matrilineal society.

When Iroquoians negotiated with each other and wished to convey respect, they used the term "uncle." If the footing were equal and neutral, the preferred form of address was "brother." European officials remained blind to such essential distinctions during the entire history of the confrontation between the white and red races. Blindly, for some two centuries, they continued to insist that the savages pay heed to their great white father. Only when one appreciates the meaninglessness of the concept for the Iroquois is one capable of hearing, in the flowery and obsequious-sounding responses, the undercurrent of poisonous sarcasm and outraged pride. One example is provided by the 1751 message from the Ohio tribes that they would confer with the Virginians at Logstown and not in Virginia: "We expect you will send our Father's speeches to us here, for we long to hear what our great Father the King of Great Britain has to say to us his poor children." Two and one half centuries later, we can at last understand what they were really saying.

Another concept that was so alien to the whites that they did not comprehend it when they saw it was the continuous and important role of women in the affairs of the clans and hence the tribes. Obviously, as the source of clan identity, an Iroquois woman would naturally enjoy higher standing in her society than an English woman in her patrilineal culture (unless, of course, the English woman was rich). But beyond that, the clan mothers were more than passive progenitors, they were active managers and policymakers.

The nominal, visible heads of the clans were the male sachems. They did what males always seem to do best—conducted councils, smoked, talked things over and decided when to go hunting or to war. But when a sachem died and his title passed to another clan member, it was not an automatic inheritance (since the lines of descent did not pass to his children, but to his nephews). Any choice among those eligible was made by the clan mother. Moreover, the clan mother could remove a sachem who displeased her. And even in wartime, when strong powers passed from the peacetime sachems to the war chiefs and emotions ran high, the women could stop a war party, or indeed a war, at any time by exercising their right to withhold provisions.

Blind to this dimension of tribal life, Washington on his way to Logstown had paid court to Shingas, but had failed to call on Aliquippa, foremost clan mother of the Senecas. When she let him know of her displeasure later, he paid the required call, but his attitude was condescending. "I made her the present of a matchcoat and a bottle of rum," he wrote, "which latter was thought much the best present of the two." The French commander whom Washington was on his way to confront had been equally dismissive when, during the first stages of his journey, he had received a delegation of Iroquois matriarchs who wanted to know whether he marched "with the hatchet uplifted, or to establish tranquility." Such questions, and the answers they received, were far from trivial.

Even had the whites been able to perceive the role of the clans and of women, they would not have been able to comprehend the nature of tribal relationships unless they had somehow found a way to stand aside from their concept of authority. In the primitive European view, authority moved in straight lines, from king to subject, from father to son. Inherited authority over lower classes could never be lost, even when inherited money evaporated. Appointive power, civil or military, might be temporary, but while held it was absolute over all lower ranks. Those who carried the king's seal gave orders, those who did not obeyed. This, to the French and English, was another immutable law of nature.

European children were given strict rules of behavior and dress and beaten into compliance. Women, servants, slaves, tradesmen, and merchants were given stern orders and watched carefully lest their natural tendencies to sloth and deception overcame them in mid-task. No work of any kind could be accomplished, it was assumed, unless someone ordered someone else to do it, supervised the manner in which it was done, and stood ready to punish laxity or error.

From such heights of civilization, one could only look down in amused disdain at the practices of savages. Shawnee parents allowed their children to behave and dress any way they wanted to, confident that they would sooner or later apprehend the ways of the tribe and conform. Within the tribes, there were no servants (although enemy captives might be enslaved and treated very badly), and no one had anything but a temporary, consensual right to tell other people what to do. The habitual tendency was not to sloth, as the whites supposed, but to work, each person gravitating toward any task that needed to be done, each contributing according to the capabilities of each. Agriculture was the specialty of the women, hunting of the men; the old did certain tasks, the young others; but instead of being directed and coerced, all were drawn to their roles, as to a fire in winter, by the gentle warmth of tribal approval.

Similarly, morality was not regarded as something that had to be imposed on a person from without, but as something that shone naturally from within. There were no constables or sheriffs, no courts or jails, no governors, administrators, or bureaucrats. This was all mystifying to the whites, who looked in vain for the person in charge. When they could not identify such a person they insisted, Columbus-like, on finding what they sought, as when they had Shingas anointed "king."

From the rigid perspective of the whites, a position such as Tanacharison's simply could not exist. He was a sachem of his tribe, the head of his clan, yet could be overruled by women who held no office. Moreover, he was not the only sachem of his tribe, there were others of apparently equal status, and in addition there were elected "pine-tree" chiefs who fulfilled certain functions, and beyond that war chiefs who took over in times of conflict. Tanacharison held a commission of some sort from the Iroquois League, with apparent responsibility for the affairs of all the Iroquois in the Ohio country, yet he never gave orders, he was always trying to persuade his subjects to do something, never with complete success. Nor was he always obedient to his overlords on the Great Council. It was all too bewildering. The English called him a half-king, derided him as an unreliable savage, and marched on toward catastrophe.

To say that the Iroquois League was more sophisticated than previously suspected is not to say that its future ever looked bright. For a hundred years, it had been grappling with a very difficult set of political problems. The English were pressing in from the east, overrunning the lands of the eastern League tribes and forever renegotiating the limits of their settlements. English traders, on the other hand, offered abundant goods at favorable rates of exchange for furs, and were reliable sources for the guns, steel knives, blankets, and pots that the Iroquois could neither do without nor provide for themselves. The French, meanwhile, filtered down from the north, appearing to respect the Iroquois lands and ways more than the English (but perhaps that was simply because there were fewer of them). The French seemed to be interested in holding the Ohio and Mississippi Rivers in order to contain the English and invigorate the French fur trade, not to enable French settlement of the land. On the other hand, they brought inferior goods, an undependable supply, and high prices.

League response to these twin threats had been to remain neutral whenever and wherever possible. When confronted by one side or the other and pressed to take a stand, the League had been conciliatory, had said whatever was necessary to get out of the predicament, had avoided above all making any irrevocable commitment until the outcome of the contest between the two powers could be foreseen.

It had been a difficult balancing act. At the turn of the eighteenth century, as England had been about to take its place as a major world power by virtue of winning the decade-long War of the Spanish Succession with France, the League had made an artful deal with both contenders. At issue was an enormous tract of land north and northwest of Lake Erie called the Beaver Hunting Ground. Recently conquered from its native inhabitants by the Iroquois, the freedom of the area—for trading, exploration, and expansion of settlement—was coveted by both the British and French. In effect, the Iroquois gave it to both.

Britain obtained a "deed" to the land (which of course meant far more to the British than it did to the Iroquois), in return for guaranteeing to the Iroquois exclusive, eternal hunting rights. From the League's point of view there was no harm in letting someone else hold onto a piece of paper as long as it retained the right to hunt on the land forever; what else, after all, was land for? At the same time, the Iroquois made a covenant with the French, promising neutrality in any future conflict in return for that country's guarantee of Iroquois hunting rights in the Beaver ground. From the French point of view, Iroquois recognition of their power to guarantee rights was tantamount to recognition of ownership.

And during the ensuing French-English war (known in America as Queen Anne's War) the Iroquois had been neutral, more or less; the eastern Mohawks fought with the British, the western Senecas with the French, while the three central tribes (the League contained only five nations until 1715) stayed out of it. In the Treaty of Utrecht ending that war, the English, in gratitude for what they knew about the Iroquois role in the war, granted the League the status of a subject nation.

Like most of the gifts brought to the red race by the white, this one turned out to be anything but a blessing. While the European courtiers of the day would unhesitatingly commit almost any barbarity to extend their power and increase their wealth, their sense of honor depended on the observation of certain legal niceties. There were, for example, only two legitimate bases for claiming enormous tracts of land outside your own country: the right of discovery or the right of conquest. As the focus of the French-English contest in the New World shifted to the Ohio country, the French quite justifiably claimed the right of discovery.

To counter this, the English legalists performed a strenuous set of logical contortions. When one claimed the right of discovery, native peoples were invisible, and the question of how one could discover a place where people were happily living was not allowed. Now, however, in order to claim the right of conquest, the English declared the natives visible. The Iroquois, they recalled, had become subjects of the British king under the terms of the Treaty of Utrecht; and the Iroquois had, by their own account at least, conquered the Ohio country. Therefore, the Ohio country was British. The only use for this silly syllogism was to fuel the self-righteousness of the English; the French were not impressed by it and the Iroquois were not informed of it.

Four decades later, when Washington first encountered the Iroquois League, it was threatened not only by the steadily increasing pressure from the French and English, but from within. In the face of the implacable expansion of the English settlements in the East, many Senecas and Cayugas had headed west, beyond the boundaries of their traditional lands, into the Ohio country. There, much like the English and French colonists dealing with official London and Paris, they found themselves in changed circumstances, far from the home government, and not always in agreement with the decisions and alliances made on their behalf back at Onandaga. These displaced tribes, who came to be known collectively as Mingos, were on the front lines of the French-English trading wars, among other displaced people. There were Shawnees in the Ohio country who had been pressed back from Pennsylvania and Virginia. There were Delawares who had been run out of Pennsylvania. To the north and west were the Twightwees of the Miami River and the Wyandots (whom Gist had visited on that memorable Christmas). All of these tribes and tribal remnants were constantly besieged by contesting representatives of England and France, Pennsylvania and Virginia, offering trade and demanding deals. The Mingos were supposedly under the direct authority of the League's Great Council; the Delawares, having been conquered in their eastern homeland by the Iroquois, were presumably a subject people; the Shawnees, driven from the Ohio country by the Iroquois in the seventeenth century, usually allied themselves with the League but ignored it when their purposes differed; the Twightwees and Wyandots were interested in the superior British trade goods but lived closer to French power and vacillated accordingly.

These strains on Iroquois authority threatened not only the League's bargaining position with the English but its continued existence. To deal with it, the Great Council had established an administrative center for the Ohio country at Logstown, and had dispatched there two emissaries. One of them was the Oneida sachem Monacatoocha (or Scaroyady), whose unenviable assignment was to supervise the fractious Shawnees. The other was Tanacharison, who in addition to his responsibilities as sachem and councillor was to oversee the affairs of the Mingos, conduct diplomatic relations with the other Ohio tribes, and steer a course for them between the French and the English. These were the complex and onerous responsibilities summarized by the English with the contemptuous term "half-king."

Neither Tanacharison nor the Iroquois League cared one whit about who won the contest between the French and the English. They cared about their own future, and in the face of twin invasions by superior numbers with overwhelming firepower, there seemed only two possibilities. One was that the powerful would bleed each other to death before they could get around to dealing with the less powerful. The other was that the Iroquois League could end up on the winning side, commanding sufficient gratitude from the winners to strike a reasonable deal. The worst case was that either the French or the English should win a decisive victory, with the League caught unequivocally on the other side. For the Six Nations and their brothers, that would be the end of the world.

As the pressure increased, indecision increased, and was more stridently expressed as disagreement among the tribes who needed unity now more than ever. The French had shown ferocity and determination in destroying Pickawillany and the Miami River Indians, and the other Ohio country tribes were impressed. The Delawares, Wyandots, and Shawnees—along with their League supervisor, Monacatoocha—had gone to a council with the Virginians at Winchester in September, then on to another with the Pennsylvanians at Carlisle; they had listened to the English case, had taken the English gifts, had drunk the English rum, had brought out their children for baptizing, and had professed loyalty, one Wyandot chief said, "as long as the sun gives light." But the Wyandots had already decided to cast their lot with the French, and the Shawnees soon followed suit. The Mingos were increasingly anxious, with those who lived closest to the French most inclined to join them despite the urgings of the Great Council to stand by the English. The Great Council was located among the English and had a far different perspective on the relative strengths of the contenders. The council, and Tanacharison as well, were losing their authority among the Mingos.

Tanacharison had needed to do something, and so he had gone north to confront the threat—and, no doubt, to assess it at first hand. He had found the French on the shores of Lake Erie, building an imposing fort at Presque Isle and preparing a portage road south to the stream known to the English as French Creek. Tanacharison had assumed his most stern, ambassadorial manner and had stated the case of the Six Nations to the French commandant, Captain Henri Marin, with complete candor. At least that is the way Tanacharison remembered it when he told the young English major about it a few months later.

"Fathers," Tanacharison began, repeating every few sentences that odious form of address, "both you and the English are white. We live in a country between. Therefore this land does not belong either to one or the other of you; but the Great Being above allowed it to be a place of residence for us. So, Fathers, I desire you to withdraw, as I have desired our brothers the English to withdraw, for I will keep you at arm's length. I lay this down as a trial for both of you, to see which of you will have the greatest regard for it; and that side we will stand by, and make equal shares with us. Our brothers the English have heard this, and I come now to tell it to you, for I am not afraid to discharge you off this land."

His answer came from the ramrod Captain Marin not in the smooth phrases of diplomacy, but in the blunt language of a soldier. Addressing Tanacharison contemptuously as "my child," Marin snapped, "I am not afraid of flies or mosquitoes, and Indians are such as those. I tell you, down that river I will go, and will build upon it according to my orders. If the river is blocked, I have forces sufficient to burst it open and tread under my feet all that stand in opposition, together with their alliances. Child, you talk foolish. You say this land belongs to you, but there is not the dirt from my fingernail that is yours. It is my land and I will have it."

Such a harsh, direct, and militant challenge of the Iroquois League was in apparent violation of the French policy of winning the League to its side. The reality may have been more complex; Marin may well have been conducting astute diplomacy of a rather hair-raising audacity. Perhaps he was challenging not the League itself, but its authority—more specifically, Tanacharison's authority—over the Ohio Mingos. If so, he was striking directly at the League's weakest spot. There was nothing Tanacharison could do but withdraw, humiliated and angry but for the moment powerless.

Now, two months later, Tanacharison was returning to confront the French again. The situation had not improved, but there had been changes. A new Frenchman was in command at Fort Buffalo, and now an English officer was here to warn him as Tanacharison had tried to warn his predecessor. More than anything else, Tanacharison was here to see if the English could stand up to this threat, and how the French reacted to it. A great deal depended on the outcome of this meeting.

CHAPTER 5

The French

"He Invited Us to Sup with Them, and Treated with the Greatest Complaisance."

DECEMBER 4, 1753

The reluctant governor of New France had understood that he must move quickly, after the unfortunate conclusion of King George's War in 1748, if his colony was not to be permanently crippled. Roland Michel Barrin, Marquis de la Galissonière, had not wanted his job—had turned it down once, then had agreed to serve only temporarily when his predecessor, the Marquis de la Jonquière, had been plucked from aboard ship into captivity by the British Navy. But while he might be serving reluctantly, he was not about to serve halfheartedly. It was not in his nature to give short shrift.

There was no doubt in Galissonière's mind that the future of New France lay to the southwest. That was the way the rivers ran, from within a few miles of the Great Lakes all the way to French Louisiana. Westward there was harsh terrain, difficult travel, and unfamiliar native tribes. To the south lay the established British colonies. But to the southwest, behind the natural barrier of the Appalachian Mountains and along the easily travelled rivers, there were friendly tribes with access to enormous quantities of pelts. The point had been driven home a decade earlier, when French forces from the Great Lakes country had swept down the Allegheny and Ohio Rivers to the Mississippi, joined others who had come up from Louisiana, and moved against some troublesome Chickasaws there. Not only was the strategic and tactical value of the river system thus confirmed, but in the process it was mapped, so that it could be used even more easily the next time.

The 1739 expedition had been important for another reason. It had been under the command of one of the colony's brightest stars—Charles le Moyne, Baron de Longueuil, scion of a French-Canadian family that had risen from poverty to glittering distinction in both commercial and military affairs. Longueuil would be heard from again, and so would a remarkable number of the young soldiers who accompanied him on the Chickasaw expedition.

Important as its riverine communications network was, the Ohio country exerted a far more powerful attraction through its fur trade. French traders and missionaries had been working the area since La Salle's descent of the Mississippi six decades before, and until the recent unpleasantness had enjoyed something close to a monopoly in the area (although a few English itinerants had been annoying them since 1726, and Croghan had become a real problem when he set up shop at the forks of the Ohio in 1741). During the war, however, Britain had used its increasingly powerful navy to throttle the flow of goods to and from New France. What few trade goods had got through had done so only at a high price. Meanwhile, the English traders had plenty of goods, and were offering them at roughly one quarter the French prices. By 1748, Croghan and his colleagues dominated trading throughout the Ohio country.

In addition to the economic damage done to the French, there had been diplomatic setbacks of major proportions. It had been bad enough that the Treaty of Utrecht, ending the War of Spanish Succession thirty-five years earlier, had stipulated that the Iroquois were British subjects. While France later had insisted that this referred only to Iroquois persons, the British had used it to legitimize their claims to all kinds of territory. Still worse, from Galissonière's point of view, was the agreement the English colonies had made with the Iroquois at Lancaster, Pennsylvania, in 1744. That treaty had averted open warfare between the Iroquois and the English, which Galissonière thought would have been handy during King George's War. Even worse, the British later claimed that the Lancaster agreement ceded the Ohio country to them. However questionable, these legal foundations of English ambition, in combination with the recent French trade setbacks, contributed to a formidable English momentum in territory vital to the French.

George Croghan and William Trent, among others, had firmly established trading businesses not only at Logstown but at such far-flung places as Pickawillany on the south shore of Lake Erie. Immediately after the end of the war, the Ohio Company had organized to claim the country around the Forks, and although Galissonière may not yet have been aware of that in 1748, he was in no doubt that unless he acted the English were coming—and not merely to trade, but to stay.

Galissonière's first step was to try to pry the Iroquois away from the English. His method was simply to explain to representative Iroquois—at a council in Montreal in November 1748—that the English were claiming them as subjects under the Lancaster Treaty. He then explained what it meant to be a British subject: that they were regarded as vassals who, whenever ordered, were "bound to go to war for the English." The Iroquois responded hotly that they were the subjects of no other power, that they had refused again and again to take up the hatchet for the English against the French. And they certainly had not ceded to anyone their lands.

Well satisfied with the setback he had thus dealt the English-Iroquois alliance, Galissonière set out to restore the French grip on the Ohio country. This would not be easy. Although Imperial France was, on the whole, richer, more populous, and more heavily armed than Imperial Britain, the situation in the New World was reversed: the French population of Louisiana and Quebec totalled fewer than 70,000, while there were 1.3 million British colonists in America—18 Englishmen for every Frenchman. Galissonière did not have the men, the money, or the matériel to take the obvious, conclusive steps—to send an occupying army into the Ohio country, fortify the key river locations, establish connections with Louisiana and the Illinois settlements, and provide security for French traders and settlers. Instead of an army, the force available to extend French Imperial power into the heart of North America consisted, its commander reported to Galissonière in June of 1749, of "one captain, eight subaltern officers, six cadets, one chaplain, 20 soldiers, 180 Canadians and about 30 Indians."

Galissonière ordered the commander of this less-than-magnificent army, Captain Pierre Joseph Cèloron de Blainville, to make a progress through the Ohio country, intimidating the tribes and any English traders he found there and reestablishing the sovereignty of France in the region. The particular method of accomplishing the latter was to conduct, at selected river junctions, an oddly furtive little ceremony involving the dedication of a lead plate announcing, on behalf of his Majesty King Louis XV, "the renewal of possession which we have taken of the said river Ohio, and of all those [rivers] which fall into it, and of the territories on both sides as far as the source of said rivers." The curious part was that this ringing pronouncement was not placed where all might read and heed it, but was buried. Nevertheless, it constituted a formal claim.

On July 29, 1749, some six weeks after his departure from Montreal, Céloron conducted his first lead-plate burial, where Conewango Creek joins the Allegheny below Lake Chautauqua. Amused natives soon dug the plaque up, and later turned it over to New York's ambassador to the Iroquois, William Johnson. Meanwhile, Céloron continued his journey down the Belle Rivière, as the French called the Allegheny and Ohio rivers. He counselled with the tribes along his way, warning them against the land-grabbing designs of the English and urging them to resume their trade with the French—at higher prices for lower quality and uncertain supply. The sachems at Venango, Chartiers Town, Written Rock, and Logstown welcomed the French, entertained them properly, gave them their full attention, gravely promised to do everything requested, and escorted them on their way.

Céloron was not deceived; he wrote in his journal that "there is little reliance to be placed in the promise of such people." But he continued to go through the motions, convening not only tribal councils, but meetings with English traders wherever he found them, during which he ordered them to leave French property. Of course they, too, assured him of their immediate compliance. Whatever his state of mind when he began these ceremonies, when he finished, Céloron was depressed. "All that I can say is, that the nations of these localities are very badly disposed towards the French, and are entirely devoted to the English. I do not know in what way they could be brought back."

On his return, Céloron found that Governor Galissonière had been replaced as planned by Jonquiere, who had been freed from captivity at last. But Jonquiere soon died, after doing little more to further French interests in the Ohio than to encourage more French traders to go into business at Logstown. The governorship of New France passed to another caretaker, who was to hold office until the King appointed a permanent successor. This caretaker was a remarkable man—the Baron Longueuil who had led the 1739 expedition against the Chickasaws. As one of the foremost French-Canadians, and now as the King's highest-ranking officer on the continent, Longueuil might have been expected to move forcefully into the Ohio. There was no reason to think him any less motivated by patriotism or by profit than his fellow aristocrats.

Certainly his co-governor, the Intendant of New France, expected it. The Intendant was responsible for the logistics of government—the taxes, the banking, the procurement of supplies, and the dispensation of services, including justice—and the current holder of the office, François Bigot, differed from his predecessors only in longevity and in an ability to carry greed to previously unimagined lengths. Bigot did not concern himself about the wisdom of the French policy in the Ohio country, or its chances for success, but he perceived at once that it would be a mother lode of graft. Therefore, he was for it.

But Bigot was shocked by Longueuil's attitude. The temporary governor, Bigot recorded, intended "to leave the Belle Rivière at peace, having a special respect and consideration for the Iroquois who live there." When the Intendant pointed out the unsuitability of this attitude, Longueuil responded with a curt lecture. "The Governor answered sharply that the English were trading there before us; that it was not just to chase them out; that at most the river belonged to the Iroquois."

It was, of course, only a temporary setback for militarism. While Longueuil never changed his position on exploiting the Ohio country, he did change jobs. On July 30, 1752, the post of governor was assumed by a man who was perfectly suited to starting a world war—

the imperious Ange de Menneville, Marquis de Duquesne. And he carried with him just the incendiary kind of orders from the Crown that facilitated such an undertaking: "Drive the English from our territory and prevent them from coming there to trade." Seize their goods, destroy their posts.

Duquesne settled on a plan that would have strained the meager resources of New France to their limits, and perhaps beyond, even if Intendant Bigot had not set himself immediately to draining off a substantial portion of those resources into his own pockets. In the spring of 1753, a force of two thousand Frenchmen (along with two hundred "of our domiciliated Indians," as Bigot put it) would march to the Belle Rivière, building two storehouses along the way, then erect three forts at key locations on a four-hundred-mile stretch of the river, leave garrison forces at each, and go on to winter in the Illinois settlements. Accomplishing such a program in the course of a single summer would have been difficult for superbly trained troops, well equipped and thoroughly supplied by their government. Given the number and the quality of the men actually available for the task, the plan was hopelessly unrealistic. But Duquesne declared it necessary and Bigot saw that it would be profitable; there was no turning back.

Duquesne appointed the leaders of his invasion force from a list of names thoughtfully provided the new governor by Bigot. A grizzled sixty-year-old veteran of the frontier, Captain Pierre Paul de la Malgue, Sieur de Marin, would command. While in charge of a post on Lake Michigan, he had been conducting on the side a busy trade in furs, the profits from which he had shared with Bigot. Michel Jean Péan would be second-in-command. He was the richest man in Canada and a frequent partner of Bigot, but may have owed this assignment to the fact that he had a beautiful wife who used her bed on his behalf, frequently—or so it was rumored—to the satisfaction of Bigot himself. Péan's cousin, François le Mercier, was put in charge of engineering and artillery. It would be a busy winter for all of them, and a lucrative one for Bigot.

In the fall of 1752, Duquesne began implementation of his plan with orders to the French commander at Fort Niagara, Claude Pierre Pécaudy de Contrecoeur (Péan's uncle and Mercier's relative). Captain Contrecoeur, a forty-six-year-old professional officer who had spent half his life in the uniform of France, was told to begin building boats, and to rush the clearing of a new portage road from his post on Lake Ontario to another above Niagara Falls. In October, Duquesne explained the orders with a confident prediction: "In the course of the month of May, I shall send from Montreal 300 soldiers [French regulars], 1700 *habitants* [French-Canadian militia] and about 200 Indians to go and seize and establish themselves on the Belle Rivière, which we are on the verge of losing if I do not make this hasty but indispensable effort." A month later, writing to Contrecoeur, Duquesne was obviously confronting some of the realities of his plan. "You know the extent of my project," he wrote, "which involves the following: 2200 men to transport; four forts to construct and all the paraphernalia which is involved in such an operation; provisions for a year. Give me your suggestions, please."

Provisions were a special problem because the crops in New France, never more than sufficient for the colony's needs, had been especially poor in 1752. Bigot merely turned to the back-door channel of trade that for years had connected the merchants of Montreal with those of New York. Through war and peace and all other vicissitudes, these tradesmen had accommodated themselves to the fact that Montreal always had more furs than trade goods, and New York vice versa. These unrealized profits yearned for each other with such irresistible pressure that the dam of national interests separating them leaked a treasonous, universally condemned, and continual traffic along the Hudson River, Lake Champlain, and the Richelieu. In 1752, this market of opportunity yielded the provisions Duquesne needed to invade the Ohio country.

During the fall and winter the contracts were made, always with a portion deducted for Bigot and his friends, and the goods were shipped to Montreal and Fort Niagara for warehousing. Unfortunate Canadians were dragooned into the militia to provide the "1700 *habitants*." In February the first detachment, under a twenty-four-year-old officer named Charles Deschamps de Boishébert, struggled west through snow and then floods to establish a post on Lake Erie from which to make the portage into the Ohio watershed.

Previous expeditions, such as Céloron's, had used the Lake Chautauqua-Conewango Creek connection to the Belle Rivière. But while Boishébert's detachment was on its way there, he received a directive from Duquesne, who was avidly following and frequently meddling in every detail of the campaign, to move farther west along Erie's shore. There, an experienced frontiersman had told Duquesne, they would find a snug harbor where they could avoid not only Erie's storms, but the reefs and rocky shores of the former landing place. From there, a portage of fifteen miles—somewhat longer, but less rugged, than the Chautauqua portage—led to the Rivière aux Boeufs (which translated roughly as Buffalo River, but appeared on English maps as French Creek).

When the main expeditionary force began leaving Montreal in mid-April, the awesome difficulty of the undertaking immediately became apparent. Negotiating the first and easiest leg of the journey took Marin's detachment twenty-three consecutive days of rowing and paddling—up the St. Lawrence River from Montreal to Fort Frontenac on Lake Ontario, then across the lake to the mouth of the Niagara River—nearly three hundred miles in all. There the truly difficult part of the journey began. All of the guns, equipment, and supplies for the army and for the building of the forts had to be carried for six miles, past Niagara Falls, to another set of boats.

A great deal of this groaning labor was done, quite willingly, by Iroquois. For some time the Niagara portage had been a major local industry, where a red man could earn some ammunition, food, or trade goods by carrying a bundle, renting a horse, or selling fresh corn and meat to the travellers. At the same time, in the time-honored way of invaded countries, the natives learned a great deal about what the invaders were doing and planning. Thus the Iroquois were the first of the affected peoples to learn that a large French army was on the move toward the Ohio.

Meanwhile the portage past Niagara became the scene of a prototypical labor dispute. The Iroquois had become so accustomed to having a franchise on the transport work there that they objected strenuously to the sight of Marin's soldiers carrying their own burdens—for free. Marin had to explain that this was an emergency, that no precedent had been set, that their unwritten labor contract would remain in force. But no sooner had the Iroquois returned to work than he faced a near-mutiny by his own troops, who refused to do for free what savages were being paid to do. The beleaguered Marin gave in and paid his men for carrying, a breach of military protocol for which he was later reprimanded.

The difficulties of the passage were prodigious. Flour got wet and was ruined, boats and oars and muskets were dropped on rocks and broken, men ran out of food, or fell ill, or deserted. But the crusty Marin did what he had to do and on June 1, thirteen strenuous days after reaching the mouth of the Niagara, he launched the last of his sixty-five boats and canoes on the voyage to Presque Isle. Eight days later he reported his safe arrival, and the rapid progress of construction of the fort there, begun by a detachment under the engineer le Mercier. "It seems that up to the present God is favoring the zeal with which I am working for the good of this colony," wrote Duquesne, as if he had been doing the work. "Every moment of the day I pray that He may deign to favor my good intentions."

Things continued to go well during June and July. The fort at Presque Isle was finished, and another begun on the Rivière aux Boeufs at the end of the 15-mile portage between Lake Erie and the Belle Rivière. Duquesne fussed over the details, but grew ever more confident. The army, he exulted in June, "is going better and better, and with gaiety in all the work in which it is employed." In July he concluded that "the bands of the Belle Rivière are returning to their villages, and not a single Englishman remains there. I am not in the least worried about the success of M. Marin, but I am a great deal concerned about the exorbitant expense of the portages."

Captain Contrecoeur also thought the show of force was having its desired effect on the native population. He reported the passage through Niagara of a frightened warrior on his way back to a village near Montreal that he had left sixteen years earlier. "He said he was coming to embrace the Christian religion with all his heart in order to get on the right road," Captain Contrecoeur reported, "and that the earth was trembling from the multitude of French who were at the Rivière aux Boeufs." And that was just the advance guard, the construction crew.

Such reports no doubt prompted the Iroquois League to take a close look at what was happening. Thus in June, a group of matriarchs confronted Marin to ask him formally, as Duquesne later reported, "whether he was marching with the hatchet uplifted, or to establish tranquility. This commander answered them that when he marched with the hatchet, he bore it aloft, in order that no person should be ignorant of the fact, but as for the present, his orders were to use it only in case he encountered opposition to my will."

Duquesne, who now fancied himself something of an expert on frontier life and tribal diplomacy, mocked the "trembling speeches of the Ladies of the Council," and reported that the Iroquois had rejected English appeals to oppose the French movement. And indeed the Onandaga Council was maintaining its careful neutrality while it awaited further developments. But the situation was more complicated than Duquesne, or even the Iroquois Council, understood, for the pressures of the French incursion were fracturing the League along its many fault lines.

The territory in the path of the French advance south from Presque Isle was Iroquois, but the people living there were Delawares and Shawnees who increasingly resented the League's attempts to supervise them and control their contacts with the French. As far as the Delawares and Shawnees were concerned, the French advance represented but one thing—jobs. The new opportunities for acquiring ammunition, food, trade goods, and liquor drew warriors from far down the Allegheny River to Marin's assistance. Of course, they told him whatever he wanted to hear, and his reports caused Duquesne to effuse, "you will be the Angel of Peace of the Belle Rivière."

The reaction of the western Mingo tribes, into whose territory the French were headed, was quite different. There would be few portages and little work for them; instead, there would be forts on their rivers and armed men in their country. The cost of trade goods, if the English were driven away, would quadruple. But the French had yet to hear from them. For the moment, Duquesne assumed that the native population was pacified, while the Iroquois League assumed that its policy of neutrality was being observed. Neither impression was accurate.

When Marin began to experience problems in mid-July, they arose not from the things he feared—the hostility of savages or the shortcomings of his troops—but from the greed of his superiors (and former partners). "All the barrels which have come to us, as well as the goods," he wrote on July 15, putting the matter as delicately as he could, "lack much more than they should of the weight they are supposed to have." He was writing to Contrecoeur, asking him to check on supplies that came through Niagara. Marin had spent winters in the wilderness, and knew the value of every scrap of provisions when survival was at stake. Later, he put the case more strongly: "Not a package, or at least very few of them, contains what is marked on the invoice."

When Contrecoeur relayed Marin's complaints to Bigot's office, the deputy Intendant responded that "Marin has a wicked mind that can only presume evil of everyone." Meanwhile Bigot did some murmuring in Duquesne's ear, and the governor reached a conclusion about the case—perhaps to his own financial benefit. He counteraccused Marin of "rejecting all the provisions that had suffered in the portage of Niagara, without considering that they were exposed to the loss of their quality in the transportation." Ignoring the fact that Marin had been complaining about quantity, not quality, Duquesne gave him a thinly veiled warning: "It is not like you to make such a difficulty, you, Sir, who were born with a hatchet in your hand and a flour sack for a diaper."

Marin quieted, and Duquesne reported on August 20 to his Minister in Paris that "there has not been, up to the present time, the least impediment to the considerable movements I have caused to be made." But out at Fort le Boeuf, impediments were piling up on Marin.

"Time is becoming dear," was the way Marin put it. If the army was to make its tour of the Ohio and get back to a base before winter—if, in other words, it was going to survive its mission—it must finish the building and get on with the marching. But as he was trying to accelerate the work, his men were wearing out. After four months of dawn-to-dark labor on a salt-pork-and-biscuit diet, living without proper shelter in unsanitary camps, the men were not only weakening but sickening. Scurvy began to take a terrible toll, and desertion and insubordination increased. The men were draftees, after all, who had expected to be soldiers, not laborers and packhorses; who in the manner of all soldiers at the outset of all wars had expected a short, triumphant campaign, not this long drawn-out affair of drudgery and disease.

Difficulties abounded. The portage road from Presque Isle to Le

Boeuf passed through swampy ground that, under heavy use, turned into a knee-deep quagmire of mud. "It was an afflicting spectacle," wrote Péan later, "to behold these debilitated men, struggling at the same time against the bad season and the difficulties of the road, broken down by the weight of their weapons and the loads which they had to carry." Meanwhile, the hot, dry weather of August withered the Belle Rivière until it was on the point of being too shallow for the laden flatboats that had to accompany the expedition. Marin, never known for his equanimity, began to flail about.

He blamed his officers. One of the best of them, Jean-Daniel Dumas, was struggling with the difficulties at Le Boeuf while Marin commanded from Presque Isle. On August 26, Marin wrote an insulting letter to Dumas concerning some rumors Marin had heard and some statements Dumas had made about the growing anxiety of the men to get back to Montreal before winter. "If there is anyone who is not pleased to continue the campaign," Marin wrote scathingly (speaking of course only of the regular officers), "you can assure them, sir, that upon any request they make of me I shall not hesitate to send them back immediately."

Dumas answered every complaint against him, then asked to be sent home: "I shall thus avoid the unpleasantness of which I am already getting a foretaste." Marin sacked him. But Péan, presumably the second-in-command, disagreed with the decision and Marin backed down as quickly as he had risen up, professing loyalty to Péan and friendship for Dumas. It was not an endearing performance.

Marin was thus a harassed and frustrated man when he received word that a delegation of Mingos from the Ohio country wanted to meet with him at Presque Isle. The word came along with a warning. Philippe Thomas de Joncaire, a principal agent of the French among the Ohio tribes since 1750, had maintained a post on the former portage route, below Chautauqua, and in late August had moved his operations to Venango at the confluence of the Rivière aux Boeufs and the Allegheny. There he took over the trading post and village recently abandoned by the British trader John Fraser. Joncaire's credentials as an intermediary were unexcelled—his father had been a celebrated expert on the Iroquois, and his mother was a Seneca. He had acted as Céloron's interpreter during the 1749 expedition and had spent a good deal of time at Logstown. At the age of forty-six, he had gained considerable wealth from his trading operations, held the rank of captain in the French militia and served as France's chief interpreter for the Six Nations. And he knew more than any other Frenchman about the Ohio tribes, about the delegation on its way to see Marin, and about its leader, Tanacharison.

Yet Joncaire's message to Marin made no contribution to understanding. It relayed no comprehension of Tanacharison's role in the Ohio country, conveyed no information about the complex dynamics in play, but merely defamed the Seneca in a manner that was sure to inflame Marin. Tanacharison, wrote Joncaire, "is more English than the English, working only against the French by continually saying foolish things. In a word, he is no good, and it is he who sold the lands to the English."

Tanacharison arrived at Presque Isle on September 2, and the account of his meetings there recorded by the French was more detailed and in many respects different from his version of events, as related to Washington. First, according to Marin, Tanacharison announced a point to which he would return again and again. Using the alien honorific that the whites seemed to like, he said, "My father, these are warriors and not chiefs who come to bid you good day." He had nothing further of substance to say that day—"business should never be hurried," he insisted—and when he began his oration on the next day it was with the same, insistent point about his credentials: "The river where we are belongs to us warriors. The chiefs who look after affairs are not its masters. It is a road for warriors and not for these chiefs."

This was a strange assertion, since Tanacharison was one of the "chiefs who look after affairs," both among the Senecas and in the Iroquois League. He seemed to be claiming the prerogative of an Iroquois war chief, the right of command separate and apart from the sachems and the councils. It may be that he was doing this to protect himself in case he was departing from Iroquois policy in confronting the French. It may be that he was leading a Mingo insurgency against the neutrality of the Onandaga Council, and explaining it to his own people in terms of the necessities of war.

Whatever he said, Tanacharison was no war chief; he was a councillor, an elder, and a wily one at that. It seems likely that he was pursuing an even more devious course of action—that he was doing exactly what the Council wanted in trying to prevent both the English and now the French from building forts and settlements in the Ohio country while encouraging them to trade there. His message to the French was essentially identical to his request of the English at Logstown—to send trade goods, "what we need, but not to build any forts."

"With this belt we detain you," he said formally to Marin, "and ask you to cease setting up the establishments you want to make. All the tribes have always called upon us not to allow it. We have told our brothers the English to withdraw. They have done so, too. We shall be on the side of those who take pity on us and who listen to us. Although I am small, the Master of Life has not given me less courage to oppose these establishments. This is the first and last demand I shall make of you, and I shall strike at whoever does not listen to us."

Marin was no diplomat, nor was he in the mood to attempt diplomacy. Moreover, if Joncaire was right, and Joncaire was the expert, Tanacharison was a scoundrel, not to be taken seriously. Marin rudely refused to accept the strings of wampum, thus rejecting everything Tanacharison had said. The Ohio country, Marin then declared, "belongs incontestably to the King," who "has ordered these establishments in order to be assured of the faithfulness of his children." After saying he did not wish to "disturb" the tribes, and saying they would remain free to trade as they wished, he progressed from rudeness to insult.

"I despise all the stupid things you have said. I know that they come only from you, and that all the warriors and chiefs of the Belle Rivière think better than you, and take pity on their women and children. I am obliged to tell you that I shall continue on my way, and if there are any persons bold enough to set up barriers to hinder my march, I shall knock them over so vigorously that they may crush those who made them."

Tanacharison responded with the dignity of a man grossly offended but unwilling to reply in kind: "I have no comment to make on what you say to me." He repeated the odd disclaimer—"you can well believe that I do not come from my chief"—then said it would be up to the nations that had sent him to decide what to do. He concluded with a point for the record: "this is the third refusal you have given me." In other words, the traditional Iroquois requirement for fair warning before hostilities had been satisfied.

The French column—extended, encumbered, and increasingly enfeebled—continued to claw its way into the wilderness. Not until September 8 were all the supplies past the Niagara portage, so that Péan with the rear guard could set out to join Marin and the main force. Duquesne remained upbeat, writing to Paris on October 3 that surely, by that time, Péan and Marin had reached the Ohio.

A few days later he learned to his chagrin that they were not even close. Péan reported that when he arrived at Fort le Boeuf, he found Marin sick and hemorrhaging, "at the last extremity" of illness. Duquesne penned a flowery letter of sympathy to Marin: "I take so keen an interest in prolonging your days that I do not hesitate to send to you Sieur de St. Pierre, whom I have ordered to assist you in every way until your complete convalescence." But the reality was that Duquesne knew he must replace Marin immediately—with an officer equally experienced and tough—or abandon the expedition. Péan could maintain the building program and keep the men moving forward, Duquesne thought, but at the head of the column must be a man who could "make himself feared and respected by the Indians." The only name that came to mind was that of Jacques Legardeur, Sieur de St. Pierre.

St. Pierre was the embodiment of everything the young Major Washington found desirable about the profession of arms. St. Pierre had carried his king's commission for most of his fifty-two years, over half the world. He had served in any number of European campaigns, had attended that country's glittering courts, and now was returning from command of a handful of rude fur-trading outposts in the western wilderness near Lake Winnipeg, in what was to become the province of Manitoba. He had lost one eye and his youth in service to France, and had been looking forward to well-earned retirement when he left the far country, only to be deflected from his homeward course by orders to go to the Rivière aux Boeufs. Ever the professional, St. Pierre sighed and set out.

Duquesne remained relentlessly optimistic about his invasion force, even as the turning leaves and freshening winds signalled the approach of winter. "The last portage is finished," he wrote brightly to Paris, and at last report Péan was "ready to leave on the 10th or

12th of October, with 180 pirogues which were all ready to enter the Rivière d'Oyo." (Apparently he was adopting frontier jargon in referring to the Belle Rivière as the Ohio.) Everything was fine, he insisted, despite the illness of the expedition commander and five hundred of his men—more than one third of the force. "The scurvy of these militia," sniffed Duquesne the vicarious frontiersman, "is seldom fatal."

As if to confirm this point, Marin rallied enough to take stock of his situation. His sadly depleted roll call was daunting enough, as was the shortage of supplies—the result of the malevolent attentions of Bigot and company, and of the sticky-fingered native workers at the portages. (The latter had not only pilfered a major part of the expedition's supply of blankets, but in one case had marched off in a hundred-man column leading a train of fully loaded packhorses toward Joncaire's forward post at Venango—and had disappeared.) Marin's subordinate officers were in a mutinous mood; Captain Legardeur de Repentigny wrote Duquesne complaining of "the slackness of the detachment," for which insubordination he was sentenced to imprisonment, when and if he got back to civilization. All this, plus the lateness of the season, might have caused Marin to relapse into illness; the state of the Rivière aux Boeufs guaranteed it.

The summer drought, which had not been sufficient to spare the men from the horrors of hip-deep mud on the portage to Fort le Boeuf, had become severe enough to diminish the waters of the creek until they could no longer float the pirogues. Both figuratively and literally, the expedition had run aground.

Marin confronted total and unavoidable failure. The army, which by now consisted of only eight hundred able-bodied men, could not advance, and with winter coming could not stay where it was. Marin ordered Péan and le Mercier to return to Montreal with all but a garrison force, which would hold the fort until another expedition could head out in the spring. As he was making these preparations, Marin received two communications.

One messenger, from upriver, brought him the prestigious Cross of St. Louis, sent to recognize, somewhat prematurely, Marin's contribution to the furthering of his king's ambitions on the continent. Along with it came permission from Duquesne to wear the Cross without awaiting formal induction into the Order. There were reports that the honor was marred somewhat when Marin's officers tried to prevent him from putting his hands on the Cross until they had a chance to tell the governor what was really going on.

The second message came from the south; it was an urgent appeal from the Delawares and Iroquois living in the Venango area. They had seen Fraser, their British supplier for more than a decade, driven off by the French and replaced by Joncaire, who, it now appeared, would have no way of getting trade goods this winter. The message began with the typical tug at the forelock: "My father, we do not doubt at all the sorrow you must feel at not being able to go among your children to comfort them." After this stab at what the Iroquois imagined the French must think a father's duties would be, there was a good deal of tongue-clucking over Marin's difficulties. And then: "We fear that the drought may prevent your coming down. Be mindful, my father, that you have driven off all the English, and that your children will be in a pitiable state if they do not see you here. Even the children are waiting for you with pleasure. Remember your promise and remember them; do not abandon them."

Marin was beyond feeling either satisfaction at his new decoration or sympathy for the imperiled tribes. He was maddened by his failure. A British deserter named Stephen Coffin who had made his way to Fort le Boeuf witnessed the commander's unraveling. "Marin, a man of very peevish, choleric disposition," Coffin later reported, "called all his officers together and told them that as he had engaged and firmly promised the Governor to finish three forts that season, and not being able to fulfill the same, was both afraid and ashamed to return to Canada, being sensible that he had now forfeited the Governor's favor forever; wherefore rather than live in disgrace, he begged they would take him—as he then sat in a carriage made for him, being very sick for some time—and seat him in the middle of the fort, and then set fire to it, and let him perish in the flames."

The men declined to participate in this showy suicide, but Marin would not return to Montreal with them. Either he could not face the shame, or he believed he would not survive the journey. Instead, he stayed with his sullen garrison, lying in his quarters contemplating his blasted hopes and failing health until, on October 29, he turned his face to the rude log wall and died.

Captain Legardeur de Repentigny, who had complained to the governor about Marin's leadership, took over temporary command of the garrison until his relative, Legardeur de St. Pierre, could arrive. And for nearly a month, de Repentigny continued to receive chatty letters from the unwitting Duquesne to the dead Marin, in which the governor was surprisingly gracious about the failure of the expedition. "Everything will be all right, Sir, if your good constitution restores itself. It is up to me to procure what you need and a whole fresh troop. That is what I am going to work on."

When the first detachment of men from the expedition made it back to Montreal, Duquesne went out to have a look at them. He was shocked by the effects of the march and the scurvy that he had dismissed as "seldom fatal." Now he realized what Marin had been talking about. "If these weakened men had set out to their destination," Duquesne marveled to his superiors in Paris, "the Rivière d'Oyo would have been strewn with dead men, because of the fevers and lung diseases that were beginning to attack this troop, and because ill-disposed Indians would not have failed to attack them when they were nothing but specters."

Now that he had accepted the gravity of the problem posed by illness, Duquesne landed on it with both feet, declaring it to be the entire cause of the failure of the expedition. As he had earlier dismissed Marin's assessment of the scurvy problem, he now dismissed the commander's assertion that the river had been too low for travel. This, Duquesne now declared, was merely "an excuse for resting his detachment." The governor assured his inquisitors at home, who were very curious about the abortive invasion, that it was to be explained only by the illness of the men and the potential hostility of the natives (despite the pleas of the local tribes for help, Duquesne remembered the solemn third warning of Tanacharison). Nothing could have been wrong with the expedition's route; after all, Duquesne had chosen that himself.

The French had little to show for their year of effort. Instead of the grand progress through the heart of the continent envisioned by Duquesne, it had taken a disheartening and agonizing struggle to get to the continent's threshold. Instead of a fortified and secure line of communications to Louisiana and the Illinois country, they had purchased, at a high price in men and treasure, a single fifteen-mile-long portage.

On December 3, Captain St. Pierre arrived at Fort le Boeuf to take command of the French invasion force, sending Repentigny north to take over the fort at Presque Isle. St. Pierre, the veteran of many explorations and campaigns, could not have failed to understand the precariousness of his situation. Those natives who had been friendly to the French advance were facing a winter of starvation as their reward; Tanacharison, of the Iroquois League, had served notice of hostile intent; and as fractious and irresolute as the British colonies had proven to be, they could not fail to respond to the French advance, now that they had been given another year in which to do it.

Joncaire, at Venango, had been doing his best to keep a good face on things. The Mingos and Delawares, whose food was already beginning to run out, were lamenting the departure of his well-supplied predecessor, John Fraser. They were facing starvation, and Joncaire, who had no way to help them, tried to make do with bluster. He called a council and declared that although the French expedition had halted because of the cold weather, it would be back in the spring. As the speech was later reported to Washington, Joncaire said "that though they had lost their general, and some few of their soldiers, yet there were men enough to reinforce them, and make them masters of the Ohio."

St. Pierre was weary, homesick, and without illusions, but he was first and foremost a professional. If his job was to represent the glory and the might of France at the head of his dispirited little band in the American wilderness, then he would do it by the book. He needed no time for reflection and preparation, and was given none; the day after his arrival at Le Boeuf, Major Washington arrived at Venango.

PART III

Action

CHAPTER 6

Contact

"They Told Me It Was Their Absolute Design to Take Possession of the Ohio, and By God They Would Do It."

DECEMBER 4, 1753

On seeing the flag of France flying over the trading post, Washington hoped he had reached his destination. But when, after an effusively polite greeting from Joncaire that did nothing to mask the underlying antagonism, Washington proffered his letter, Joncaire waved it aside, saying that the commander to whom such matters must be addressed was another sixty-five miles upstream, at Le Boeuf. He offered dinner—the French outpost was suffering none of the privations that would kill scores of natives that winter—and liberal doses of the diplomatic lubricant much favored by Frenchmen in the wilderness—brandy. Despite all the difficulties of supply, brandy was the one commodity of which neither the French, nor the tribes within their reach, ever seemed to run short.

What the French succeeded in lubricating more than anything else on the night of December 4, was their own tongues. In the warm, after-dinner glow of the fire and the brandy, they dropped all pretenses and all caution. They had a right to the Ohio country, they declared (perhaps in halting English, or for approximate translation by Washington's struggling interpreter, Jacob van Braam), their man La Salle had discovered it six decades earlier. The English outnumbered them, but moved too slowly to stop them, they grinned to their English guests. Finally, boozily, they showed their whole hand to the young major, who recalled, "They told me it was their absolute design to take possession of the Ohio, and by God they would do it."

Among the expansive French imperialists at the party was a man who apparently made no impression at the time on either Washington or Gist, whose accounts did not mention him. He was Michel Pépin, a skilled interpreter and diplomat to the tribes who had been appointed French commissary for the upper Ohio and who was on his way downriver to prepare the Mingos for the approach in the spring of the French main force. Pépin's nickname on the frontier was La Force, and although Washington did not particularly notice him now, he would meet him under fateful circumstances later.

For all their reputation as crafty frontiersmen, Joncaire and his comrades appear not to have been very bright. By the time Washington left their company, despite his lack of knowledge of any of the languages being spoken around him, he had a complete and accurate picture not only of French intentions, but of their timetable and the location and size of their fortifications, supplies, and garrisons. The slightest attention to security could have kept this greenhorn completely in the dark, yet all the information he could want was presented to him as if in an open book.

His Mingo escort, by contrast, was presented with an open bottle. When Europeans wanted to distract natives from some course of action, they often found that presenting alcoholic beverages would muddy any situation beyond saving. And this one was already tangled, in ways that Joncaire appreciated and Washington did not even begin to comprehend.

The tenacious Tanacharison was trying to make good his threat made to Captain Marin three months earlier at Presque Isle, but he was having trouble bringing it off. He had failed to organize an impressive escort for Washington, and now he could not even get the tribes on his route to serve notice on the French that their invasion was not appreciated. The method he was trying to use was one that had deep meaning in Iroquois diplomacy, although it was little regarded by whites. Tanacharison wanted to return to the French all the wampum belts they had sent to the tribes as notification of their advance into the Ohio country. Return of the belts would signify that their recipients had rejected the message.

The business of the belts soon descended into comic opera. Joncaire refused to accept the Mingo belts Tanacharison had brought with him; like Washington's letter, he insisted, they must go to the commander at Le Boeuf. When Tanacharison demanded that Custaloga, a leading sachem of the Delawares living near Venango, turn over his belt, Custaloga temporized. Hungry as his people were becoming, he apparently could not see any sense in antagonizing the French, who were close by, simply to do a favor for the British, who were far away. Tanacharison insisted that he had brought orders from Shingas, but Custaloga remained mulish, saying that if Shingas had wanted the belt returned, he should have sent a speech along, so that Custaloga would know exactly what to say. Thus frustrated, Tanacharison perhaps had more reason than usual to embrace the forgetfulness of liquor during the expedition's stay at Venango—a stay extended to three days by a long, cold, torrential rain.

It was not until midday on December 7 that the party finally began the last leg of its outward journey, northward from Venango. The next four days were hellish, a succession of what Washington recalled as "excessive rains, snows, and bad travelling through many mires and swamps." They could not have felt confident. They now had a French force at their back as well as to their front, and were well aware that the French had taken to scooping up isolated Englishmen found along the Ohio tributaries and taking them to Montreal in captivity. Tanacharison remained a steadfast friend, but his ability to command—even to influence—the loyalty of the tribes among whom they were traveling was becoming more and more questionable.

On the evening of December 11, the ragged little band of adventurers and diplomats, far from home and friends, drew themselves up as well as they could and rode into the presence of the beleaguered little company of soldiers and conscripts huddled in Fort le Boeuf, far from home and friends. Imperial Britain was at last face to face with Imperial France in the heartland of North America.

* * *

On the morning of December 12, Washington mustered his most imposing manner and entered the presence of Captain St. Pierre. Both men had reason to be tense, and there would have been little to choose between Washington's habitual iciness and St. Pierre's professional flintiness. St. Pierre began by saying he was not ready to talk. He would not rely on a British interpreter, and must have his own, but the nearest person who "knew a little English" was his relative Legardeur de Repentigny, at Presque Isle. He had been sent for. Would the major mind waiting a few hours?

The young major had no choice, and spent the time wandering about, studying the fortification and counting men. It was late afternoon before he was summoned back into St. Pierre's presence, and then it was only so that he and van Braam could read and confirm the French translation of Dinwiddie's letter. If he expected confrontation and impassioned argument—as he well may have, since he had no experience in diplomacy—he was disappointed. In all the delay, and debating of verb tenses, the letter lost its intended whiff of gunpowder.

Dinwiddie had taken his most haughty tone: "I must desire you to acquaint me by whose authority and instructions you have lately marched from Canada with an armed force, and invaded the King of Great Britain's territories. It becomes my duty to require your peaceable departure." The sharp words and unmistakable intent might have raised the hackles and the heartbeat on first reading, but after two labored translations it was just another sentence. Now that everyone agreed on how it should be said in French, St. Pierre smiled, thanked Washington, and said he would need a day or so to frame a suitable reply.

St. Pierre spent the day trying to pry Tanacharison from his apparent alliance with the British. The French commander displayed his fort, his soldiers, and his stock of gifts and liquor, emphasizing by contrast the poverty of the representatives of Britain. Tanacharison was a willing listener—and eater and drinker. Washington, meanwhile, obeyed his other instructions from Governor Dinwiddie and indulged in some espionage, with startling results. He found, drawn up on the banks of French Creek near the fort, no fewer than 220 canoes, with more being built daily. It was nothing less than an invasion fleet, poised to carry a large force of French regulars into the American heartland in the spring.

Now Washington had to wonder whether the French intended to allow him to return with his intelligence. In due course, however, St. Pierre handed over a reply to Dinwiddie and proffered canoes laden with supplies to speed the first leg of Washington's return journey. Tanacharison, smiled the French officer, would be staying behind.

Now there appeared the first glimpse of tempered steel in the character of the young militiaman. Washington ordered his men out of the canoes. He found Tanacharison and asked for an explanation, which was that St. Pierre had bribed the sachem to stay awhile, in order to receive some presents. Washington angrily confronted the oily St. Pierre, accusing the Frenchman of a serious breach of diplomatic courtesy. Somewhat taken aback, St. Pierre agreed to deliver the promised presents to Tanacharison the next day and do nothing more to impede the departure of Washington's party. But when all was done on the following day and once again it was time for Washington to go, the devious Frenchman laid out one more offering—of copious amounts of brandy. To warm you, he smiled at the Iroquois sachem, on your journey.

From recent experience, Washington knew that Tanacharison, like many people not inured to alcohol by frequent imbibing, would be incapacitated in minutes. And so he did an unthinkable thing. He confronted the proud sachem in front of the assembled onlookers, forbade him to touch the brandy, and ordered him into a canoe. There was a long, pregnant pause. If Tanacharison considered himself insulted by this challenge, the shaky British alliance with the Iroquois League could be shattered. The harm to the British cause could be incalculable. "I can't say that ever in my life I suffered so much anxiety as I did in this affair," Washington would recall.

But at length Tanacharison gave a brief nod and turned to go with the Virginians. Instead of being angered, he appeared to be impressed by Washington's spunk; he soon ceremonially adopted the young man as a brother to the Seneca with the tribal name Caunotaucarius, meaning Town-taker.

Having got away, Washington needed to get back to Williamsburg with the French response, and news of the impending invasion, as fast as possible. What should have been an easy beginning—the sixty-five-mile run downstream to Venango, where they had left their horses—turned into an agony of frustration. The stream was so low that their heavily laden canoes repeatedly grounded and "obliged all hands to get out and remain in the water half an hour or more, getting her over the shoals," Washington recorded. "In one place the ice had lodged and made it impassable by water. Therefore we were obliged to carry our canoe across a neck-land a quarter of a mile over." Because of the low water, the ice, and the winding of the stream—"I dare say the distance between the fort and Venango can't be less than 130 miles to follow the meanders"—it took them six days, until December 22, to get to Venango.

Leaving Tanacharison and the other red men there, Washington and his servitors struggled on. Their horses were weak, barely able to carry the essential supplies, so everyone had to walk. The going was hard, wrote Washington. "The cold increased very fast, and the roads were getting much worse by a deep snow continually freezing." He decided to leave the horses and his escort, leave the trails, and with Gist strike out across the country on foot, taking the most direct possible route back to Williamsburg. Gist, who had done this sort of thing before, knew the difficulties of such a journey, and was, he wrote in his journal, unwilling to undertake such a journey with Washington, "who had never been used to walking before this time. But as he insisted on it, I set out with our packs, like Indians, and travelled 18 miles. That night we lodged at an Indian cabin, and the Major was much fatigued. It was very cold. All the small runs were frozen, that we could hardly get water to drink."

They moved on, according to Gist, at 2:00 A.M. on Thursday, December 27, into a day of high adventure. Washington related the startling events with becoming modesty and brevity: "We fell in with a party of French Indians, which had laid in wait for us, one of them fired at Mr. Gist or me, not 15 steps, but fortunately missed. We took this fellow into custody, and kept him until about 9 o'clock at night, and then let him go."

What Washington described in his journal—which was also his official report to Governor Dinwiddie—was an ambush laid by a crafty foe. "Fell in with" was common parlance for "engaged in battle," and the "party" had "laid in wait for us." But Gist described the incident quite differently in his private diary. At a village called Murdering Town, Gist recorded, "we met with an Indian whom I thought I had seen at Joncaire's at Venango when on our way up to the French fort. This fellow called me by my Indian name, and pretended to be glad to see me." Gist was suspicious of the man, but nevertheless engaged him as a guide to the most direct way to "the forks of Allegheny."

What follows, in Gist's journal, is a most curious story, curiously told. It demonstrates once again Gist's remarkable tendency to accept without curiosity the most bizarre behavior by savages. It also casts a different, albeit frustratingly insufficient, light on Washington's version of the same events. For these reasons it is worth considering in its entirety:

> We set out, and the Indian took the Major's pack. We travelled very brisk for eight or 10 miles, when the Major's feet grew very sore, and he very weary, and the Indian steered too much north-eastwardly. [This is indeed odd, for the direct course from the vicinity of Venango to the forks of the Ohio is due south.] The Major desired to encamp, to which the Indian asked to carry his gun. But he refused that, and then the Indian grew churlish, and pressed us to keep on, telling us that there were Ottawa Indians in these woods, and they would scalp us if we lay out; but to go to his cabin, and we would be safe. I thought very ill of the fellow, but did not care to let the Major know I mistrusted him. But he soon mistrusted him as much as I. He said he could hear a gun to his cabin, and steered us more northwardly. We grew uneasy, and then he said two whoops might be heard to his cabin. We went two miles further; then the Major said he would stay at the next water, and we desired the Indian to stop at the next water.
>
> But before we came to water, we came to a clear meadow; it was very light, and snow on the ground. The Indian made a stop, turned about; the Major saw him point his gun toward us and fire.

A collection of curiosities. All along, Gist had been relating what the Major did and said, what the guide did and said. Now, suddenly, after describing the excellent visibility, Gist described the dramatic highlight of the story through the Major's eyes, not his own: "the Major saw him point his gun toward us." Why this attribution? Had Gist, despite his suspicions, let the guide get out of his sight in that clear meadow with the good light, so that only Washington saw what happened? Or did Gist see, but have some doubt about the man's action or intention? His account was of course set down later, by which time Gist knew of Washington's insistence that this had been a hostile act. Was Gist shrugging to himself over a harmless exaggeration?

Gist's journal at this point becomes quite lyrical.

> Said the Major, "Are you shot?" "No," said I. Upon which the Indian ran forward to a big standing white oak, and to loading his gun; but we were soon with him. I would have killed him, but the Major would not suffer me to kill him. We let him charge his gun; we found he had put in a ball; then we took care of him. The Major or I always stood by the guns; we made him make a fire for us by a little run, as if we intended to sleep there. I said to the Major, "As you will not have him killed, we must get him away, and then we must travel all night." Upon which I said to the Indian, "I suppose you were lost, and fired your gun." He said, he knew the way to his cabin, and 'twas but a little way. "Well," said I, "do you go home; and as we are much tired, we will follow your track in the morning; and here is a cake of bread for you, and you must give us meat in the morning." He was glad to get away.

Small wonder that this, apparently one of the most incompetent savages in history, was glad to be told to go home. Here was a warrior who not only tried to ambush two armed men at close range with one bullet, who not only failed to hit either six-foot-two-inch target from a distance of "15 steps," but then, having commenced hostilities, allowed himself to be overtaken while reloading his weapon a short distance away. These and other improbable details and exchanges—why, for example, did they "let him charge his gun"?—make the entire episode incomprehensible. If Gist was trying to record the truth with hints and clues, he failed; if he was simply making a private record of Washington's tendency to portray events to maximum personal advantage, he may have succeeded.

When their mysterious companion had disappeared into the woods, Washington and Gist "set our compass, and fixed our course, and travelled all night," just in case there were other, more capable assailants nearby. They continued all day as well, not resting until Friday night. The next morning they reached the Allegheny River a few miles above the Forks. It was a daunting sight. "We expected to have found the river froze," wrote Washington, "but it was not, only about 50 yards from each shore; the ice I suppose had broken up above, for it was driving in vast quantities. There was no way for us to get over but on a raft, which we set about with but one poor hatchet, and got finished just after sunsetting after a whole day's work.

"We got it launched, and on board of it, and set off," Washington recalled, "but before we got half over, we were jammed in the ice in such a manner that we expected every moment our raft would sink and we perish. I put out my setting pole to try to stop the raft, that the ice might pass by, when the rapidity of the stream threw it with such violence against the pole that it jerked me into ten feet of water, but I fortunately saved myself by catching hold of one of the raft logs. Notwithstanding all our efforts we could not get the raft to either shore, but were obliged, as we were pretty near an island, to quit our raft and wade to it. The cold was so extreme severe that Mr. Gist got all his fingers and some of his toes froze, and the water was shut up so hard that we found no difficulty in getting off the island on the ice in the morning, and went to Mr. Fraser's."

Gist corroborated this part of the story, but did not lavish on it anything like the detail of the previous adventure. He wrote simply that they "made a raft, and with much difficulty got over to an island a little above Shanopin's Town. The Major having fallen in from off the raft, and my fingers frost-bitten, and the sun down, and very cold, we contented ourselves to encamp upon that island. It was deep water between us and the shore; but the cold did us some service, for in the morning it was frozen hard enough for us to pass over on the ice."

About this incident there was undoubtedly less to be said than Washington recorded, and more than did Gist. Two things about Washington's immersion need to be noted: that it was probably not total, since the letter he was carrying from St. Pierre to Dinwiddie survived untouched by water; and that it probably made him no wetter than Gist, who also had to launch the raft and wade ashore on the island. What neither man described was the agony of that long night, which can be appreciated by anyone who has made camp in freezing weather. Without a fire, built promptly and fed all night, and shelter of some kind, both men could have died. It was fortunate, indeed, that Gist was an experienced woodsman who knew what had to be done and how to do it. Building a fire in snow and ice, for example, was not something for which Washington had demonstrated any special aptitude. Small wonder that it was Gist, and not his companion, who in Washington's words had "all of his fingers and some of his toes froze."

They came now into more familiar and settled territory. They took shelter at Fraser's, at the mouth of Turtle Creek ten miles up the Monongahela from the Forks, and while waiting for horses to be brought for them, heard news of a massacre of white settlers far to the south on the Great Kanawha River, and visited the clan matron Aliquippa at her home three miles away. Washington heard that she was upset because he had not called on her on the way to the French fort, and decided to humor her since it involved almost no effort. Gist still thought she was a Delaware, although Conrad Weiser knew her to be Seneca despite her use of a Delaware name. Neither man had the faintest idea of her power.

On January 1, Washington and Gist left Fraser's, heading up the Youghiogheny to Gist's plantation, and after a day's rest continued toward Wills Creek. Before arriving there on January 6, Washington recorded, "We met 17 horses loaded with materials and stores for a fort at the Forks; and the day after a family or two, going out to settle." That is all he had to say about crossing paths with the Ohio Company's fateful initiative to grasp the Ohio country. He made no mention of encountering the expedition's leader, William Trent.

Washington did not record how long he stayed at Wills Creek, only that he arrived at Belvoir on January 11 and rested there one day, arriving in Williamsburg on January 16, where he immediately conveyed St. Pierre's letter. The French commander had told Dinwiddie that the question of French "rights" to the Ohio country and of British "pretensions" thereto could be taken up only by the Marquis de Duquesne, to whom St. Pierre had forwarded Dinwiddie's complaint and warning. "As to the summons you send me to retire," St. Pierre continued, "I do not think myself obliged to obey it. Whatever may be your instructions, I am here by virtue of the orders of my general; and I entreat you, sir, not to doubt one moment but that I am determined to conform myself to them with all the exactness and resolution which can be expected from the best of officers."

The next day Washington and Dinwiddie reported to the executive council, and on the 18th Washington submitted his written journal, which to his professed surprise was soon thereafter printed and given wide distribution in the colonies and in England, affording him his first measure of fame. In a preface to the published version, Washington demurred that he had had but one day to work on his notes, that the result contained "numberless imperfections," and that "nothing can recommend it to the public but this: those things which came under the notice of my own observation, I have been explicit and just in a recital of; those things which I have gathered from report, I have been particularly cautious not to augment."

CHAPTER 7

Command

"I Could Enumerate a Thousand Difficulties."

May 18, 1754

It must have been with some relief that Robert Dinwiddie turned, in late January of 1754, to the relatively straightforward business of preparing for world war. He was by that time ensnared in a quite different and mundane controversy that, to his considerable mystification and growing anger, was spiraling out of his control.

It had seemed a simple matter of imposing a normal fee for a government service. But the proposal proved to be a match tossed into a powderkeg House of Burgesses, and the resulting explosion left more than a whiff of rebellion hanging in the colonial air. It marred at the outset, and cast a long shadow over, Dinwiddie's efforts to respond vigorously and decisively to the French threat to the Ohio country. And it cast a strong light on the limitations of Dinwiddie's arrogant style of governance, a style that served for a time as George Washington's only model, a style that was to lead them both into the depths of catastrophe before the year was out.

"The people here are too much bent on a republican spirit," Robert Dinwiddie once declared, speaking of Virginians whose ranks included the likes of the young Thomas Jefferson, Patrick Henry, and George Washington. He did not like to see the authority of the English Crown challenged the way that the gentlemen planters of Virginia so frequently did. Dinwiddie was not an aristocrat, but was a believer in the rights of aristocracy; not English, but a fervent champion of England's empire; not Anglican, but a staunch defender of the established Church of England.

He was first a merchant—the son and grandson of merchants—born in 1692 a Scotsman and a Presbyterian. He had come of age and learned the trade in Glasgow, where his father had done well enough to provide an ample country house and a university education for his sons. Robert had learned how to turn a profit in Glasgow just as that city's flourishing trade with America was beginning, and in 1720 had taken his knowledge to the colony of Bermuda. There, for the eighteen years that followed, he had worked hard, married well, and become wealthy. But he wanted more.

The year 1738 had marked a turning point in Dinwiddie's life. At the age of forty-six, he had been a successful man: a merchant prince directing a thriving trade throughout British America and the Caribbean; a public man who for thirteen years had held the post of Collector of Customs and for eight a seat on the Council of Bermuda; a man of society connected by marriage to the island's leading families; and, somewhat belatedly, a family man whose first child, a daughter, had been born into modest luxury the same year that Dinwiddie's brother lost the family home and took up residence in a Glasgow poorhouse.

His minor post had offered few opportunities for displaying his mettle to London officialdom, but Dinwiddie had not let the smallest one get past him. He had submitted to the Board of Trade—the powerful advisory body in London that studied the commerce of the Empire with a view to wringing ever more revenue out of it—several solid ideas for improving the control of maritime trade, for a better ship registry, for a colonial currency. He had established and carefully cultivated extensive and impressive contacts in London, the center of his universe.

In 1738, his patient work had been rewarded with an appointment as Surveyor General, or supervisor of customs, for a vast territory including the coast of British America, the Bahamas, and Jamaica. It was the kind of imperial post for which every bureaucrat hungered; not only did it pay well for light work, but the commission was for life, and meant permanent security. It was customary to dispatch hirelings to perform—often, indifferently—the duties of such offices, but Dinwiddie was not only industrious, but conscientious. Unlike the aristocrats whose circles he was now approaching, he was driven to justify himself by works—he was not convinced that the good things of life were permanent, and held by right of birth. He had seen his father lose his grip on life toward the end, and knew where his brother was living.

And so Dinwiddie embarked on an intensive round of inspections. He toured the ports of Virginia and North Carolina, investigated widespread fraud among British agents in Barbados, reported his findings in person and in detail to London, and in 1741 took up temporary residence in Norfolk, Virginia, one of the busiest seaports under his charge. There he no doubt had dealings with a subordinate collector in his domain, William Fairfax.

And there, prophetically, Dinwiddie was soon embroiled in a contest of wills with the leaders of the colony. He startled the members of the august Council of Virginia by announcing that the Surveyor General was entitled to a seat on the council of every colony in his jurisdiction. His predecessors had made no such claims, but Dinwiddie knew from his service in Bermuda what the Council was—the upper house of the bicameral legislature, the governor's cabinet, the court of last appeal in the colony, and perhaps more importantly than anything else the ultimate gentleman's club. Dinwiddie was determined to have his place on the council of the largest and fastest-growing colony in British North America.

The Council members were not pleased at the prospect of admitting into their fraternal circle any such stranger and lowborn functionary. They demanded proof of his claim. Dinwiddie was not in the habit of carrying his commission around with him, and it took time to get it. When it arrived and confirmed his claim, the Council grudgingly appointed him a councillor extraordinary, qualified to give advice to the governor when asked, but denied any legislative or judicial authority. Dinwiddie insisted on full membership, appealed his case to London, and won. The right of the Crown government to make even trivial decisions in and for the colonies, and to overrule any colonial authority, had once again been upheld. Dinwiddie and his royalist colleagues would win many such battles in the succeeding three decades, in the course of losing a continent.

Having established his right to serve, Dinwiddie appeared to be uninterested in serving. Two years passed, during which he travelled about his district and to England, before he ever appeared at a meeting of the Council. He took the oath of office in April of 1745, attended meetings for a few months, then returned to London for six years. He seemed to have lost all interest in Virginia, selling his position as Surveyor General to Peter Randolph and relinquishing his membership in the Council.

But Dinwiddie's interest in the colony flared anew when he learned of the resignation, late in 1749, of Governor Gooch. It took Dinwiddie eighteen months of manipulating every contact he possessed, but he won appointment, on July 4, 1751, as lieutenant governor. The governorship went to William Anne Keppel, Earl of Albemarle, a dissolute courtier who required £3,300 a year from Dinwiddie as consideration for the right to do all the work of governing the colony. This fee, about three quarters of the total stipend for the position, helps account for Dinwiddie's interest in other sources of income.

Dinwiddie had a merchant's mind attuned to trends that presented opportunities for profit, and he had quickly grasped that the most lucrative prospects in Virginia were in the land business. He had become an investor and partner in the Ohio Company on March 27, 1750, more than a year before his appointment as lieutenant governor had come through.

London would remain focused on the colonial exports of furs, tobacco, and timber, but Dinwiddie and a growing number of colonial businessmen were becoming entranced with land. The uninitiated valued land for the things that could be harvested from it; the smart money was now harvesting the land. One way to wealth in real estate, as shown by Lord Fairfax's former agent King Carter, was simply to reserve large blocks of wilderness land, under the casual procedures designed to make it easy for settlers, and then hold them until rising demand increased their value. That increase, in a colony whose population was in the process of growing from 115,000 in 1730 to 340,000 in 1760, was assured.

Dinwiddie the experienced bureaucrat immediately spotted in

this situation an opportunity of a different kind. To be legal, a patent for a tract of land required the governor's seal. Other governors charged a nominal fee for this service, and Dinwiddie saw no reason to deny himself this source of income. In April 1752, just five months after Dinwiddie's arrival in the colony, his Council obligingly approved a charge for this service of one pistole—a Spanish coin in wide circulation in the currency-starved colonies, valued at almost one pound sterling, the approximate price of a cow. As he moved to begin collecting this fee, which was neither backbreaking nor trifling, he also served notice that he expected land grants to be patented promptly. Speculators had not been bothering to patent their holdings until they were about to transfer them, for the simple reason that once raw land was patented, annual quit-rents were due. Dinwiddie was delivering a double blow, and the speculators, most of whom were also members of the House of Burgesses, struck back.

William Stith, chaplain of the House and president of the College of William and Mary, insisted that the fee was "against law," and "subversive of the rights and liberties of my country." Here again was an expression of the curious set of ideas that had figured in the arguments over the Fairfax proprietary—that Virginia was a country whose citizens held definable rights. Dinwiddie's country was England, and all property was held first by the sovereign, who dispensed it as a privilege. Dinwiddie simply did not comprehend the idea behind the toast proposed by Stith and soon chanted as a powerful, inflammatory slogan: "Liberty, property, and no pistole." Among the scores of voluble opponents who agreed with that sentiment were such personages as House speaker John Robinson, the influential planter Landon Carter, and the colony's attorney general, Peyton Randolph.

The situation became so rowdy, and the required confirmation of the fee by the House appeared so unlikely, that Dinwiddie delayed convening the Burgesses and appealed to the Board of Trade. That body of course confirmed his right to impose the fee, and so informed him the following year, 1753. Armed with that, the governor called the House into session on November 1, the day after Washington's departure on his mission to French Creek.

Instead of compliance, Dinwiddie was greeted by a renewed firestorm. The Burgesses denounced the fee as illegal, contrary to the English constitution, and inimical to the growth of the colony. They gave sympathetic hearing to appeals from six counties for repeal of the fee. Wary of Dinwiddie's right to prorogue the legislature should it become too troublesome, the Burgesses met secretly in December, framed an appeal to the Privy Council (the senior assembly of king's advisors, of which the Board of Trade was one committee) in London, and passed a resolution declaring that anyone who paid the fee would be betraying "the rights and privileges of the people."

The case was to be argued before the Privy Council in June of 1754. The Burgesses sent the colonial attorney general, Peyton Randolph, to represent them, armed with a fee of £2,500 and a guarantee of a lifetime pension should Dinwiddie fire him, which Dinwiddie promptly did. The Earl of Halifax, president of the Board of Trade, prepared to argue on Dinwiddie's side, but not without expressing his vexation that the controversy had reached such unbecoming proportions. The Privy Council would eventually uphold Dinwiddie's rights in the face of what one lawyer called this "puny House of Burgesses" that had "boldly dared to do what the House of Commons in England never dared to attempt." But the victory would be far from complete, would heal no wounds, and in January, Dinwiddie could not know how a distressingly messy situation would be resolved.

On January 21, five days after Washington's return from French Creek, Dinwiddie did what many another leader has done in the face of an intractable domestic problem: he brandished the threat of war. His Council agreed to call the House of Burgesses back into session and meanwhile, as an emergency measure, to recruit one hundred men from Frederick and Augusta Counties and send them to the frontier under the command of George Washington, with William Trent recruiting perhaps one hundred more from among his fellow "traders and other friends, to annoy the enemy."

In the succeeding week or so, the governor made these rather vague plans more explicit. He ordered Major Washington to Frederick County, where he would receive fifty men from Lord Fairfax, whom Dinwiddie had ordered to "direct the militia of Frederick to be drawn out." Washington was also to receive fifty militiamen from Augusta County, led by James Patton, and take the entire force to

Alexandria. There, with the assistance of a newly appointed commissary of stores and provisions—William Fairfax's son-in-law and Dinwiddie's fellow Scot John Carlyle—Washington was to provision and train his men "in the best manner you can." Having somehow accomplished this, Washington was to "use all expedition in proceeding to the Fork of the Ohio" to complete and defend "the fort which I expect is already there, begun by the Ohio Company." To William Trent, who was on his way to the Forks to begin building the fort, Dinwiddie dispatched a captain's commission and instructions to recruit one hundred men "in the pay of this government," to await reinforcement by Washington's one hundred and in the spring perhaps four hundred more.

In this, even more than in the pistole controversy, Dinwiddie had the vigorous support of his superiors in London. Along with the bristling communiqué for the French commander at Le Boeuf, they had sent thirty cannons for the defense of the Ohio country (Dinwiddie appreciated the thought, but had to confess they were "much too large to be transported so great a distance by land, and in bad roads," and asked for something smaller). And they ordered three independent companies of British regulars—two from New York and one from South Carolina—to march to the aid of Virginia.

There was far less enthusiasm from Dinwiddie's fellow governors. He wrote them in January to report the French aggression and his own response, and to ask for their support. The governor of Maryland, Horatio Sharpe, responded that his assembly had resolved that "the exigencies of affairs was not such as required any aid or support from them." That would not change, he thought, until and unless Maryland was actually invaded. The governor of Pennsylvania, James Hamilton, supported Dinwiddie in principle but could not actually do anything; his Quaker-dominated assembly would not consider spending money for warlike purposes. For the time being, Virginia was on its own in defending the King's dominion over the Ohio country. For the moment, this struck Dinwiddie as more of an opportunity than a problem.

It became more of a problem when the House of Burgesses went into session on February 14 and immediately, flatly refused to enact a supply bill to pay for the measures Dinwiddie had ordered. Dinwiddie was incredulous. Trent and Christopher Gist had arrived at the Forks to begin construction of what they intended to call Fort Prince George. Hostile French forces would soon be on the way toward them, the militia was being alerted, yet the Burgesses were digging in their heels, having the scent of the pistole still in their nostrils.

It was only after a week of what Dinwiddie described as "great application, many arguments, and much difficulty" that the House faced up to its duty. On February 22, it voted to authorize £10,000 for defense. But it was not an appropriation, simply authority for the treasurer of the colony to borrow money whose disbursement would then be overseen by a committee of ten burgesses and four councillors. As difficult as it had been to get the approval, the additional steps required—finding lenders to provide funds, then wrangling with the committee to get approval for expenditures—during the months to come would drive Dinwiddie continually to distraction.

In addition to his troubles with the burgesses, Dinwiddie was having difficulty raising soldiers. He had been given the authority to call up the militia, but found that his subjects were fully as suspicious of his motives as were his legislators. From the viewpoint of the men receiving the urgent messages to muster and prepare to march away from their farms and families, Dinwiddie appeared not as a patriot gathering forces against the enemy, but as a businessman protecting his interests to the last drop of other peoples' blood.

These feelings were intensified by an important difference between the Tidewater aristocrats and the Valley farmers. An established planter could leave his estate at any time he chose, for a trip to England or a sojourn in the back country, comfortable in the knowledge that there were plenty of slaves at home to do the work, and if not sons then a wife to oversee it all. But if the principal male of the frontier farm left the property, chances were that the labor required for survival, let alone prosperity, simply could not be done by those remaining. The idea of marching away in January or February, and possibly not returning in time for spring planting, was hardly a matter of indifference to the operator of a family subsistence farm.

Moreover, many ordinary people held the belief, as Washington recalled years later, that the whole notion of a French threat to the Ohio country, and the entire report of his journey to and confrontation on French Creek, were merely "a fiction and scheme to promote the interest of a private company by many gentlemen that had a share in government. These unfavorable surmises caused great delays in raising the first men and money." A poem popular at the time expressed this populist view of Dinwiddie's motives: "You promised to relieve our woes/ And with great kindness treat us;/ But whorf; awaw! each infant knows/ Your whole design's to eat us."

For these reasons, the duly summoned militia refused to muster in the numbers required. As their excuse, the citizens of Frederick and Augusta who knew about such things pointed to the law creating the militia. It was designed expressly to defend each county, they said, and the spirit of the law, if not the letter, was clearly that militia forces could not be used outside their home county. Certainly they were not to be taken outside their colony, and no one knew for certain whether Virginia or Pennsylvania had jurisdiction over the forks of the Ohio.

Dinwiddie was reduced to enticing volunteers to enter the service for money, and to this purpose he applied much of the £10,000 appropriation. But he knew he would need something more than the measly pay of a private soldier—eightpence, or fifteen pounds of leaf tobacco, per day—to attract the number of men he needed. And so, while the Burgesses were still in session, he sweetened the pot for the volunteer considerably, with a proclamation "for encouraging men to enlist in his Majesty's service for the defense and security of this colony." This proclamation announced that two hundred thousand acres of prime land on the east side of the Ohio River had been reserved for later grants to "such persons who by their voluntary engagement and good behavior in the said service shall deserve the same." That the parcel described in this proclamation sounded like the same land granted to the Ohio Company for the moment escaped notice. As subsequent events would reveal, no one was more intrigued by the prospect of later wealth for present duty than George Washington.

For the present, however, Washington was preoccupied, and not only by the urgency and difficulty of his mission. His recruiting efforts in Frederick County had been an abject failure, and in Alexandria had not gone much better. Supplies were scarce and the required teams and wagons nonexistent. But none of this could distract Washington from his campaign for higher rank.

On February 24, his commission as major of the Virginia Regiment took effect. It was most decidedly not enough. He conveyed this news promptly not to Dinwiddie, but to an influential family friend and member of the Governor's Council, Richard Corbin. Washington was forthright in stating his disappointment: "You gave me some room to hope for a commission above that of major, and to be ranked among the chief officers of this expedition." With due modesty he disclaimed interest in overall command. "It is a charge too great for my youth and inexperience to be entrusted with," he wrote. "I have too sincere a love for my country to undertake that which may tend to the prejudice of it."

Having disavowed interest in a position that he had no right to expect, Washington staked his real claim: the rank of lieutenant colonel. As he had when applying for the post of adjutant, he seemed to recognize that he was reaching rather far, but promised Corbin he would grow into the job. "I flatter myself that under a skilful commander, or man of sense (which I most sincerely wish to serve under), with my own application and diligent study of my duty, I shall be able to conduct my steps without censure, and in time, render myself worthy of the promotion that I shall be favored with now."

Washington did not make such demands directly of Dinwiddie. Instead, he began what was to be very nearly his life's work—wheedling from politicians the practical necessities required to achieve their stated goals. When he did manage to collect a few men, they proved to be not the firm-jawed patriots he had in mind, but mostly "loose, idle persons that are quite destitute of house and home, and many of them of clothes." Once enlisted, they remained vagabonds, for as Washington complained to Dinwiddie, gently at first, not wanting to be a bother, there were no tents, no "cutlasses, halberds, officers' half pikes, drums etc," no pay schedule and no uniforms.

In his first and mildest list of needs, written at Belvoir on March 7th, 1754, Washington's concerns were naively theoretical. The need for officers' half pikes, for example, would not seem important for long, and did not impress Dinwiddie at all. "Picks, cutlasses, or halberds, none in the magazine," the governor responded brusquely, "the officers must head their companies with small arms." And the need for the uniforms, Washington explained, was based on "my acquaintance with these Indians, and a study of their tempers that has in some measure let me into their customs and dispositions." What Washington had learned was that "it is the nature of Indians to be struck with and taken by show, and this [that is, dressing the men in brightly colored uniforms] will give them a much higher conception of our power and greatness."

Two days later, the pretensions were already dropping away. Then Washington repeated his request, not for decorations to impress the savages, but for clothing, without which his men would be "incapable of the necessary service, as they must unavoidably be exposed to inclement weather." The uniforms could be provided at no expense to the government, Washington pointed out, by withholding their cost from the soldiers' pay. He was learning fast.

Dinwiddie responded first to Washington's first concern: the matter of his rank. Dinwiddie conveyed the good news offhandedly, well into the body of a letter written just over two weeks after the date of Washington's appeal to Corbin for the rank of lieutenant colonel. Dinwiddie must have felt that the young officer was pushing a bit hard, for his granting of the boon was at the same time casual and waspish: "Mr. Muse was with me this day and will soon be at Alexandria. I have appointed him major at 10 shillings per day; and enclosed you have a commission for lieutenant colonel, pay 12 shillings per day, without any trouble of commanding a company."

Washington's response was effusive: "I hope my future behavior will sufficiently testify the true sense I have of the kindness; and as I intend strictly to adhere to all the proper rules (as far as it is in my power) and discipline of the profession I have now entered into; I am vain enough to believe I shall not be quite an unfit member for it; but in time, shall be able to recompense for the present indulgences."

With that out of the way, Dinwiddie had more serious business to conduct in his letter of March 15. He had been startled, he said, to learn from the letters of William Trent and Christopher Gist "that the French are so early expected down the Ohio." Trent had learned of a speech made to assembled Mingos at Logstown by the French diplomat and commissary called La Force. Apparently he was no longer being diplomatic, for he had reportedly castigated the Mingos for assisting the Virginians and according to Trent had delivered a dire threat: that "neither they nor the English there would see the sun above 20 days longer."

The response had been firm: "We are ready to receive you in battle but not in peace." But the Mingos, and the Virginians in their remote and exposed position, were worried. So was Dinwiddie. He ordered Washington to march for Wills Creek immediately with at least part of his force. He was to widen and improve the trail from there to Redstone Creek, then reinforce and defend the Forks.

There were by then six companies in the Virginia Regiment. In place of William Fairfax, who was too ill to take command as expected, Dinwiddie had selected (around March 1) Colonel Joshua Fry, the county lieutenant for Albemarle County. Fry, fifty-four years old, was a teacher of mathematics at the College of William and Mary who had assisted Peter Jefferson with his 1751 map of Virginia. It is not apparent why Dinwiddie thought this overage, unwell teacher with no significant military experience was the right choice to lead a critical and grueling expedition into the wilderness. All the governor could say in praise of his new commander was that Fry was "a man of good sense and an able mathematician." Dinwiddie may have thought that Fry's training as an engineer and experience as a mapmaker fitted him for the command, but Washington privately pronounced Fry unfit for the job by reason of weight and age.

The six captains serving under Fry and Washington were the Ohio Company's William Trent; the fencing teacher and interpreter from Fredericksburg, Jacob van Braam; a scion of one of Augusta County's first families and partner in the Greenbrier Company, Andrew Lewis, thirty-four (whose six-foot frame, martial bearing and heavy tread were as impressive as Washington's); a flamboyant twenty-eight-year-old Petersburg merchant named Robert Stobo, who brought with him ten "servant mechanics" and a wagon bearing his personal supplies, including 126 gallons of Madeira wine; and two Scotsmen, fifty-one-year-old Peter Hog from Edinburgh and thirty-year-old Adam Stephen, a former surgeon on a British hospital ship who had been practicing medicine in Frederick, Maryland. George Muse, thirty-four, a veteran of the Cartagena expedition and adjutant of the Middle Neck, served as Washington's aide, while another Scot, twenty-four-year-old James Craik, held the post of regimental surgeon.

Washington was in interesting company here. In August of 1745, when Prince Charles Edward Stuart had returned to Scotland to lead the climactic battle in his family's long struggle to reclaim the British crown, Peter Hog and Adam Stephen were on his side. That did not necessarily mean that they were devout followers of "Bonnie Prince Charlie," for by that time every malcontent in Scotland's highlands had gravitated to the Jacobite cause for lack of another. What it did mean was that they had been malcontents, willing to take up arms against the British Empire. It also meant that they had special reason to remember the savage reprisals of the British army that defeated the Jacobites at the Battle of Culloden in April of 1746, and then unleashed a holocaust of murder, rapine, torture and destruction on not only their surviving enemies but the civilian population of the entire area. Even in those violent times the events were so shocking to the British public that they ever after referred to the British commander as "the Butcher." They were speaking of William Augustus, Duke of Cumberland, the favorite son of King George II (although William's older brother was the Prince of Wales and would become King George III) and now the captain-general of the British army, the leading proponent of a new war with France, and a major policymaker for the colonies of British North America.

Similarly, Jacob van Braam had served in the army of the Netherlands, which had been at war with England off and on for decades. And Andrew Lewis, as an adolescent, had seen his father kill his aristocratic Ulster landlord in a pitched battle over rack rents, a favorite method of the English overlords of Ireland. The killing had been an obvious case of self-defense, but John Lewis and his family had been required to flee for their lives to the backwoods of America to avoid British vengeance on those who took up arms against their betters.

This was quite different company from that to be found riding to hounds at Lord Fairfax's Greenway Court or at William Fairfax's Belvoir. These were not men given to drinking teary-eyed toasts to their king. They were to be Washington's closest companions for the next four years.

Another constant companion was to be frustration, which

dogged Washington from the beginning as he marched westward from Alexandria at noon on April 2, 1754. It took the two incomplete companies under captains Hog and van Braam the rest of that day to march four miles, where they camped virtually within sight of their starting place. Thereafter they picked up the pace, and covered in another eight days the remaining sixty-five miles to Winchester, where Captain Stephen's company was waiting. Not to be found there, however, were the wagons and teams that had been promised. After a week of fuming and searching, Washington was able to collect only ten more. The lengths to which he was prepared to go were indicated by a warrant for his arrest on a charge of trespassing, issued by the Frederick County court clerk on April 15. The sheriff tried to serve the warrant, but noted on its reverse side that "the within-named George Washington would not be taken. He kept me off by force of arms."

A few days later, Washington and his men left Winchester for the eighty-mile march to Wills Creek, where he would again find none of the teams, wagons, or supplies that Dinwiddie had been promised by George Croghan, that ever-helpful agent of Pennsylvania. Dinwiddie had engaged Croghan as an assistant commissary and had appointed Croghan's frequent companion Andrew Montour as chief scout and recruiter of native help. (Montour, whose father was an Oneida sachem and whose mother was a French-Algonquian mix, was a rare synthesis of the white and red cultures, appearing to a German who met him in 1742 as quite European except that he had "around his whole face an Indianish broad ring of bear fat and paint, and both ears braided with brass and other wire like a handle on a basket." Montour gave excellent advice to all comers, but had no loyalties to one colony over another.)

There was soon worse news than the lack of supplies, and it came into Wills Creek with a haggard Ensign (second lieutenant) Edward Ward, who was supposed to be in garrison at the forks of the Ohio. His story confirmed everyone's worst fears about French intentions and capabilities.

On April 13, Ward had happened to see a copy of a letter written by John Davison, an interpreter with the party at the forks, to a trader named Robert Callender, a partner of George Croghan who was operating three trading posts in the area. Ward had been keenly interested to read what Davison had confided: that a French force would arrive at the Forks within a few days.

Ward had been at that point an extremely lonely second lieutenant. His captain and commander, William Trent, was off at Wills Creek looking for reinforcements and food. His lieutenant was John Fraser, the trader who had been driven from Venango by the French. Fraser was not letting his commission prevent him from conducting business as a trader at his new establishment on Turtle Creek, ten miles upriver from the Forks. Indeed, Fraser had only accepted the commission after Trent had agreed to his terms—that he should not be required to go to the fort more than once a week, or as he thought necessary. When Ward found him on the 14th and displayed Davison's letter, Fraser did not see any need to bestir himself, but asked with a shrug, "What can we do?" When Ward suggested the obvious—that as ranking officer, Fraser should get to the fort and prepare a defense—the lieutenant responded that "he had a shilling to lose for a penny he should gain by his commission at that time, and that he had business which he could not settle [in] under six days with his partner."

Ward, according to his own later account to Dinwiddie, answered hotly "that he would immediately go himself and have the stockade fort built, and that he would hold out to the last extremity before it should be said that the English had retreated like cowards before the French forces appeared."

Although he lacked orders and supervision, Ward was as good as his word. By the morning of April 17th, with the help and encouragement of Tanacharison, Ward and his men had affixed the gate to a rude stockade enclosure, just in time to watch from within it a truly daunting sight. Down the broad Allegheny River came a dark phalanx of three hundred canoes and sixty bateaux, each canoe carrying four men, the bateaux laden with supplies and eighteen cannons. The stockade must have seemed suddenly flimsy to the 41 men within it, watching this massive advance.

The French force, commanded by Claude Pierre Pécaudy de Contrecoeur, former commander at Niagara, landed just above the fort, formed up, and marched to within gunshot range. A detachment led by the engineer François le Mercier advanced briskly to demand surrender and give Ward one hour to respond in writing. Ward turned to Tanacharison for advice, and the Iroquois suggested a ploy he had seen the French use on Washington: Ward should say that he did not have the authority to negotiate with them, and that they should await the arrival of the proper officer. At the deadline, Ward went to the French lines and tried out his line on Contrecoeur. The French commander listened politely, then told Ward to decide what to do, instantly, or be attacked.

Ward surrendered, and Contrecoeur immediately became the gracious host. After all, there had not yet been any casualties in this confrontation. Not only might Ward take away all his people, but all his possessions including weapons and tools, which he did at noon on April 18th. When for some reason he camped for the night only a few hundred yards from the fort, Contrecoeur invited him to return for supper. By his own account, Ward stoutly resisted Contrecoeur's polite requests for information about "English governments" and his repeated pleas to purchase some of the detachment's carpentry tools.

Washington heard Ward's doleful story on April 20, sent Ward on to Williamsburg with the news, and began thinking about what he was going to do next. His meditations were soon disrupted when the rest of Trent's company straggled in. Trent had promised them the daily wage of two shillings, a fact that did not sit well with men who, bearing the same rank and doing the same work, were being paid one third that amount, a mere eight pence per day. Moreover, there was confusion about whether Trent's men had or had not been sworn in as militiamen, and if they had, whether or not they were required to take orders from Washington in his capacity as commander of a nonmilitia volunteer force, which moreover was now located outside of Virginia (there might be disagreement about jurisdiction over the Forks, far to the northwest, but Wills Creek was clearly within the boundaries of Maryland). These men had not been well led so far, and their disgust at a command that could not decide what it was paying its men or what it wanted them to do was not entirely unreasonable. Washington could neither impress nor control them, and eventually he was forced to report tersely to Dinwiddie that they "dispersed, contrary to my positive orders."

Washington called a council of war on April 23 to consider his detachment's situation. As he reported in the formal minutes of what must have been a tense wilderness gathering, it was obvious that 150 men could not wrest possession of the Forks from a thousand. Retreat was also unacceptable; not only would it be embarrassing, it would endanger the alliance with the Iroquois. In the absence of higher authority, Washington and his officers defined a new, limited mission for their detachment: to proceed to the Ohio Company storehouse at the confluence of Redstone Creek and the Monongahela. "We will endeavor to make the road sufficiently good for the heaviest artillery to pass," Washington wrote to Dinwiddie, "and when we arrive at Redstone Creek fortify ourselves as strongly as the short time will allow." There they could cache their supplies and ammunition, and when the rest of the regiment arrived could proceed to the Forks by water. It was a good compromise and a solid-sounding plan that was heartily approved by Dinwiddie and his council.

Someone in camp was advising Washington well, because he now became worried about Tanacharison, who had accompanied Trent to the forks, had helped to lay the first log of the Virginia fortification there, and by Ward's account had "raged greatly at the French" while Ward surrendered. Tanacharison's loyalty appeared to be firm, but the French show of power at the Forks might well have shaken him.

Perhaps Washington was beginning to pay closer attention to Tanacharison's words. After translation by Englishmen with little knowledge of the language or appreciation for the person speaking, after being copied and related by people with even less sensitivity to the situation, Tanacharison's messages could be read as the halting words of a simple savage dealing clumsily with his betters. But if the missives were regarded as communications from a highly intelligent ambassador of an alien but sophisticated government, then the glint of hard purpose could be seen among the soft and simple words.

Thus, in a letter to Washington borne by two warriors who accompanied Ward in his retreat from the Forks, Tanacharison said blandly, "Have good courage, and come as soon as possible; you will find us as ready to encounter with them as you are yourselves. We have sent these two young men to see if you are ready to come, and if so, they are to return to us, to let us know where you are, that we may come and join you." An inattentive reader might see that as unqualified encouragement from a solid ally. But anyone who knew Tanacharison would catch the important qualification of his being "as ready as you are yourselves," and the unstated emphasis on the question of whether the English were, in fact, "ready to come."

Washington dispatched an answer immediately. It began by thanking Tanacharison "from hearts glowing with affection for your steadfast adherence to us." It described Washington's command as but "a small part of our army advancing toward you, clearing the roads for a great number of our warriors that are immediately to follow with our great guns, our ammunition and our provisions." The letter was masterful, for it sounded all the right notes: it used Iroquois terms of affection and address, Iroquois nicknames ("Buck's brother" for Ward, who was half-brother to George Croghan, known among the tribes as Buck) and names (Esscruniata for Scaroyady); avoided invoking any great white father; and concluded by offering "a string of wampum that you may thereby remember how much I am your brother and friend." It was signed with Washington's Iroquois name, Caunotaucarius, but Washington could not have written this letter unassisted. Neither before nor afterward did he display such an easy familiarity with Iroquois ways. (The unacknowledged advisor may have been John Davison, a veteran of the French Creek expedition, who by May 22 or so was with Tanacharison, interpreting messages to Washington.)

After the near-mutiny and resignation of Trent's men, the Virginia regiment was down to five companies. The promised supplies and wagons still had not shown up. Pay was irregular, communications uncertain, and directives unclear. On May 1, hard and unremitting work was added to the list of difficulties, as the regiment began its road-building task. For the ensuing three weeks, they crawled northwestward from Wills Creek. "The great difficulty and labor that it requires to amend and alter the roads," Washington recorded, "prevents our marching above two, three or four miles a day." He hoped the Youghiogheny would prove to be a viable water route to the Forks, but his eager exploration when he reached it showed it to be far too shallow and rugged.

By mid-May, Washington could no longer contain his frustration. He had seized both rank and opportunity, he was commanding a military force on a historic mission, but instead of the crisp certainties any novice would have expected in such a position he found himself in a swamp of imponderables. This was more comic opera than an imperial expedition—it did not even resemble his recent mission to French Creek. In that case the objective had been clear, the instructions specific, and his companions as responsible and motivated as he. Now nothing was clear, and whatever he tried to do he found his officers and men sullen and unwilling. Even more vexing, he was not getting the basic support of his government. He was being sent into hostile country with a large force of men without being given the means sufficiently to clothe, feed, equip, arm, or pay them. No amount of trying or complaining had been able to produce the wagons and teams for what should have been a substantial baggage train. Nothing in his thinking about the attractions of a military profession had prepared him for this.

Yet when he blew, as he did with an incendiary letter to Dinwiddie on May 18, it was not over these issues. He had complained repeatedly about all of them, but always in patient and respectful terms. What put him into a rage was the issue of officers'—which is to say, his own—pay. And it is important to note that he did not start this particular round of the fight, but was propelled into it by his subordinates. These fractious and unrepentant rebels against British authority were in no more mood now than they had been in Scotland, Ulster, or Holland to accept demurely mistreatment by the British Crown. There had been from the beginning a lack of clarity about officers' pay, confusion over their legal status, the manner of funding, their exact mission, the amount and nature of help to be expected from the other colonies and from England, and a score of other variables. Dinwiddie might have been forgiven, too, for thinking that Virginia gentlemen might be prepared to meet this dire threat to their country without undue concern for their daily wages. If that is what he thought, he was soon corrected.

Washington was, at the outset of his letter, merely adding his support to a list of complaints about pay and allowances drawn up by his subordinate officers. But what could have been merely a letter of transmittal gradually changed as he took up point after point. He was obviously at war with himself as he wrote. On the one hand, he was deeply angered by what he saw as outrageous treatment of an officer; on the other hand, he had not become an officer by raging at the governor of Virginia. On the one hand, it seemed to him that something had to be done, and that he had no alternative but to press the matter; on the other, he worried that Dinwiddie might perceive the problem to be a malcontent named Washington, and the solution to be the malcontent's removal. As a result, Washington's letter was an odd combination of flaring anger and sudden obsequiousness, as when he wrote of his officers: "Nothing prevents their throwing down their commissions (with gratitude and thanks to your Honor, whose good intentions of serving us are well assured of) but the approaching danger, which has too far engaged their honor." He raged in another passage, "I could enumerate a thousand difficulties that we have met with, and must expect to meet with, more than other officers who have almost double our pay"; then, backpedaling, "but as I know you reflect on these things, and are sensible of the hardships we must necessarily encounter, it would be needless to enlarge."

In a similarly ambivalent passage, he proceeded jerkily from fawning to fury: "Giving up my commission is quite contrary to my intention. Nay, I ask it as a greater favor, than any amongst the many I have received from your Honor, to confirm it to me. But let me serve voluntarily; then I will, with the greatest pleasure in life, devote my services to the expedition without any other reward than the satisfaction of serving my country; but to be slaving dangerously for the shadow of pay, through woods, rocks, mountains,—I would rather prefer the toil of a daily laborer, and dig for a maintenance, provided I were reduced to the necessity, than serve upon such ignoble terms; for I really do not see why the lives of his Majesty's subjects in Virginia should be of less value than of those in other parts of his American dominions."

His summation was similarly divided against itself: "I find so many clogs upon the expedition, that I quite despair of success; nevertheless, I humbly beg it, as a particular favor, that your Honor will continue me in the post I now enjoy."

The sprouts of some new ideas poked from the verbiage of this letter: a questioning of authority, for one thing, along with certain incendiary notions about justice and implied rights. Whether or not Dinwiddie recognized the omens, his response was crushing: "The first objection, to the pay, if made at all, should have been made before engaging in the service. The gentlemen very well knew the terms on which they were to serve and were satisfied then. [Indeed, Washington's pay as lieutenant colonel of volunteers had been specified in a March 15 letter; he had noted the pay scale of the entire regiment in April; but had not sent Dinwiddie his bitter complaints until May.] The hardships complained of in the last article are such as usually attend on a military life and are considered by soldiers rather as opportunities for glory than objects of discouragement. They might easily have been foreseen and avoided, but would be now the worst reason in the world for quitting the service." The first cracks were appearing in the increasingly strained relationship between two men who expected instant obedience from subordinates and instant appreciation from superiors.

CHAPTER 8

First Blood

"I Heard Bullets Whistle, and Believe Me, There Was Something Charming in the Sound."

May 28, 1754

Around May 24, Washington arrived at a place called Great Meadows, halfway between Wills Creek and Redstone Creek. He liked what he found there, not least because of the lush grass, a scarce commodity in the mountains. The meadow was two to three hundred yards wide and about two miles long, with low hills, covered with massive oak trees, rising to either side. The hollow was traversed by Great Meadows Run, a weedy, convoluted stream that was sometimes ten feet wide, and by the smaller, equally marshy Indian Run. Near their confluence, their shallow beds formed what Washington thought were ready-made entrenchments. He had water, grass for his pack animals, rudimentary earthworks; it would be, he wrote to Dinwiddie, "a charming field for an encounter."

Two Mingo warriors soon arrived at Great Meadows with a warning from Tanacharison that a French force was on the march toward Washington and that "they intend to fall on the first English they meet." The messengers seemed little impressed by the French, reporting that they had small parties floundering around in all directions, unable to find the English force because the Mingos had refused to guide them. Moreover, the Mingos reported, many of the Frenchmen were ill.

Christopher Gist came into camp on May 27, and confirmed the approach of the French. Gist reported that La Force, with fifty French soldiers, had visited his plantation nearby and "would have killed a cow and broken everything in his house if they had not been prevented by two Indians" acting as guards. In fact, Gist reported, he had seen signs of the French force within five miles of Washington's. Washington dispatched Captain Hog and seventy-five men, nearly half his force, to try to catch the French before they could get back to their canoes at the mouth of Redstone Creek.

It was a warm, humid evening, with thick clouds threatening rain and contributing to the feeling of tension in the camp. It was almost full dark when a Mingo messenger known as Silverheels came into Great Meadows to report that Tanacharison, on his way to join Washington, had come across tracks that had led him to the French encampment. Eagerly, Washington assembled a detail of forty men, under Captains Stephen and van Braam, and followed Silverheels on a six-mile march to Tanacharison's camp through "heavy rain, and a night as dark as it is possible to conceive—we were frequently tumbling over one another, and often so lost that 15 or 20 minutes search would not find the path again." They lost seven men, nearly 20 percent of the force, in the dark.

In the murky light of the waterlogged dawn, Washington's men found Tanacharison's camp, and learned the extent of their reinforcements: Scaroyady and a mere handful of warriors, "but seven Indians with arms," a disappointed Washington recorded, "two of which were boys." One of them was probably Scaroyady's eleven-year-old son. While two scouts went out to reconnoiter the French camp, the Virginians ate their rations, dried and primed their flintlocks, and prepared themselves for action. When the scouts returned, the detachment set out for the enemy camp, marching, Washington recorded in his diary, not in column but "one after the other, in the Indian manner."

The French were supposedly professional soldiers, on a dangerous mission deep in enemy country. Yet they had no sentries out, and hours after sunup were leisurely going about the business of breakfasting and dressing. They were bivouacked in a cramped, boulder-studded ravine, apparently to stay out of sight, yet had given no thought to the fact that they were surrounded by high ground whose rocks and trees provided dense cover to any enemy. On reaching the ravine, Captain Stephen took his men to the left, and Washington deployed on the right, while Tanacharison, Scaroyady, and their braves circled to the enemy's rear.

Apparently someone in the French camp caught sight of Washington or one of his men as they were moving into final position, and called out a warning. At the shout, some of the French ran for their stacked muskets. "I ordered my company to fire," Washington reported, and Stephen's men echoed the volley. Stunned by the onslaught, seeing their comrades dropping all around them, the surviving French tried to run away from the concentrated fire—only to confront the fearsome Iroquois, who were shrieking, brandishing tomahawks, and charging. Thoroughly panicked, the French turned and ran toward the Virginians again, waving their hands desperately in the air. Before Washington could get down to the floor of the ravine to accept their surrender, the Iroquois began tomahawking the wounded and collecting scalps. Washington stopped the killing, took custody of twenty-one survivors (one of them wounded), and then had to face down the heated demands of the Iroquois to be given the prisoners (to the Iroquois, they were the most valued spoils of war).

There were ten mutilated bodies on the field. One of them was that of the expedition's commander, Lieutenant Joseph Coulon de Villiers de Jumonville.

The French survivors were insistently trying to get something across to their captors. It must have taken a while for the heat of battle to subside, for the murderous Iroquois to be placated, for the realization to dawn that there was something to the French cries beyond the expected chagrin of a defeated and captured party, for van Braam to make sense of what they were saying and relay it to Washington. They were carrying a message, they said, from the government of France. When Washington grasped what they meant, he was severely shaken.

The next day he wrote his report of his first battle—of the first battle deaths, gunshot wounds, and scalping he had ever seen, much less caused—in prose that was crisp and orderly. But when he got to the issue raised by the French prisoners, his composure evaporated and his syntax fractured. If the French were telling the truth, what Washington had just done would not be hailed as a bold military victory, but condemned as an act of murder.

The French insisted that their mission had not been military, but diplomatic. They had been sent not to attack the English, but to warn them, just as Washington had gone north to warn the French, about encroachment. They had been looking for Washington's force in order to deliver their message, and had camped in the ravine to be near water, not to escape detection. Washington's ambush of a peaceful embassy, the French now declared, was barbaric, contrary to every principle of international relations. That his attack had killed an officer who was well known and well connected in France would seal Washington's infamy in Europe as well as the colonies.

"The absurdity of this pretence is too glaring," Washington assured Dinwiddie, but his supporting argument was sweaty and garbled. "Their whole body moved back near two miles, sent off two runners to acquaint Contrecoeur with our strength, and where we were encamped etcetera now 36 men would almost have been a retinue for a princely ambassador, instead of petit, why did they, if their designs were open, stay so long within five miles of us without delivering his embassy, or acquainting me with it . . . " and so on. Later in the day he dispatched a second message, warning Dinwiddie not to be swayed by the arguments of the French prisoners being sent to him. "I doubt not but they will endeavor to amuse your Honor with many smooth stories, as they did me, but were confuted in them all and by circumstances too plain to be denied almost made ashamed of their assertions."

Washington had a better argument than he was at first able to express. The French had had every opportunity to make a peaceful overture; by instead scouting the English camp, sending runners back to their headquarters at the forks, and lurking nearby without communicating, they had taken what amounted to hostile military action and had forfeited any claim to diplomatic status. As time went on, Washington would grow more assured in making his case, but there can be no doubt that he suffered greatly from wondering, for a troubled few days in the wilderness, whether his first battle had made him a hero or a criminal.

Dinwiddie apparently was not too sure about the matter either. In a report to the Board of Trade in London written more than two weeks later, he depicted the incident as a "little skirmish by the Half-king and their Indians, we were as auxiliaries to them." Then, just in case the notion did not take that this had all been the fault of savages, he put a little more distance between himself and young Colonel Washington: "My orders to the commander of our forces [were] to be on the defensive."

Washington's May 29 report to Dinwiddie did not begin with his account of the skirmish and his troubled defense against the charge of murder; they occupied the second half of the bulky missive. Dated on the day after the first battle of Washington's life and the opening engagement of a great war to come, the first thousand words laboriously scratched on paper in a wilderness camp in hostile territory were a treatise on the increasingly sore subject of officers' pay.

Stung by Dinwiddie's previous, reproachful letter, Washington nevertheless would not yield on a single point of contention about what officers were allowed for their "table" and uniforms, how the volunteers' pay compared with that of British regulars, and so on. In a firmer, less emotional, and better organized tone than that of his previous letter on the subject, Washington plodded through the particulars, insisting on the rectitude of the complaints, his refrain being his point of honor that he preferred to serve with no compensation than to be insulted by inadequate compensation. But he felt it necessary to hedge on his honorable position. "For my own part, it is a matter almost indifferent whether I serve for full pay, or as a generous volunteer; indeed, did my circumstances correspond with my inclination, I should not hesitate a moment to prefer the latter." Read with proper weight given to the qualifiers, that sentence says that he was not indifferent to whether he was paid or not, that his circumstances did not correspond with his inclination, and that he did indeed hesitate to prefer serving without pay.

Washington's intransigence on the question of pay was wearing on his governor, who was beset by many difficulties. In late May,

Dinwiddie had progressed with the members of his Council to Lord Fairfax's Greenway Court to conduct a full-dress conference with the Ohio tribes, none of whom showed up. After sitting on his hands for sixteen days, Dinwiddie returned disgruntled to Williamsburg, whence he wrote Washington on June 2, "I heartily wish that yourself and officers had not at this time discovered an uneasiness on account of your pay, especially as the long delay of Colonel Fry's detachment in not yet joining yours gives me too much concern." He had not yet learned that Joshua Fry had died on May 31 from injuries suffered in a heavy fall from his horse.

Nor would he learn for some time that the Privy Council in June decided the matter of the pistole fee in his favor, but with some irritating codicils: he was not to collect the fee for properties west of the Alleghenies, he was to limit grants there to one thousand acres per person, and he was to restore Peyton Randolph to his post as attorney general.

More irritating news was soon to come from Albany, New York, where a conference of colonial officials gathered on June 14 to discuss ways in which the colonies and the Iroquois League could cooperate in defending their territories. Dinwiddie had already proposed, to the proper colonial authorities in London, creation of a northern and southern district, each having a council to coordinate the interests of the adjoining colonies. Thus Virginia disdained to send representatives to Albany, and had nothing to do with the approval there of an ambitious plan of colonial union proposed by Benjamin Franklin. The plan was of course angrily rejected by the authorities in London.

Meanwhile, at Great Meadows, Washington recovered his poise a few days after his skirmish, put the French accusations out of his mind, and began to think of himself as quite the hero. "I had scarcely 40 men under my command," he wrote to his younger brother John Augustine, or Jack, "nevertheless we obtained a most signal victory." The more he thought about it, the more impressed he became with his own role, finally writing a postscript that fairly glowed with self-satisfaction: "I fortunately escaped without a wound, though the right wing where I stood was exposed to and received all the enemy's fire and was the part where the man was killed and the rest wounded. I can with truth assure you, I heard bullets whistle, and believe me there was something charming in the sound." The remark caused much hilarity when it gained currency along with accounts of later events. Even King George was moved to some heavy Hanoverian humor, observing that anyone who thought the sound of bullets charming could not have heard many. A more somber epitaph, penned by Horace Walpole, placed the brawl and the young major in a cause-and-effect relationship with what was about to become history's first war of global proportions: "The volley fired by a young Virginian in the backwoods of America set the world on fire."

Unaware of having said anything funny, the young Virginian set about improving his situation at Great Meadows. Assuming that the French would move against him in retribution for his ambush of Jumonville, Washington had his men dig a circular trench about fifty feet in diameter and chop down about seventy-five oak trees in the surrounding hills. They cut the trees into ten-foot logs, which they then split lengthwise, sharpened at one end, and erected in the trench, sharp end up. In the center of the circle thus enclosed, they built what one soldier described as "a small house to keep our provisions and ammunition in" that was "covered with bark and some skins and might be about 14 feet square." About twenty feet outside the walls of this unorthodox structure, Washington ordered entrenchments dug. He was quite satisfied with the result, writing Dinwiddie on June 3, "We have just finished a small palisaded fort in which with my small numbers I shall not fear the attack of 500 men."

Tanacharison came to review these preparations with eighty Mingos, only a few of whom were fighting men, saying that Scaroyady soon would bring more warriors from the Ohio country. Washington, obviously deprived for the moment of competent advice about such things, decided this was a good time to propose that the Iroquois women and children be sent from the Ohio country to the interior of Virginia, where they could "imbibe the principles of love and friendship in a stronger degree," or in other words become civilized. Ever the diplomat, Tanacharison made no response to this insulting offer, saying merely that he would have to consult Scaroyady. Washington may have realized that he was not deepening any friendships with such clumsy initiatives, for he soon wrote to Dinwiddie that "Montour would be of singular use to me here at this present, in conversing with the Indians. For want of a better acquaintance with their customs I am often at a loss how to behave and should be relieved of many anxious fears of offending them if Montour was here to assist me."

Montour and Croghan, who had been at the abortive Winchester conference, soon arrived at Great Meadows, along with the companies of Andrew Lewis and Robert Stobo. They brought the news that Colonel Fry was dead and that Washington was promoted to full colonel, in temporary command of all 110 men and nine swivel guns. He would bear this responsibility only until the arrival of Colonel James Innes and three hundred regulars from North Carolina.

In his letter transmitting Washington's new commission, Dinwiddie tried to head off yet another problem he saw coming. The relationship between Colonels Innes and Washington was clear and acceptable to all parties, but that was not true of the relative rank of the provincials and Innes's subordinate officers. The first of them, Captain James Mackay, would soon reach Washington with his company. "The captains and officers of the Independent Companies, having their commissions signed by His Majesty, imagine they claim a distinguished rank and, being long-trained in arms, expect suitable regards. You will therefore consult and agree with your officers to show them particular marks of esteem, which will avoid such causes of uneasiness as otherwise might obstruct His Majesty's service."

If Dinwiddie thought he had thus preempted the problem, Washington's 3600-word response soon corrected him. Washington would be happy to be courteous to Captain Mackay, he declared, but "should have been particularly obliged if your Honor had declared whether he was under my command, or independent of it." And he certainly hoped that "Captain Mackay will have more sense than to insist on any unreasonable distinction." He promised to be "studious to avoid all disputes that may tend to public prejudice," then explained how unavoidable such disputes were going to be: "This will be a canker that will grate some officers of the regiment beyond all measure—to serve upon such different terms when their lives, their fortunes and their characters are equally, and I dare say as effectually, exposed as those who are happy enough to have the King's commission." He was grateful for the promotion and for Dinwiddie's approval of his actions, but "now I shall not have it in my power to convince your Honor, my friends and country of my diligence and application to the Art Military, as a head will soon arrive to whom all honor and glory must be given."

Mackay and his company arrived, in fact, while Washington was still writing the letter, around June 15. Washington apparently liked him on sight—his first appraisal was of "a very good sort of a gentleman." Nor did Mackay have any problem with the young colonel on a personal level. But when it came to the punctilio of their respective ranks, the two officers were prickly in the extreme. Washington was a colonel of Virginia troops, but he lacked experience and his men did not have even the status of militia. Mackay was a mere captain of North Carolina forces, but he held a commission from the King and his men were not farmers carrying muskets, but trained regulars.

Mackay had his men move off a short way and set up a camp separate from the Virginians, in the manner of aristocrats edging away from contact with commoners. When evening came, Washington courteously sent a messenger to give Mackay that night's password for the sentries. Mackay responded that as the holder of a King's commission he could not properly receive any orders, even on such a trivial matter, from a colonial. "Then who is to give it?" Washington fairly shouted in his letter to Dinwiddie. "Am I to issue orders to a Company? Or is an Independent Captain to prescribe rules to the Virginia Regiment? This is the question, but how absurd is obvious."

Washington had at long last encountered the embodiment of his ideal—a contemporary holding a commission from the King. Mackay was not some London aristocrat at the head of a regiment of the Coldstream Guards, but a provincial like Washington, from the new and undeveloped colony of Georgia, who for seventeen years had been commanding his fellow colonists in Georgia, Florida, and now South Carolina. Nor was Mackay what enlisted men call a lifer—he would resign his commission within the year. Yet Washington, contemplating this example of his highest ambition realized, saw behavior he could only call absurd.

The next day, it got worse. Washington intended to resume work on the road, improving it from Great Meadows to Redstone Creek as he had done from Wills Creek to Great Meadows. But when he proposed this to Mackay, the icy response was that regular soldiers did not perform labor unless paid an extra shilling a day. Washington, whose men were making only eight pence a day, could not pay or promise such money. Neither could he stand the thought of the South Carolinians marching "at their ease while our faithful soldiers are laboriously employed." Somehow, without giving or receiving orders, Washington and Mackay agreed to separate, Mackay staying in camp at Great Meadows while Washington moved out to continue work on the road.

Two days later, at Gist's plantation thirteen miles to the north, Washington convened a conference at which he hoped to solidify the support of Tanacharison's Mingos and recruit the Delawares to take the field with him. It was a serious mistake to meet with them while his forces were divided and his ill-equipped and poorly supplied regiment was grubbing a road through the woods—especially since several of the Mingos present had just come from Logstown by way of the impressive French installation at the Forks, now known as Fort Duquesne, and said they had seen there more than two thousand fighting men. These Mingos were openly pugnacious, telling Washington they had heard that the English were going to attack the villages of the tribes who did not march with them, and vowing to report everything they saw to the French on their return. The Delawares were noncommittal, and the Shawnees present apparently had nothing to say at all.

Washington drew himself to his full height and lied through his teeth. He was the vanguard, he said, of "an army to maintain your rights; to put you in possession of your lands, and to take care of your wives and children, to dispossess the French, to support your prerogatives, and to make that whole country sure to you; for those very aims are the English arms actually employed; it is for the safety of your wives and children that we fight; and as this is the only motive of our conduct, we cannot reasonably doubt of being joined by the remaining part of your forces, to oppose the common enemy."

Not surprisingly, the results of this ill-considered council were disastrous. Washington not only failed to recruit the Delawares and to deflect the Shawnees from their already established tendencies to favor the French, but he lost the support of Tanacharison, who now politely refused to go anywhere near the Virginians. Tanacharison later told Conrad Weiser that he thought Washington was "a good-natured man but had no experience." Now the Virginians had no native scouts to watch for the enemy. The men continued to labor on the road, becoming first weak and then ill on their diet of parched corn and lean, fresh-killed beef. Washington waited tensely at Gist's for word that the blow was about to fall.

Word came late on Thursday, June 27, when a messenger from Scaroyady reported that the French at Fort Duquesne were preparing to march against the Virginians. Washington called in his road crews and put them to work preparing Gist's for attack, and sent carefully phrased word to Mackay conveying the thought that it would be awfully nice if the latter could manage to arrive there, really quickly, to help in the defense. To his credit, Mackay did not stand on ceremony, but marched immediately.

Scaroyady's intelligence was accurate. The next day, June 28, at 10:00 A.M., Captain Louis Coulon de Villiers, half-brother to the slain Jumonville, left Duquesne with six hundred French and Canadian troops and one hundred native allies, under orders to march against the English and "chastise them for having violated the most sacred laws of civilized nations." The French had found a *casus belli*. Meanwhile Mackay was marching to Gist's from Great Meadows. He arrived at 2:00 A.M., just as a runner came in from the opposite direction with a report on the large French force coming up the Monongahela. Now that Mackay's and Washington's forces were united, it appeared they were in the wrong place. The chronic shortages of provisions now became critical; there was not enough meat, salt, or bread to sustain them for more than a few days. The enemy could simply sever their supply lines and starve them into submission, or await their inevitable retreat and hack them to pieces at leisure on the long march south. The officers agreed unanimously that they should get back to what they were now calling Fort Necessity, where supplies and reinforcements had surely arrived by now.

With the Virginians weakened and ill and the North Carolinians weary from their forced march out, it took them two days to march the thirteen miles back to Necessity. Captain Stephen wrote that during the entire time, Mackay's troops "refused to lend a hand to draw the guns, or help off with the ammunition; nor would they do duty as pioneers, which had an unhappy effect on our men, who no sooner learned that it was not the proper duty of soldiers to perform these services than they became as backward as the independents." Many of the Virginians, and virtually all of the remaining Iroquois scouts, disappeared into the woods. Those who had not deserted wished they had when at the last extremities of exhaustion they stumbled out of the woods at Fort Necessity to find no fresh supplies, no reinforcements, and no hope. They would have kept marching all the way back to Wills Creek if they had been able, but they were not.

Total despair was averted by the arrival, later on that July 1, of a shipment of flour from Wills Creek, along with word that another independent company, from New York, was on the march and should reach them soon. Washington dispatched a plea for help and set his weary men to work on perfecting their trenches and setting up their swivel guns. Mackay's men dropped their aversion to work long enough to help position the guns. Tanacharison wandered in, surveyed the sorry scene, advised Washington to get away from there, and took his own advice.

That night the French force camped along the road the Virginians had been working on, near Gist's plantation. The French commander was every bit as demoralized as Washington. Villiers had had to leave his heavy guns and supplies behind at Redstone Creek, making him feel even more vulnerable this deep in enemy country. His French and Canadian troops were in reasonable shape, but his native warriors were extremely nervous about being so far from help. Some Algonquins had already left him, and those who had stayed were thinking about going. From somewhere came a report that five thousand English reinforcements were on their way to Washington's relief. On top of everything else, it was raining, and appeared ready to do so for days. Villiers was seriously considering giving up and heading back when a deserter from Adam Stephen's company came into the French camp and told in great detail how bad conditions were at Fort Necessity.

Energized by the realization that his seven hundred men outnumbered the English defenders by almost two to one, Villiers moved the next day to within striking distance of the Meadows. "We marched the whole day in the rain. I stopped at the place where my brother had been assassinated, and saw there yet some dead bodies." None of the corpses had been buried. A severed head had been left stuck on an upright stick.

Early on the morning of July 3, a scouting party rushed into Fort Necessity to shout that they had encountered an approaching enemy force just four miles away, that it was "a heavy, numerous body, all naked." Washington kept his men at work improving their entrenchments, digging feverishly in the mud, until three columns of French soldiers (fully clothed) came into view at about 11:00 A.M. They were marching along the wagon road from Gist's plantation, which approached Fort Necessity from the southwest. Then, as the French commander deployed a skirmish line, Washington and Mackay formed their men in front of their trenches.

For all the unorthodoxy of their situation and preparations, Mackay and Washington apparently expected the enemy to use ordinary linear tactics, approaching in ranks (the men standing shoulder to shoulder) and firing in volleys until their bayonets could be brought into play. "We drew up on the parade," recalled one of the Virginians, James Wood of Winchester, and "saw the French and Indians coming down the hill." Just to the east of the French line of approach, a neck of woods extended to within sixty yards of the fort. Wood thought that the purpose of the "parade " was "to take possession of a point of woods," although no one else mentioned that objective. Apparently no one recognized the significance of those woods until it was too late.

Now, long before the two lines came within range of each other, the first Englishman cracked. According to Wood, Major George Muse "called to halt, the French would take possession of our fort and trenches, ran back in the utmost confusion, happy he could get into the fort first." Throughout the battle Muse would huddle in the supply house within the fort, and not long afterward, in disgrace, he would resign his commission.

From a distance of six hundred yards—at least six times the effective range of their muskets—the French fired their first volley. Captain Stephen responded with fire from the swivel guns, which was equally ineffective. According to the joint report of Mackay and Washington, the French then "advanced in a very irregular manner" until they reached the point of woods, where they fired another volley. Exhibiting better discipline than their opponents, the English held their fire and now saw a strange thing. Instead of continuing their advance, the French scattered into the woods.

"Finding they had no intention of attacking us in the open field, we retired into our trenches, and still reserved our fire," Mackay and Washington reported. Washington admired the coolness with which Mackay's men took their positions under fire, selecting for themselves the most exposed trenches. "We expected from [the enemy's] great superiority of numbers that they would endeavor to force our trenches; but finding they did not seem to intend this neither, the Colonel gave orders to fire, which was done with great alacrity and undauntedness."

Now the battle was joined, but hardly in the manner either side had expected. From the rising ground on all sides of the fort, and especially from the cover of the nearby woods, the French poured in a withering fire on the encircled English. Not only did this fire take a steady toll of human casualties, it soon killed all the cattle and horses in the encampment, along with most of the dogs. It was difficult to maintain the firing in the steady rain that resumed and intensified during the afternoon, dribbling into the gunpowder, cartridge boxes, and especially the priming charges on the exposed pans atop the muskets. Return fire was even more difficult for men huddled in trenches that were knee-deep in mud, filling with water and reddening with the blood of the wounded and the dead.

The defenders' problems with wet gunpowder were compounded by a mystifying shortage of a critical piece of equipment. If a muzzle-loading musket misfires, the lead bullet and powder charge has to be removed to make the weapon usable again. The only way to accomplish this is by applying a device called a worm—an indispensable part of the kit of any hunter or soldier. The worm screws onto the end of the ramrod and, when inserted into the barrel and twisted against the seated lead ball, pierces and grips it with two small coils of hardened wire so that the bullet can be withdrawn. According to an account of the battle written by Stephen for the *Maryland Gazette* of August 29, 1754, there were in the entire English force during the defense of Fort Necessity only two worms. No explanation was ever offered by the principals for this inexplicable deficiency, if it existed as Stephen described.

As evening came on, the situation in Fort Necessity was worse than desperate. Thirty men were dead, another seventy wounded, another hundred too sick to fight. They were surrounded, outnumbered, exposed, wet, and hungry. Wet powder had disabled many of their weapons. There were "only a couple of bags of flour and a little bacon left for the support of 300 men," wrote Adam Stephen. "What was still worse, it was no sooner dark, than half of our men got drunk." Expecting to die that night, they saw no reason to waste the camp liquor supply. "We determined not to ask for quarter," Washington wrote of those terrible evening hours, "but with our bayonets screwed, to sell our lives as dearly as possibly we could. From the numbers of the enemy, and our situation, we could not hope for victory."

Washington did not know that Villiers was feeling just as desperate as he was. The French had suffered fewer than twenty casualties, with three of those dead, but they were close to despair nevertheless. They, too, were struggling with the effects of three days of marching and fighting in incessant rain, including useless powder and weapons. They, too, were running short of food and ammunition, with no hope of resupply. They had no cannon with which to reduce the English fortifications. They were deep in enemy country, and Villiers was convinced that five thousand English reinforcements were on the way to Great Meadows. Their native allies, restless as always in any protracted engagement, were threatening to leave.

Washington, preoccupied with the prospects of doom, was too startled to respond when, at about 8:00 P.M., a voice called out of the dark woods, "*Voulez-vous parler?*" A second and third time the shouted question came: "Do you want to talk?" Unable to conceive that the French would be willing to negotiate, Washington decided this must be a trick to reconnoiter his situation. No Frenchman would be allowed within English lines, he had someone call out. Then send a representative to ours, came the answer. Captain van Braam and Ensign William La Peyroney, Washington's adjutant, were detailed to go out and receive the message.

"I told him," Villiers recorded, "that as we were not at war, we were very willing to save them from the cruelties to which they exposed themselves on account of the Indians; that we consented to be favorable to them at present as we were come only to avenge my brother's assassination, and to oblige them to quit the lands of the King our master."

Washington had trouble believing that he was being offered a reprieve. He asked to see the terms in writing. Villiers promptly complied, but according to Stephen, "we were obliged to take the sense of them by word of mouth: it rained so heavily that he could not give us a written translation of them; we could scarcely keep the candle light[ed] to read them; they were wrote in a bad hand on wet and blotted paper so that no person could read them but van Braam who had heard them from the mouth of the French officer." The paper explained, van Braam told Washington and Mackay under these difficult conditions, that Villiers had not intended an act of war, but revenge for the killing of Jumonville. That being accomplished, "we grant leave to the English commander to retire with all his garrison and to return peaceably into his own country."

Washington and Mackay signed, and by agreement struck the English colors. At dawn the Virginians and the North Carolinians who could still walk, carrying their dead and wounded, trudged out of Fort Necessity between the ranks of victorious French soldiers. A short distance away they halted to bury the dead and organize for their long march. They watched their fort burned to the ground, and fended off a few pugnacious intrusions by excited braves. Then, leaving Captains van Braam and Stobo as hostages, at midmorning they marched away from the scene of their humiliation.

"Mr. Washington was very sad company," according to James Mackay, on their long march back to Wills Creek and Winchester. He was even sadder when, on reaching Williamsburg at midmonth, he discovered that the articles of capitulation referred not to the death or killing of Jumonville, as he had understood them, but to an "assassination." Washington had signed what amounted to a confession that his ambush of Jumonville had been an act of murder, not warfare. Washington blamed van Braam for failing to translate the document properly. "The interpreter was a Dutchman, little acquainted with the English tongue," he wrote years later, his anger still apparent.

Robert Dinwiddie supported his defeated commander in public, but nursed private doubts and resentments. "Washington's conduct was in many steps wrong," he wrote to a friend in March 1755, "and did not conform to his orders from me, or he had not engaged till the other forces had joined him." Dinwiddie did not make clear, of course, to what orders he referred, or how Washington could have avoided engaging. Once again, however, he had put some distance between himself and his young lieutenant, at least in his own mind.

Another who was backing away from Washington as far and as fast as he could was Tanacharison. The sachem was devastated by the defeat and determined not to be dragged down by association with so weak a force and so ineffectual a leader. Washington would not listen, Tanacharison complained: "He took upon him to command the Indians as his slaves, and would have them every day upon the scout and attack the enemy by themselves, but would by no means take advice from the Indians." In summary, Tanacharison thought, "The colonel was a good-natured man, but had no experience." For his part, Tanacharison was despondent. He spent a few months living with George Croghan, sending appeals to the Mingos to remain loyal to the British. They ignored him, and he was no longer convinced he had chosen the right path. His health steadily declined, and in late October he died. His long struggle on behalf of his people over, he was buried by white strangers.

The fort at the forks of the Ohio was firmly in the hands of the enemy. The Virginia regiment had been decimated and humiliated. The English alliance with the Iroquois had been shattered. Washington was deeply shamed, and would for the rest of his life regard the fourth of July as his most unhappy anniversary.

CHAPTER 9

Braddock's Road

"He looks upon the country, I believe, as void of both honor and honesty; we have frequent disputes on this head."

June 7, 1755

Governor Robert Dinwiddie appeared to have lost touch with reality. "Considering the present state of our forces," he wrote to George Washington on August 1, 1754—not yet a month after the latter's devastating defeat at Fort Necessity—"the forces should immediately march." The governor ordered Washington, who was then at Winchester, to bring his Virginia regiment quickly back up to its authorized strength of three hundred men and take it to Wills Creek. There he was to meet Colonel James Innes and the three independent companies, which were also to be at full strength. This force was then to march westward across the Alleghenies and "either dispossess the French of their fort, or build a fort in a proper place."

Washington was incredulous. What Dinwiddie had referred to as "the present state of our forces" was the very reason they could not march immediately, would not make it to Wills Creek if they tried, and most certainly could not dispossess the French. They would be outnumbered, "we should be harassed and drove from place to place at their pleasure," Washington protested—venting his feelings first to William Fairfax, not the governor—and would be unable to hold any fort: "Scarcely a man has either shoes, stockings or hat. These things the merchants will not credit them for; the country has made no provision; they have not money themselves; and it can not be expected that the officers will engage for them again, personally, having suffered greatly already on this head; especially now, when we have all the reason in the world to believe they will desert whenever they have an opportunity. There is not a man that has a blanket to secure him from the cold and wet."

Dinwiddie had ordered Washington to bring the regiment up to strength, but, Washington raged in his letter to Fairfax, "not a sixpence is sent for that purpose. Can it be imagined that subjects fit for this purpose, who have been so much impressed with and alarmed at our want of provisions (which was a main objection to enlisting before) will more readily engage now without money than they did before with it!" Dinwiddie had given bland assurances about provisions, but Washington insisted that even if they could be obtained—and the traders "are not to be depended upon"—by the time they could be delivered, winter would be imminent, "a season in which horses can not travel over the mountains on account of snows, want of forage, slipperiness of the roads, high waters, etc. Neither can men, unused to that life, live there without some other defense from the weather than tents: this I know of my own knowledge, as I was out last winter."

Washington wrote more judiciously to the governor, presenting his problems in an organized, crisp way. There were no more vacillations from rage to servility. The anger was there, but under tight, formal control. He requested pay and provisions for his men, proper commissions for his officers, and legal means to deal with deserters. "There is scarce a night or opportunity but what some are deserting, and often two or three or four at a time," he reported, and the only way to deal with the problem was to hang some of the offenders. "Give me some written orders and indemnification; otherwise I cannot give my assent (as I am liable for all the proceedings) to any judgement of the martial court that touches on the life of a soldier." Could his regiment get beyond Wills Creek, Dinwiddie's point of departure for the new expedition? "I fear we can not, were we to attempt it; and, at that place, for want of proper conveniences, we could not remain. I have the honor to be, etc., Geo. Washington."

The situation, bad as it was, soon was made worse. The governor's Council, at Dinwiddie's insistence, rejected a House of Burgesses appropriation of £20,000 for defense because it included £2,500 to pay for the services of Peyton Randolph in arguing the pistole-fee case before the Privy Council. "Instead of augmenting our forces," William Fairfax wrote on September 5, "the Governor perhaps will have some difficulty to get means for the pay and maintenance of the few we now have." A bill stipulating capital punishment for mutiny and desertion also failed. In disgust, Dinwiddie prorogued the assembly until October. Fairfax was pessimistic. "All our efforts to promote the public service have miscarried. In short our prospect is gloomy. I wish that you may be able to enjoy the fruits of that philosophic mind you have already begun to practice."

When the Burgesses reconvened on October 17, desperation had made Dinwiddie a more pliable man, albeit not a more honest one. He announced to the Burgesses that London had approved £20,000 for the defense of Virginia, and had already dispatched half of that amount along with a shipment of two thousand muskets. Surely, he argued, the Virginia assembly could spend as much for their own defense, especially since he was now willing to sign a separate appropriation repaying Peyton Randolph for his London expenses. Dinwiddie did not think it appropriate to reveal to the burgesses that the money from London was not a grant to the colony but a loan, to be repaid from the proceeds of the tax on tobacco. The burgesses approved £20,000 for defense, as requested, but not to be dispensed at Dinwiddie's sole discretion. The money was to be disbursed by a committee of burgesses and councillors chaired by Speaker Robinson.

Two days after the session began, Dinwiddie held a conference in Williamsburg with the governors of two neighboring colonies. Arthur Dobbs had just arrived from Ireland to take up his new duties as lieutenant governor of North Carolina. And Horatio Sharpe, who had been serving as lieutenant governor of Maryland for a year, had been commissioned a lieutenant colonel and appointed commander-in-chief of the British American forces to be sent against the French. The governors agreed that Sharpe would raise seven hundred men and march on the French fort at the Forks as soon as possible, presumably in the spring.

Dinwiddie was considerably energized by this influx of cash and allies, and with vigor attacked the problems that had bedeviled him for a year. He now had money to solve the supply and pay problems, and the will to deal with the manpower problems. He resolved to disband the Virginia regiment and replace it with no fewer than ten independent companies of regulars, on the model of the one commanded by James Mackay. Not only would he thus put one thousand men under arms, he wrote elatedly on October 25, but he would put an end to the "disputes between the regulars and the officers appointed by me." Henceforward, all of his officers would carry the King's commission, and none would have enough rank to argue about; "there will be no officer above a captain." He saw himself as the only field-grade officer of this military force, assured London that all the present officers would be happy to serve under him, and assumed they would be as grateful to receive royal commissions as the Crown would be willing to give them. He confidently requested that a bundle of royal captain's commissions, the names left blank for him to fill in, be sent out forthwith. He reminded the colonial authorities that this was precisely what had been done to mount the expedition to Cartagena thirteen years earlier.

Dinwiddie had some trouble selling this concept to James Innes, who eventually swallowed hard and agreed to it. Washington, on the other hand, would have none of it.

Late in October, Washington resigned his colonel's commission and retired from the military profession. It was not a very large or noble principle that impelled his action; in fact it had more to do with ego than any broader concept. But for the first time he openly and unflinchingly rebuffed Dinwiddie in a way that could not be mistaken or ignored.

Washington explained his action in detail to the man around whom he had maneuvered for his first military post—William Fitzhugh, who eighteen months earlier had refused to yield to Washington the adjutancy of the Northern Neck. Fitzhugh had become important to Washington again when he was appointed second in command to Horatio Sharpe. Fitzhugh had tried to dissuade Washington from resigning, without success. Washington explained his intransigence in terms that managed to be blunt, uncompromising, and yet not quite offensive: "If you think me capable of holding a commission that has neither rank nor emolument annexed to it, you must entertain a very contemptible opinion of my weakness, and believe me to be more empty than the commission itself."

Washington's foremost concern was that officers whom he had once commanded could, in Dinwiddie's new organization, command him. "In short, every captain bearing the King's commission, every half-pay officer or other appearing with such commission, would rank before me." It was intolerable, and it made him feel exceedingly sorry for himself. "I choose to submit to the loss of health," he wrote, "and the fatigue I have undergone in our first efforts, than subject myself to the same inconveniences and run the risk of a second disappointment." Obviously, no threat of any foreign power arrayed against England and Virginia, no appeal to patriotism or loyalty or duty, could make it bearable.

It seemed appropriate, on departing the military life forever, to pen an epitaph: "I shall have the consolation of knowing that I have opened the way when the smallness of our numbers exposed us to the attacks of a superior enemy; that I have hitherto stood the heat and brunt of the day, and escaped untouched, in time of extreme danger; and that I have the thanks of my country for the services I have rendered it."

This much was true. Washington had faced the frustrations of command and the rigors of battle in the wilderness with unflinching courage and unyielding purpose. The high principles he had applied to most of his dealings had in large measure made up for his inexperience, and he had grown in the service.

It would have been a good place to end his summation, but Washington had not yet resolved things as completely as he was trying to suggest. After some muttering about being the victim of plots in London and treachery from James Mackay, all misguided, he compulsively cracked the door he had just so firmly slammed shut. At the end, one sentence stood by itself, unqualified, casting its shadow over all that had been said before, illuminating what was to come.

"My inclinations are strongly bent to arms."

For more than two years, Washington had been without a home. He had been in camp, at headquarters in Winchester, on duty in Alexandria or Williamsburg, and occasionally at ease at Belvoir. His farm at Fredericksburg was occupied by his mother, and her fierce attentions were such that he spent as little time there as possible. Apparently he never considered taking up residence at his Bullskin Creek property in Frederick County, where a small cabin served as an overnight shelter or overseer's shack.

Nor had he been comfortable at Mount Vernon, preferring to stay at Belvoir when he was in the area. Lawrence's widow, Ann, had remarried five months after Lawrence's death, and had moved to the estate of her new husband, George Lee. She maintained Mount Vernon, without much interest, because it was to become her daughter's.

However, shortly after Washington left the Virginia Regiment late in 1754, Sarah died. Ann decided to lease the entire estate—2,298 acres, a grist mill, the house and buildings and eighteen slaves—to Washington for her lifetime, after which, according to Lawrence's will, a life tenancy would pass to Washington. Until and unless he had children, he would never own Mount Vernon outright, but as of December 17, 1754, he had a home. With considerable relish, he absorbed himself in the minutiae of preparing for the spring planting and of maintaining and expanding the estate that was now, mostly, his.

Meanwhile the great engines of empire in London and Paris groaned toward renewed war. The complaints and alarms of the British governors were arriving from colonies not just in America, but from the Caribbean and India as well. The road to war was familiar, worn smooth with use, the protocols executed with the practiced ease of experienced dancers: claim and counterclaim, insult given and offense taken, rage and outrage, violence begetting more violence until the climactic confrontation of armies brought release.

The war party in England was that of the royalists, led by none other than the Butcher of Culloden, the Duke of Cumberland. Wrapping himself in the flag of his country as all war-lovers do, he thus draped with the bright colors of patriotism a barbaric lust for battle and dictatorship. Thus he intimidated into abashed silence the Whigs and others who looked for an alternative to war, who suspected that the American colonies might make productive use of a degree of independence in their political and economic affairs. Cumberland had more difficulty with another opponent of war with

France—his father and sovereign, King George II, who feared what the French might do to his native Hanover in the event of renewed hostilities.

Two imperial offices had primary authority over the American colonies. One was that of the Lords Commissioners for Trade and Plantations, the so-called Board of Trade; the other was the Secretary of State for the Southern Department, who served under the First Lord of the Treasury. The president of the Board of Trade since 1748 had been George Montagu Dunk, Earl of Halifax, a devoted follower of Cumberland's warlike ways and an old friend of Robert Dinwiddie. By 1755, Halifax was convinced that the only way to resolve the increasing difficulties in colonial policy was for London to take direct charge of all dealings with both the French and the tribes. The only function of the colonial governments, in his view, was to do what they were told and pay for the war.

Halifax's views were not shared by his cousin, the First Lord of the Treasury. Thomas Pelham-Holles, Duke of Newcastle, who had served for twenty-two years as Secretary of State for the Southern Department, was a moderate Whig. In the winter of 1754-55, he had offered France a compromise, much to the disgust of Cumberland: Britain would confine itself to the eastern half of the Ohio Valley, and the French could settle the western portions. But the French government was as eager for war as Cumberland's party, and rejected the overture. Newcastle still did not want war, but wanted to threaten war in order to discourage the French from following up on their defeat of Washington. He proposed sending two British regiments to America, but in order to overcome George II's aversion to any provocation of France, Newcastle sought the advice and help of the captain-general, Cumberland, and immediately lost control of the situation.

Cumberland won approval from his father for the troops to be sent, but not to assist the colonies; they would be commanded by a British general of Cumberland's choosing, they would implement London's strategy at Cumberland's direction, and the colonial governors and assemblies would keep out of the way and pay the bills. This was the way to solve not only the French problem, but to nip in the bud the colonies' emerging tendencies toward union and independence. Benjamin Franklin's plan of union, drafted at Albany in 1754, had been read with profound distaste in London.

Why Edward Braddock should have been selected by Cumberland for the fateful command in America was a mystery. During his forty-three-year career with the Coldstream Guards he had plodded to the rank of lieutenant colonel, and had been required to leave the regiment to go higher. He had taken command of the 14th Regiment of Foot in Gibraltar in 1753, and in April of the following year had made major general. Ten months later, on February 19, 1755, he stepped heavily ashore in America to conduct the campaign of his life.

Within the week, he received a request from a young planter named Washington, who was not quite as absorbed with the spring fieldwork as one might have expected. On March 2, Captain Robert Orme of Braddock's staff replied from Williamsburg that "the General, having been informed that you expressed some desire to make the campaign, but that you declined it upon some disagreeableness that you thought might arise from the regulation of command, has ordered me to acquaint you that he will be very glad of your company in his family, by which all inconveniences of that kind will be obviated." By "family," Orme meant Braddock's staff.

Washington, having recently at great expense found his voice when dealing with Dinwiddie, reverted to his earlier obsequiousness before a distinguished veteran of the vaunted Coldstream Guards. Clumsily, he played the reluctant bride. He did not want a command, he wrote, but was interested in serving as a volunteer: "I wish for nothing more earnestly than to attain a small degree of knowledge in the military art." But there was a problem, which he defined this way: "The inconveniences that must necessarily arise, as some proceedings in a late space (I mean before the General's arrival) had, in some measure, abated the edge of my intentions and determined me to lead a life of greater inactivity, and into which I was just entering at no small expense; the business whereof must greatly suffer in my absence." Whatever this was all about, as Orme and Braddock must have wondered, Washington offered to discuss when Braddock reached Alexandria, Virginia, the main staging area for the spring offensive.

What Washington wanted, he explained at Braddock's Alexandria headquarters early in April, was permission to join the expedition when it reached Wills Creek, and to leave it during any periods of inaction, so that he could take care of his new plantation. He would engage his brother Jack to manage affairs at Mount Vernon, but wanted to be both a soldier and a planter. "These things, sir," he wrote haltingly to Orme, "however unreasonable they may appear [he crossed that out, and substituted "in whatever light they may appear"], I hope will not be taken amiss [he thought better of that, too, and changed it to "will not I hope be thought unreasonable"], when it's considered how unprepared I am at present to quit a family and estate scarcely settled and in the utmost confusion." Orme, who must have been bemused by this unmilitary arrangement, nevertheless conveyed Braddock's permission for Washington to join his staff when the army reached Wills Creek, and to leave it "whenever you find it necessary to return."

On April 13, Washington attended a meeting of colonial governors convened by Braddock to review the strategy for the summer's campaign. Washington came away "perfectly charmed" by the martial politician Governor William Shirley of Massachusetts, who pressed his own ideas of what to do. But the Duke of Cumberland had given detailed instructions, and Braddock made it clear that proposed amendments were not welcome. The campaign was to begin as soon as weather permitted, and it was to begin with an attack on Fort Duquesne. At about the same time, Shirley would take two thousand men against Fort Niagara; William Johnson, New York's emissary to the Iroquois, would lead 4,400 New England and New York provincials against the French fort at Crown Point, on the southern tip of Lake Champlain; and Lieutenant Colonel Robert Monckton would invade Nova Scotia with two thousand New Englanders. Braddock's force would consist of two regular regiments of infantry shipped from Ireland for the purpose—the 44th, commanded by Colonel Sir Peter Halkett, and the 48th, under Colonel Thomas Dunbar. In addition, he commanded three independent companies of regular troops raised in the colonies, a detachment of Royal Artillery, and 463 provincials—eight companies from Virginia and one each from Maryland and North Carolina—for a total complement of just under 1,800 men.

The governors soon realized that they had not been brought together to give advice but to receive orders and to pay the bills. Previously, they had been assigned quotas for their contributions to Braddock's war chest. Now they reported that they had asked their assemblies for the money but had been refused. Braddock would have to get his money from England. He was not pleased.

Braddock did not comprehend the enormity of the issue gradually taking shape under his fretful gaze. He did not understand any better than his masters in London that by prodding the colonies to unify in support of the war effort, they were in fact causing the colonies to unite in opposition to the Imperial government. He had neither the ability nor the time to get beyond the boundless frustrations of his logistics.

Braddock had already begun the transport of supplies and equipment toward his forward staging area at Wills Creek. And it had already proved far more difficult than expected to procure supplies and equipment, even when he had money, and now the demands of the move itself instructed Braddock on the truly daunting dimensions of his problem. He was determined to haul his enormous artillery train over the mountains for the siege of Fort Duquesne. But in those rugged woods there was nothing for horses to eat, so for every horse required to haul a cannon or a baggage wagon, he would need another to haul feed. "I am to expect numberless inconveniences and obstructions from the total want of dry forage, and from being obliged to carry all our provisions with us which will make a vast line of baggage." The arithmetic indicated that he would require two hundred wagons and 2,500 horses. He ordered them found and delivered to Wills Creek by May 10.

In addition to these practical difficulties, there developed an enormous political and economic controversy. Obviously, Braddock would have to build a great road to get his army and its trains out west, and among the army of land speculators watching these proceedings there was not one who failed to realize that when Braddock was gone, the road he built would remain, and would become an artery of trade and expansion. The route he chose, then, had far more than military import; to the governors and land speculators of the colonies of Virginia, Pennsylvania, and Maryland it was a major factor in their future.

Thus Dinwiddie, Washington, and the gentlemen of the Ohio Company were dismayed to learn that half of Braddock's army would march not through Virginia, but through Maryland, proceeding up the northern banks of the Potomac. The idea was apparently conceived by Braddock's quartermaster general, Sir John St. Clair, who had scouted the area in January and February.

St. Clair was an unusual combination of competence and arrogance. He had the training and the intelligence to devise practical solutions to complex problems, along with complete intolerance for those who were slow to acknowledge his brilliance. The cost of maintaining his unbounded self-confidence in the chaotic conditions of the American West would take a heavy toll, but would not quite destroy him. A sympathetic observer would write of St. Clair a few years later, "his appearance was somewhat grotesque, a long beard, blanket coat, and trousers to the ground. But he gave so good an account of what he went about, that I could have kissed him, and freely forgave his oddities, as who is without. He carried our artillery and wagons smoothly along, although in very broken sentences, intermixed with full stops, and sometimes stares, that in faith I was once or twice afraid that he was going to leave them, or to turn them back. But at length on he went, making every difficulty disappear."

Having looked over the country, St. Clair reasoned correctly that it would be easier to impress the needed horses and wagons from the local residents if the burden were spread over two colonies. It made eminent sense to him to move part of the army through Pennsylvania. The Virginia speculators did not care about lost horses and wagons, they cared about the danger to their plans if a more northerly route to the West replaced the Virginia road.

The danger became obvious when Braddock's men began their march in mid-April. The 44th Regiment headed for Winchester along the well-established Virginia route, but the 48th stayed north of the Potomac and marched to Frederick, Maryland, and thence to the confluence of the Potomac River and Conococheague Creek. This strategic site, thirty-five miles northeast of Winchester, was the location of an Ohio Company warehouse and was linked to Philadelphia by a wagon road. Across the Potomac, in Virginia, a man named Evan Watkins operated a ferry from a place called Maidstone.

Braddock accompanied the 48th through Maryland. On arriving

at Frederick, he was told that when he reached Wills Creek he would find waiting not the two hundred wagons for which he had contracted, but twenty; not the 2,500 horses he had ordered, only two hundred. Braddock's rage at the unreliability of colonials was utterly unavailing. His expedition was saved by the Postmaster General of America, who came to the army ostensibly to improve the delivery of the general's dispatches. But Benjamin Franklin was also a member of Pennsylvania's General Assembly, and in fact had been sent there to improve the general's regard for that colony ("our assembly apprehending," Franklin wrote, "that he had conceived violent prejudices against them").

Braddock's rage at the scarcity of wagons gave Franklin a chance to observe that it was a pity the army had not landed in Pennsylvania rather than in Virginia, because in his state "almost every farmer had his wagon." Furthermore, Franklin knew how to produce the needed vehicles and horses. On April 26, he published an advertisement offering fifteen shillings a day for the rental of a wagon and four-horse team, and two shillings a day for a horse with pack saddle. "You have an opportunity of receiving and dividing among you a very considerable sum," perhaps £30,000, "which will be paid to you in silver and gold of the King's money." A month later, Braddock had at his service 150 wagons, teams, and drivers, along with 1,500 packhorses. It was accomplished "with great punctuality and integrity," Braddock wrote on June 5, providing "almost the only instance of ability and honesty I have seen in these provinces." The significance of the fact that it had been accomplished by making an offer, instead of issuing an order, was lost on Braddock.

Franklin on one occasion during his visit presumed to caution the general about the possibility of being ambushed in the wilderness. The general, who had never been in a battle, "smiled at my ignorance," Franklin recalled, and replied, "These savages may indeed be a formidable enemy to your raw American militia; but upon the king's regular and disciplined troops, sir, it is impossible they should make any impression."

Braddock also discovered at Frederick, apparently to his surprise, that no road continued westward. Instead, the 48th Regiment would have to cross the Potomac and march south to near Winchester in order to strike the road to Wills Creek. Washington joined the fuming Braddock on May 1 and accompanied him to Winchester, where more disappointment awaited; contrary to his expectations, there were no Cherokee and Catawba scouts waiting to serve him.

While the groaning army wrestled its guns and wagons westward, Braddock and his escort trotted their horses to Wills Creek in three days, Braddock complaining all the way. "From Winchester to this place, which is 70 miles, is almost uninhabited but by a parcel of banditti who call themselves Indian traders, and no road passable but what we were obliged to make ourselves with infinite labor," he wrote. "I have ordered a road of communication to be cut from Philadelphia to the crossing of the Youghiogheny, which is the road we should have taken, being nearer, and through an inhabited and well cultivated country."

Washington apparently did not know about these orders, for he was gloating in his letters at the discomfiture of the general, and those who had promoted the Maryland route, when they discovered they had to shift south to the Virginia road. Washington thought the experience had given Braddock "a good opportunity to see the absurdity of the route, and of damning it very heartily," which gave Washington "infinite satisfaction." He did not understand that Braddock was damning the Virginia route, not the Maryland portion.

Washington's mood seemed to vary from day to day. On leaving Mount Vernon, he had taken obvious satisfaction in explaining to his most influential acquaintances that he had been "importuned to make this campaign by General Braddock," when in fact it was the other way around. All he could expect for his trouble, he complained in a way that made it appear a boast, was the gratitude of his country: "I expect to be a considerable loser in my private affairs." On arrival at Wills Creek, however, he complained bitterly that, contrary to his prior stipulation, it appeared he would be there with nothing to do for a month or more. "I dreaded this (before I came out) more than every other incident that might happen in the campaign," he wrote to his special friend Sally Fairfax. But on the other hand, his status on Braddock's staff satisfied him immensely, as he explained to his brother Jack: "I am thereby freed from all command but his, and give orders to all which must be implicitly obeyed. I have now a good opportunity, and shall not neglect it, of forming an acquaintance which may be serviceable hereafter if I can find it worth while pushing my fortune in the military way."

Washington's fears of boredom at Wills Creek—which, with its new stockade and importance, was now dubbed Fort Cumberland in honor of the captain-general—were soon alleviated. Braddock urgently needed cash, and on May 15 he dispatched Washington to get £4,000 from a British agent in Hampton. Washington was to waste no time getting there, to stay "no longer than two days," and to return "as speedily as may be." Twelve days later, he was back in Winchester with the money, after a ride of about four hundred miles. "I am fatigued and a good deal disordered," he recorded, "by constant riding in a drought that has almost destroyed this part of the country." He was delayed at Winchester, which he referred to as "this vile hole," because he needed an escort for himself and the money on the dangerous trail to Fort Cumberland. The mounted escort he expected to be waiting for him was not there, and he could not raise a militia detachment: "You might as well try to raise the dead to life again, as the force of this county."

On May 28, in the midst of his urgent mission and of the delay in getting a guard, Washington wrote to Jack about an entirely different matter, to which he had obviously given considerable thought. The House of Burgesses was considering a bill to divide Fairfax County, creating a new county and two new seats in the House. "Major [John] Carlyle mentioned it to me in Williamsburg in a bantering way and asked how I should like to go,"—that is, stand for election as a burgess—"saying at the same time he did not know but they might send me when I knew nothing of the matter for one or t'other of the counties. I must confess I should like to go for either, but more particularly for Fairfax, as I am a resident there." He asked Jack to "fish out Colonel Fairfax's intentions, and let me know if he purposes to offer himself as a candidate. If he does not I should be glad to stand a poll." In addition, Jack was to approach a detailed list of the most influential residents of Fairfax County to "discover their real sentiments without disclosing much of mine." Jack was to conduct himself "with an air of indifference and unconcern" until he found out which way the wind was blowing. (In the event, Fairfax County was not divided, George Fairfax did run, and was elected in December along with the incumbent John West.)

Washington left Winchester the next day and arrived at Fort Cumberland on May 30, where he found Braddock's bad mood getting worse. The hope of much-needed scouting help from the tribes had twice bloomed and twice died. George Croghan had brought in fifty reluctant Mingo warriors, but Braddock ordered their families to leave camp because the presence of women was disrupting camp discipline. Shingas came in with a delegation of Delawares, Shawnees, and Mingos to offer Braddock their help, but was instead mortally insulted. According to Scaroyady, Braddock declared that "no savage should inherit the land" to be liberated from the French; only the English would "inhabit and inherit" the land. Some of the warriors present were so angry they immediately joined the French. Only Scaroyady and seven of his warriors remained with Braddock. "He was a bad man," Scaroyady would recall later. "He looked upon us as dogs, and would never hear anything what was said to him." The sachem thought the general was full of "pride and ignorance."

Washington did not think much of Braddock either: "The General, by frequent breaches of contracts, has lost all degree of patience, and for want of that consideration and moderation which should be used by a man of sense upon these occasions will, I fear, represent us home in a light we little deserve; for instead of blaming the individuals as he ought, he charges all his disappointments to a public supineness; and looks upon the country, I believe, as void of both honor and honesty; we have frequent disputes on this head, which are maintained with warmth upon both sides especially on his, who is incapable of arguing without, or giving up any point he asserts, let it be ever so incompatible with reason." This defense of provincial honor was written by a man who had expressed contempt for the back country and its inhabitants ever since first seeing it seven years before; who had just two weeks earlier described Winchester as a vile hole and compared the Frederick militia to dead people.

His defense of the character of his countrymen, moreover, did not extend to Pennsylvanians. Washington had just learned of the road being built, on Braddock's orders, to connect "Pennsylvania with the French fort." Realizing full well what such a road meant to the economic hopes of the Ohio Company, he fulminated that it would "give all manner of encouragement to a people who ought rather be chastised for their insensibility to their own danger, and disobedience of their sovereign's expectation. They are to be the Chosen people, because they furnished what their absolute interest alone induced them to do."

It is small wonder, with all these vexations, that Washington was somewhat brusque with George Fairfax, who was moved to get in touch with his old friend because the military authorities had confiscated two of his horses and a servant. Quite put out by this unscheduled contribution to the country's defense, George Fairfax wrote a rare letter to Washington expressing his dismay and requiring assistance. Washington replied that there were a great many horses with the army, that he would see what he could do, but that he was "just at this time a good deal hurried."

Washington was also as abrupt as filial duty permitted with his mother, who wrote to upbraid him for not visiting her on his dash to Williamsburg, and to demand that he procure for her a Dutch servant and some butter. Washington apologized for neglecting her and observed without apparent sarcasm that neither Dutchmen nor butter were available to him in the wilderness. He was, he reported dutifully, "in tolerable health though something fatigued with the journey."

For three days beginning on June 7, Braddock's army lumbered westward from Fort Cumberland. By the fourth day they had not yet gone a dozen miles, and Braddock held a council of war to see what they could do to speed things up. "What was looked on at home as easy," wrote quartermaster St. Clair, "is our most difficult point to surmount, I mean the passage of this vast tract of mountains. Had we a country we could subsist in after we get over them, the thing would be easy." Braddock and his officers sent a few guns and mortars back to Cumberland, lightened the loads on the wagons, and used more packhorses. Then they continued as before. The line of march was nearly five miles long, and each evening the rear guard camped near the ground the vanguard had left that morning. Wagons broke down with maddening regularity, Captain Orme recalled, and "the horses grew every day fainter, and many died." The men were weakening, too, from "the constant and necessary fatigue, by remaining so many hours under arms."

It took ten days for the entire army to move twenty miles, to Little Meadows, northwest of Fort Cumberland. There Washington, who was now ill with dysentery and suffering "violent fevers and pains in my head," attended another council of war on the subject of speed. He "urged it in the warmest terms I was master of, to push on; if we even did it with a chosen detachment for that purpose, with the artillery and such other things as were absolutely necessary." One reason for haste, he said, was that the French could not resupply or reinforce the fort during the continuing severe drought. Governor Dinwiddie and his council had recently proclaimed a day of fasting and prayer, "there having been no rain for two or three months, and all sorts of grain near perishing."

Braddock took the advice, after a fashion. He assembled eight hundred of his best troops, left most of his baggage train behind, and moved out. But he still had thirty wagons and thirteen guns with him, and the first day's march covered all of four miles. "Instead of pushing on with vigor, without regarding a little rough road," fumed Washington, "they were halting to level every mole hill and to erect bridges over every brook; by which means we were four days getting 12 miles." At that, Colonel Dunbar's division was slower, because he was left with twice as many wagons and pack loads as he had horses to move them, and had to move by two-stage advances.

By June 23, Washington recorded, "my illness was too violent to suffer me to ride, therefore I was indebted to a covered wagon for some part of my transportation; but even in this I could not continue, for the jolting was so great that I was left upon the road with a guard and necessaries, to await the arrival of Colonel Dunbar's detachment, which was two days march behind. The general giving me his word and honor that I should be brought up before he reached the French fort; this promise, and the doctors threats that if I persevered it would endanger my life, determined my halting."

Day after day the segmented army lumbered toward Fort Duquesne, hacking at the road before it, heaving the thirteen guns and thirty wagons over the roots and runs and rocks, clattering through the deep silent forest that seemed to have no end. Braddock's division gradually outdistanced Dunbar's, until the latter as it inchwormed along was three days' march behind the former. At least Dunbar's men were spared the bloody harassment that started about June 25.

On that day, three officers' servants and a wagoner looking for stray horses in the woods beyond the picket line were ambushed. The batmen were killed and scalped, the wagoner mortally wounded. From that day forward, the tension of awaiting sudden attack never eased. No doubt the boys from Ireland and Philadelphia were regaled by the frontiersmen of Virginia with stories about how their savage foes took scalps and applied exquisite torture. The dread and loathing, the consuming fear of the possibility of being taken alive by the savages, had plenty of time to take hold.

CHAPTER 10

Massacre

"The Virginian companies behaved like men, and died like soldiers."

July 9, 1755

The attacks on Braddock's lumbering columns (a few more Englishmen were picked off from the rear guard and a flanking party on July 7) were the tactics of a desperate enemy. Captain Contrecoeur had been in command at the forks of the Ohio since evicting Ensign Ward from his stockade and building the much larger Fort Duquesne. It was an impressive structure, its 150-foot-long walls bristling with fifteen cannons, but Contrecoeur knew it could not withstand bombardment by the artillery being hauled toward it by the English. His garrison had been reduced to fewer than three hundred men the previous winter, and because of the severe drought and low rivers, reinforcements under Captain Daniel Liènard de Beaujeu had only just reached him. At that, he had only about six hundred French and Canadian troops with which to meet Braddock's force of nearly two thousand.

In addition, of course, Contrecoeur had perhaps eight hundred warriors, most of them old friends of the French from the Great Lakes country—Wyandots, Ottawas, Chippewas, and Pottawatomies—along with some Shawnees and a smattering of Delawares and Mingos, including the group recently infuriated by Braddock. But the closer the English army came, the more scouts came into Fort Duquesne with alarming, exaggerated reports of three thousand, even four thousand enemy troops, of scores of cannons. Contrecoeur's native allies began to melt into the woods. To hold them, he tried to appear stronger than he was, braver than he felt. Without them he was lost.

As always, alliances with the tribes depended on appearances, and at the moment the English looked good. However slow its advance, the army was an impressive spectacle, its masses of red and blue uniforms moving in orchestrated cadences, looking for all the world as if it knew what it was doing. To an impartial and footloose observer, the French did not look nearly as confident. As Shingas later explained, a few of his people were openly committed to the French, "but the greater part remained neutral till they saw how things would go between Braddock and the French in their engagement, and they made it their business to draw nigh the place where the engagement happened that they might see what passed at it."

Contrecoeur's second in command, Captain Beaujeu, confronted the deteriorating situation on the night of July 8. Beaujeu's family had served the French military for seven centuries and he was a career officer, but he was not a hidebound traditionalist. His manner of communicating with his native allies was a far cry from that of a Braddock or a Washington. In council that evening he made his argument—that it was necessary not to await attack, but to go out and ambush the English before they had a chance to begin their siege. Then, as a witness reported, he "began the war song." Beaujeu knew that the warriors expressed their opinions not with pen and ink but with their voices and feet, dancing and chanting their agreement, and he very nearly succeeded in winning them over. "All the Indian nations immediately joined him," a French witness to the council reported, "except the Pottawatomies of the Narrows, who were silent. Which occasioned all the other nations to desire not to march until the next day." As Beaujeu understood, such decisions had to be unanimous. Far into the night he labored to get his plan of attack approved by the few holdouts.

On the morning of July 9, General Braddock knew that one more day's march would put him within striking distance of the fort, eight miles to the northwest. He would face his greatest danger of a preemptive attack this day, but he did not think it would happen. According to his handful of scouts, Fort Duquesne was defended by no more than three hundred troops and some savages. (The reports were correct at the time they were made; the scouts had not seen the fort since the arrival of Captain Beaujeu and his three hundred reinforcements.) To confront this meager force, Braddock had 1,300 fighting men and thirteen guns, and he was suffering no doubt about the outcome.

To get there, the army first would have to bear to the right, around an eastward curve in the Monongahela River, and march past the mouth of Turtle Creek. The trail was rough and was crowded against the river by high ground close on the right, perfect for an ambush. The banks of Turtle Creek were too steep for the wheeled vehicles, and would require hours of work before they were passable. All this could be avoided, scouts told Braddock, by crossing the horseshoe instead of going around it: by fording the Monongahela twice and taking a straight-line course to the site of John Fraser's trading post just downriver from Turtle Creek (the one he had built after being run out of Venango by the French, where Washington had stayed on his trip to French Creek in November of 1753, and that had been burned to the ground by the vengeful French). Christopher Gist, just back from scouting the vicinity of Fort Duquesne, reported that the drought-starved river was low, barely knee-deep, and the banks gentle. Braddock agreed to the plan.

The first elements moved out at 3 A.M. on July 9. Washington, having been hauled to the vicinity by wagon on the previous day, attended his commander mounted gingerly atop a generously padded saddle, feeling "very weak and low."

Christopher Gist was wrong about the terrain of the second river crossing. Instead of the easily surmounted banks he had described, the men confronted twelve-foot bluffs jutting from the water's edge. It took several nervous hours for the working party to cut and pack a slope gentle enough for the wagons and guns, and then, at midday, the army crossed the last natural barrier between it and Fort Duquesne.

"A finer sight could not have been beheld," wrote Thomas Walker, commissary to the Virginia forces, "the shining barrels of the muskets, the excellent order of the men, the cleanliness of their appearance, the joy depicted on every face at being so near Fort Duquesne, the highest object of their wishes. The music re-echoed through the mountains." It seemed a great day to be an Englishman.

As experienced by the men, however, the reality was considerably different from the picture sketched by the good Dr. Walker. According to a report made later, the men were by their own description "harassed by duties unequal to their numbers, dispirited by want of sufficient provisions, with nothing to drink but water, and that often scarce and bad." One of their number recalled that morning's breakfast: "Where there was one that had anything to eat, there was 20 that had nothing. Some men had nothing most of the day before." Nevertheless, even abused, weary, and exhausted men can experience a momentary lift in spirits, especially when the end of their travail is at hand.

The army had formed a line of battle at the lower ford, but returned to column as it headed up from the river and into the woods. The scouts, including George Croghan, Christopher Gist, and Scaroyady's handful of warriors, rode immediately in front of the twenty-man vanguard of the advance party. About fifty yards back came the advance party itself, Lieutenant Colonel Thomas Gage at the head of perhaps three hundred men. Then came the working party—the bridge-builders and road-cutters of the expedition—under Colonel St. Clair, followed by their two-hundred-yard line of wagons bearing tools and ammunition. The van of the main body was a hundred yards back—twenty-nine light horse, or cavalry, under Captain Robert Stewart, veteran of Fort Necessity, with sailors and pioneers. After another one-hundred-yard interval came the main body, Braddock riding at its head with his aides Orme and Washington. Then came Colonel Ralph Burton with two columns of regulars, each about 250 strong, one on either side of the main wagon train, and flanked in their turn by herds of cattle and horses. It was another hundred yards to the rear guard, Sir Peter Halkett commanding, consisting of about a hundred men, including the Virginia Regiment under Adam Stephen.

From one to two hundred yards to either side of the line of march were scattered two dozen small flanking parties. And among the wagons and the columns were found another 250 souls—the personal servants of the officers, soldiers' wives, sutlers, wagoners, and volunteers. (Among the wagoners was the young neighbor lad who had been inspired by Christopher Gist's tales of the West—Daniel Boone.) All of them on that warm July afternoon were headed not for war, but for camp; Braddock's orders were to march until 3 P.M. and then bivouac. They would knock on Fort Duquesne's gates tomorrow.

As they marched up from the river, they passed the burned-out ruins of the unfortunate Fraser's trading post, passed through some young woods with tangled underbrush, and then stepped into a majestic forest of mature hardwoods. St. Clair marveled that "this wood was so open that carriages could have been drove in any part of it." Enormous trunks spired into the sky, holding aloft a dense canopy that lent a muted, blue-green cast to all below. Light and sound took on a weird, alien quality.

Yet the soldiers continued to be in a euphoric mood, as if their campaign were over. Such moods in armies are communicated by the officers, and Braddock and his lieutenants had convinced themselves that Fort Duquesne was going to be a pushover. They were so confident that here, only seven miles from the fort and its defenders, they sent no scouts out to see what the enemy was doing. Instead, the scouts were riding along within sight of the vanguard, which now was without the two guns it had been hauling along as a precaution. On making the second river crossing, Colonel Gage had waved them off with the comment, "I do not think we shall have much occasion for them." When the head of the column was about a mile from the second ford (meaning that the rear guard was just then leaving the river), it approached a ridge rising to its right. Neither Gage nor Braddock did anything about it.

This is especially remarkable given Braddock's reaction to a similar situation the previous day, when contact with the enemy was less surely imminent. Harry Gordon, one of Braddock's four engineers, recalled that on that occasion the army had entered "a narrow valley, at its widest a quarter of a mile, very much commanded on both sides by steep hills. In this march every proper precaution was taken to secure us." Braddock had first "ordered 350 men to take possession of the heights on each side," then had ordered the advance guard to check out the rising ground in front. When they had found no sign of an enemy, the main party had marched through. But on this day, miles closer to the fort and the enemy, the rising ground commanding their route of march drew hardly a glance. Braddock would later be heavily criticized for sticking to orthodox methods, but orthodoxy required securing that hill, as well as obtaining scouting reports from the vicinity of the fort. Braddock's conduct of the march was not conventional, it was sloppy.

It was, however, a model of organization compared with what his enemy was doing at that moment. Long after sunup, Captain Beaujeu had still been trying to get his native allies to join him in ambushing the British army. Only when he declared in desperation that he was going to attack by himself, with or without help, did the impressed warriors decide to go along. By then it was very late in the day for an ambush, and Beaujeu, stripped to the waist, was leading his 108 French regulars, 146 Canadians, and six hundred Indian warriors in a run toward the Monongahela in the desperate hope that the usual English lassitude would permit him enough time to find a position and get into it.

At approximately 1 P.M., Beaujeu's time ran out. His headlong advance came to a shuddering halt at the sight—a few score yards away through the trees—of the English advance.

An English eyewitness said that on catching sight of the enemy, one of Braddock's guides "immediately discharged his piece, turned round his horse and cried, the Indians was upon us." The scouts galloped back to the advance party, which "Colonel Gage ordered to form," engineer Harry Gordon recalled. "Most of them did, with the front rank upon the ground, and began firing, which they continued for several minutes." It was the standard response to the approach of an enemy force, it was done with dispatch and precision, and it was effective. The approaching warriors were dismayed by the roar of musketry, so much so that some of them insisted later that artillery fired on them, although there was none with the British vanguard. Many Frenchmen and warriors fell in the first few minutes of this unplanned, helter-skelter engagement. Among the first to die was Captain Beaujeu.

Had the French and their allies maintained European discipline and advanced in a group, allowing the British to apply their training, they would have been slaughtered in minutes. But their response was reflexive and utterly mystifying to the British regulars: they dispersed, taking cover behind trees not only to the front, but along both sides of the British column. "Immediately they began to engage us in a half moon, and still continued surrounding us more and more," a British witness recorded. Harry Gordon concurred: "They divided themselves and run along our right and left flanks." While doing so they drove in, or cut off and killed, the small British flanking parties on the slopes to either side of the column.

Colonel Gage's advance party now began taking intense fire. He ordered them forward, but, the colonel later fumed, "not one platoon could be prevailed upon to stir from its line of march, and a visible terror and confusion appeared amongst the men." This was hardly surprising, given that their worst nightmare was coming true: they were among the savages, and were being butchered. They had been trained to volley—to direct a mass of bullets at an enemy formation without paying much attention to the flight of any single bullet. (In fact, the argument had been made that while a volley was an act of war, aiming one's musket at an individual was an act of murder.) They volleyed now, but with no organized formation at either end of the volley, it was a waste of gunpowder. Worse than that, as Colonel Gage recorded, "this fire killed several of our men on the flanking parties, who came running in on the detachment, as did also the vanguard, which completed our confusion."

In the spreading panic, Harry Gordon retained his engineer's eye for terrain: "The Indians making their appearance on the rising ground to our right, occasioned an order for retiring the advanced body 50 or 60 paces." But the soldiers did not fall back far enough, and when "they confusedly formed again a good many of their officers and men were killed and wounded by the Indians, who had got possession of the rising ground on the right." Within minutes, fifteen of the eighteen officers and half of the three hundred men in the advance were dead.

St. Clair ran forward from the working party to see what was happening. He had barely taken a glance when a bullet smashed into his chest. He staggered to Braddock and "begged him for God's sake to gain the rising ground on our right to prevent us from being totally surrounded," then fainted. Braddock had no time for the rising ground. He ordered Colonel Burton to take a portion of the main force forward to the support of the beleaguered advance party, leaving the rest to guard the baggage. In the noise and smoke of battle, with his columns separated on either side of the train, with panicked flankers coming in, horses and cattle milling about, and apprehension growing, Burton had his hands full trying to gain some semblance of control.

He did manage to get a force under way, but it was still in line of march. For the British army, this was the equivalent of being attacked with one's pants around one's ankles. They were trained to fight from line of battle, but they had no room or time to form a line of battle. As Colonel Burton's men came within range of the rising ground, they came under intensified fire. As they watched their comrades picked off one after the other, the survivors began to huddle into their formation, became increasingly deaf to orders, and grew ever more distracted by the thought of a slow death by fire and knife. Burton apparently decided that it was pointless to continue to try to advance under such a disadvantage, and in Orme's words he was "forming his men to face a rising ground upon the right," in other words trying to get his troops organized to charge it, when the remains of the advance party, all cohesion lost and panic rampant, crashed into his formation.

By now Washington was on the scene. He had never seen British regulars in action before, although given his longstanding lust for a King's commission, he must have envisioned the scene many times. He had commanded men under fire twice, once in a brief ambush and once under attack like this, although on that occasion he had been in entrenchments. His physical courage under fire was beyond question; he had the soldier's knack of fatalism that permitted him to ignore the bullets and remain focused on the situation. It was with keen interest, then, that he regarded the British army in action.

He was immediately, irrevocably disappointed. The vaunted regulars "were immediately struck with such a deadly panic that nothing but confusion and disobedience of orders prevailed amongst them. The officers in general behaved with incomparable bravery." This was his reaction to what he saw. He had not seen the brave beginning, when the vanguard volleyed as it had been taught to do. He saw the soldiers huddled and mulish under the fearful onslaught, acting, as men do in such circumstances, as if ducked heads, hunched shoulders, and raised elbows could deflect this deadly leaden hail. By contrast he saw the officers standing erect or dashing about on horseback bellowing orders, and they struck him as brave. And of course they were.

The problem was that they were bravely trying to do the wrong thing. As they had been trained to do, they were ordering their men to maintain and perfect their formations, to respond to this unbelievable situation with parade-ground drill. The enemy was supposed to do likewise, and present itself in a proper compact mass for the volley. As Adam Stephen later declaimed, "The British troops were thunderstruck to feel the effects of a heavy fire, and see no enemy; they threw away their fire in a most indiscreet manner."

All the Virginians were contemptuous of this huddled mass of soldiers standing brutishly, allowing itself to be slaughtered. The British, on the other hand, were amazed by the colonials' lack of discipline, and blamed it for making things worse. "At the first of the firing," a regular soldier reported, "the American troops, without any orders, ran up immediately, some behind trees, and others into the ranks, and put the whole into confusion." The Virginians, for their part, thought it obvious that a man in this situation must immediately get down, take cover, select a target, aim, and fire. Some must have said so, others demonstrated.

In all of this, the most bravely stupid man was Braddock himself, who dashed continuously up and down, ordering his men to organize themselves into platoons and fire proper volleys. "The colors were advanced in different places," Orme recalled, "to separate the men of the two regiments. The General ordered the officers to endeavor to form the men, and to tell them off into small divisions and to advance with them; but neither entreaties nor threats could prevail."

Washington was doing this work, riding from officer to officer in the constant hail of bullets, giving useless orders to frenzied commanders who repeated them to terrified men. It was the men who earned his contempt. This despite the fact that, as he must have known, many of the troops took to heart the advice of the Virginians and other frontiersmen and demanded that they be allowed to "take to the trees," as Colonel Dunbar later related it, "which the General denied and stormed much, calling them cowards, and even went so far as to strike them with his own sword for attempting the trees." To Braddock, leaving formation and taking cover was the same thing as desertion. "Some of the irregulars (as they were called) without directions advanced to the right, in loose order, to attack," Washington recalled. "But this, unhappily, from the unusual appearance of the movement being mistaken for cowardice, a running away was discountenanced." He did not record whether this movement was "discountenanced" with the flat of a sword or with a musket.

Here was a microcosm of the titanic, unseen, and largely unremarked clash of cultures taking place within British America, even as it grappled with its enemies. Here, in an army under severe stress, the dispute reached flash point, with fatal consequences. On the one hand were the British officers, Eastern aristocrats, attempting to impose their will on events and people, insisting on obedience and discipline before all else, certainly before common sense and even before survival. On the other were the provincials, Western pragmatists, deaf to orders that made no sense, alert to effective methods and eager to implement them. In the middle were the pawns, the riffraff of the Irish and American waterfronts who had been swept into the British army, told to obey orders no matter what, and who were now standing like cattle before the sledgehammer, not knowing what to do.

They were dangerous pawns. "If any got a shot, the fire immediately ran through the whole line, though they saw nothing but trees." They were also panicked, and in that condition made no subtle distinctions. To them, anything that moved or fired in the woods was an enemy. When the Virginians and the others who had taken to the trees fired their weapons, it made no impression that they had taken cover on the British side of the trees and were firing at the enemy. One of Braddock's men saw an officer lead 170 Virginians "up to where the enemy was hid and routed them. But O unhappy! Our infatuateds, seeing a smoke, fired and killed him with several of his men." Dr. Alexander Hamilton of Annapolis wrote afterward that "many more of our men were killed by their own party than by the enemy, as appeared afterwards by the bullets that the surgeons extracted from the wounded, they being distinguishable from those of the French and Indians by their size." For every enemy bullet in the front of the body, Dr. Hamilton claimed, the surgeons found two English bullets, "chiefly on the back parts."

At length, Braddock's men got their artillery into action, but like the infantry they had no targets. Nevertheless they banged away, wasting powder and shot, and drawing the most intensive fire on their positions. "The Indians, whether ordered or not I can't say, kept an incessant fire on the guns," a soldier reported, "and killed the men very fast." Even worse, St. Clair's men had abandoned the two field pieces that Gage had declined to keep with the advance party, and the French soon deployed them with terrible effect on the mass of British troops. Meanwhile the warriors in the woods, delighted at their ability to fire with virtual impunity, worked their way along both sides of the compacted British mob until they had almost closed the circle. One of those in the column "expected nothing but death for every one of us, for they had surrounded all but a little in the rear, which they strove for with all their force." In fact, the British expected worse than death at the hands of the savages. "If it was not for their barbarous usage which we knew they would treat us, we should never have fought them as long as we did, but having only death before us made the men fight almost longer than they was able."

In their ultimate agony, Braddock's men not only fought the enemy as best they could, but became infinitely more dangerous to the officers who had been berating and punishing them for months and who now were screaming orders that made no sense, about advancing into those deadly woods. "One or two officers were killed by their own platoon," one soldier reported, and an officer confirmed the fact: "Numbers ran away, nay fired on us that would have forced them to rally." It worked the other way, as well, according to a contemporary who heard that the officers "killed some of the men for not standing, so it became a fight between the men and officers."

Two hours passed. For all that time, the British and Americans fell in droves before both enemy and friendly fire, at war with the enemy, each other, and their own emotions. Most of the officers were dead or wounded, with the remarkable exception of Braddock and Washington, each of whom had exposed himself constantly to the worst of the firing, each of whom had had several horses killed under him. The Virginians had demonstrated that at the slightest initiative the enemy melted away, that given the slightest cover a man could be relatively safe—from his enemies at least. If Braddock had seen, he did not comprehend, and as his officers and men died in heaps he continued to try to do the same things: Form up, get in line, stand at attention, and die.

Once again, at about 4:00 P.M., he ordered Burton to try to take the rising ground to the right that never should have been yielded. Burton tried again, and again it came to nothing. Now Burton's time was up; he went down wounded. So was Braddock's. There would forever be doubt about who fired the shot. Many legends would have it that one of his own men pulled the trigger, and several claimed the credit, although none convincingly. Whatever its source, the bullet found him and lanced him through the right arm and side, lodged in his lungs, and dropped him helpless to the ground.

With the bellowing voice and the flat of the sword no longer there to keep them, the survivors immediately broke and ran for the river. Now confusion and fear turned to blind, animal panic. With his customary contempt, Washington described how the men "broke and run as sheep before the hounds, leaving the artillery, ammunition, provisions and every individual thing we had with us a prey to the enemy. And when we endeavored to rally them in hopes of regaining our invaluable loss, it was with as much success as if we had attempted to stop the wild bears of the mountains."

The enemy, one witness wrote, "pursued us, butchering as they came, as far as the other side of the river; in crossing it they shot many in the water, both men and women, scalping and cutting them in a most barbarous manner." The nightmare now was not to die, but to live long enough to feel the attentions of the enemy. "The yell of the Indians is fresh on my ear, and the terrific sound will haunt me until the hour of my dissolution."

There was charity between comrades, but it took unexpected forms. "I was wounded in one leg, and the other heel, so could not go," one soldier wrote, "but sat down at the foot of a tree, praying of every one that run by that they would help me off. An American Virginian turned to me. Yes, countryman, says he, I will put you out of your misery, these dogs shall not burn you. He then levelled his piece at my head. I cried out and dodged him behind the tree, the piece went off and missed me, and he run on." Soon others carried the wounded man to safety.

Virtually no one was interested in helping anyone else, much less their despised commander. They left him on the field. Orme recalled trying to bribe some men to help Braddock, but money held no interest for them. Only Washington, Orme, Stewart, Croghan, and a few others retained their sense of duty. They loaded Braddock into "a small covered cart which carried some of his most essential equipage," and took him to the lower ford. There Braddock insisted on trying to rally the hundred men they found there.

The panic was by no means over. One of the men remembered "expecting every moment to have our retreat cut off (which a half a dozen men would very easily have done) and a certainty of meeting no provisions for 60 miles." They could not know yet that there was to be no pursuit. As far as the victorious warriors were concerned the battle was over, and it was time to gather up scalps, prisoners, and spoils of war. Most of the French-Canadian militia had fled at the first shots, and the remaining French regulars, perhaps a hundred in number, were afraid of Dunbar's reserves, which they knew to be on the march behind Braddock. They had no way of knowing how far away Dunbar really was.

Washington galloped to the upper ford to try to stop the continuing headlong flight of the men and found Gage already there doing just that. Washington turned and headed back to Braddock. At sunset, he found the commanding general, in pain and despair, deserted by all but a handful of his men, being carried to the rear in a litter. Gradually it was becoming clear that the army had suffered not merely defeat, but slaughter. As later counts would show, of about 1200 fighting men, at least half were dead or wounded; of eighty-six officers, only twenty-three were able to walk away. Croghan later said that Braddock begged him in vain for the use of one of his pistols, that he might "die like an old Roman."

Braddock sent Washington into the night woods to find Dunbar, fifty miles away, and order him to advance six miles to Gist's plantation and there prepare to help the wounded. On the first part of his difficult journey, Washington found himself among those who most needed help, hundreds of wounded men whom panic had carried for a mile or two along the road to the rear, but who could go no farther. "The shocking scenes which presented themselves in this night's march are not to be described," Washington wrote later.

"The dead, the dying, the groans, lamentations and cries along the road were enough to pierce a heart of adamant. The gloom and horror of which was not a little increased by the impervious darkness." His two guides from time to time had to identify the trail "by groping on the ground with their hands."

Triumphant warriors ransacked the battlefield, claiming as prizes thirteen cannons, five hundred head of cattle and horses, thirty wagonloads of ammunition, and provisions and equipment including Braddock's personal papers and his war chest containing thousands of pounds in currency. And of course there were the scalps from the dead, the rum, and the prisoners. A British prisoner, captured before the battle, saw from confinement in Fort Duquesne a party of warriors "coming in with about a dozen prisoners, stripped naked, with their hands tied behind their backs, and their faces and parts of their bodies blacked." This was an indication that the prisoners had already been presented to the tribal matrons; those who had been selected for adoption had had their hair shorn, those destined for burning had their faces blackened. "These prisoners they burned to death on the banks of the Allegheny river, opposite to the fort." The fate of one was typical: "They tied him to a stake, and kept touching him with firebrands, red-hot irons, etc., and he screamed."

Having had their fun and having defeated their enemy, most of the warriors left Fort Duquesne during the next few days, leaving Contrecoeur to worry about what Braddock's army was going to do once reinforced by Dunbar. As it turned out, he need not have been concerned. On July 11, Braddock arrived at Gist's plantation, murmuring after a day of silent agony, "Who would have thought it?" On the evening of July 13, Braddock declared, "We shall better know how to deal with them another time." Then, to the surprise of many who had thought his wound not that serious, and much to his own surprise, he died.

"We buried him in two blankets in the high road that was cut for the wagons," one of his soldiers recorded, "that all the wagons might march over him, and the army, to hinder any suspicion of the French Indians. For if they thought he was buried there, they would take him up and scalp him." Washington later reported that he had directed the burial. If he was at all affected by the high tragedy of Braddock's end, the deep symbolism of this anonymous grave in which was dumped the embodiment of the British Empire, he did not say.

Nor did he have anything to say about what Colonel Thomas Dunbar did with the command that fell on his shoulders with the death of Braddock: Dunbar ordered a general retreat, not only from Gist's plantation, but from Fort Cumberland, where he first destroyed the enormous store of ammunition and supplies so painstakingly assembled there, and then marched east to Philadelphia. As John Carlyle acidly observed from Alexandria, "they are determined to go into winter quarters in July (brave English men)." Before long, Dunbar would continue his retreat, leaving Philadelphia and then the continent itself. Contrecoeur's impoverished and depleted band was left in triumphant and undisturbed possession of Fort Duquesne.

What did Washington make of this most climactic and historic battle, and what did it make of him? It was to date the worst defeat suffered by British arms in America. It meant the loss of the heartland of the continent to the French, the destruction of the designs of the Ohio Company, the deferment yet again of his personal hopes for a King's commission and a regular command.

Yet Washington was to maintain for the rest of his life a most curious ambivalence about what he saw on the banks of the Monongahela. In his writings immediately afterward he clung for the most part to a most bland and conventional view—that the officers behaved very well, but the "English soldiers" panicked and brought on defeat. He wrote to his mother a week after the battle that the "dastardly behavior of those they call regulars exposed all others that were inclined to do their duty to almost certain death." He never questioned the appropriateness of what the officers were trying to do, and he never condemned Braddock, even many years later when he reflected, "true, true, he was unfortunate, but his character was much too severely treated. Even in the manner of fighting he was not more to blame than others—of all that were consulted, only one person objected to it."

His attitude contrasted strangely with the blunt words of Adam Stephen, one of Washington's principal lieutenants and the commander of the Virginia Regiment in the battle. Stephen was also contemptuous of the regulars' performance under fire, but his strongest feelings were reserved for Braddock. "His excellency found to his woeful experience, what had been frequently told him, that formal attacks and platoon-firing would never answer against the savages and Canadians. It ought to be laid down as a maxim to attack them first, to fight them in their own way, and go against them light and naked, as they come against us."

Stephen knew what he was talking about. Before the battle, he had been assigned to escort one hundred cattle and one hundred packhorses from Dunbar's detachment to Braddock's force. During the fifty-mile march his hundred men were "dogged night and day by the Indians; but by vigilance, which is the only thing that can secure one against such an enemy, joined the general four days before the battle without the loss of a man or a bullock. We beat them out of their ambushes, and always had the first fire on them." By contrast, he pointed out acidly, "the British gentlemen were confident they would never be attacked." Stephen knew enough about the tribes to know that the French had been forced to attack before Braddock got to the fort, because "the French must lose the use of their Indians if they did not. They had collected a body of them, and they would not be cooped up in the fort."

Washington had learned all these things, too. More than a year earlier, he had worried that Captain Mackay, encountering an enemy force, would order "a regular attack, which would expose us to almost immediate death without hope of damaging them, as the French all fight in the Indian method which we have got some experience in." But he could not bring himself to state the obvious conclusions about the quality of Braddock's leadership. About as close as he came was to say that during the battle he had asked permission (and even here he did not name Braddock) "to head the provincials and engage the enemy in their own way; but the propriety of it was not seen until it was too late for execution."

The bitterness that Washington did express, while his countrymen raged at Braddock's defeat and Dunbar's disgrace, was entirely personal. His efforts to pursue a military career had been, in his view, entirely unrewarding. He vented his frustration on August 2, a week after his return to Mount Vernon, in a letter to his elder half-brother Augustine: "I was employed to go a journey in the winter (when I believe few or none would have undertaken it) and what did I get by it? My expenses borne! I then was appointed with trifling pay to conduct a handful of men to the Ohio. What did I get by this? Why, after putting myself to considerable expense in equipping and providing necessaries for the campaign—I went out, was soundly beaten, lost them all—came in, had my commission taken from me or in other words my command reduced, under pretence of an order from home. I then went out a volunteer with General Braddock and lost all my horses and many other things. I have been upon the losing order ever since I entered the service, which is now near two years."

In this frame of mind, Washington waited at Mount Vernon to hear what Virginia and the other colonies were going to do. He was still adjutant of militia, and it was obvious to everyone that in the aftermath of Braddock's army being driven from the western frontier, the militia was going to be needed. He alerted his county lieutenants to expect an inspection during September. It was also obvious that some kind of expedition against Fort Duquesne would have to be attempted, by someone, sometime. As one of the few who had escaped Braddock's defeat with his reputation unharmed—in fact, it was enhanced—Washington was a likely choice to command such an expedition, if it was organized by the colonies and not the Crown. Once again, Washington expressed deeply ambivalent feelings, declaring to his mother on August 14 that "if it is in my power to avoid going to the Ohio again I shall, but if the command is pressed upon me by the general voice of the country, and offered upon such terms as can't be objected against, it would reflect eternal dishonor upon me to refuse it."

Besides, he added, "at present I have no proposals." But if he did get one, he explained in detail to one friend, he would apply strict conditions. He would demand the right to name his own officers, and he would need a ready supply of cash. However, he went on, there were not enough competent officers, there were not wagons and horses, and the prospects for any such expedition in the foreseeable future were dismal. Worse, if he attempted it and failed, "I should lose what at present constitutes the chief part of my happiness—the esteem and notice that my country has been pleased to honor me with."

Obviously, seeking command of such an expedition was out of the question. "But if the command should be offered, the case is then altered." Perhaps, too, the case was altered somewhat by the fact that another man had offered to take the job—none other than William Fitzhugh.

Meanwhile, the House of Burgesses convened in special session. Washington pointedly stayed away from Williamsburg to avoid the appearance of applying for an appointment. The burgesses appropriated £40,000 for a reinvigorated Virginia Regiment, to be strengthened to a thousand men, and to be commanded by George Washington if he would do it. On August 23 the assembly was prorogued. On August 27, Washington arrived in Williamsburg to confer with Dinwiddie. On September 1, his appointment was confirmed as colonel of the Virginia Regiment and commander-in-chief of the Virginia forces.

Washington had little to say by way of explaining his ready acceptance of what he had vowed to avoid. "The solicitations of the country," he shrugged, "overcame my objections."

CHAPTER 11

The Outrages

"I am distracted what to do!"

April 24, 1756

Captain Adam Stephen tried to keep the terror from his official communication, but he was not successful. "Matters are in the most deplorable condition at Fort Cumberland," he wrote Washington on October 4, 1755. "By the best judges of Indian affairs, it's thought there are at least 150 Indians about us—they go about and commit their outrages at all hours of the day and nothing is to be seen or heard of but desolation and murders heightened with all barbarous circumstances and unheard-of instances of cruelty. The smoke of the burning plantations darken the day and hide the neighboring mountains from our sight."

The time forever to be remembered as "the Indian outrages," a years-long series of attacks on frontier families and military detachments, had begun. It had come to Thomas Jemison's prosperous farm near Carlisle, Pennsylvania, for example, on a beautiful morning as his wife and six children, along with a visiting neighbor family of five, were getting ready for breakfast. The Jemisons had lived there for a dozen years, since coming to the New World from Ireland in 1743. They had heard the stories of savage depredations on the frontier, but none had occurred close to them, and Thomas believed that if they could get safely through one more year, Washington's army (with whom his brother John had served, and died, at Fort Necessity) would repel the threat.

"Father was shaving an axe-helve at the side of the house," Mary Jemison recalled years later (she was twelve at the time); "mother was making preparations for breakfast; my two older brothers were at work near the barn; and the little ones, with myself, and the [neighbor] woman and her three children, in the house." The neighbor had just set out on horseback for his house to get some supplies.

There was a sudden, appalling crash of gunfire, a glimpse of the neighbor and his horse lying dead in the yard, and then a rush of bronze bodies. "They first secured my father, and then rushed into the house, and without the least resistance made prisoners" of them all. The raiders, "six Indians and four Frenchmen," grabbed all the food they could carry and, "in great haste, for fear of detection," drove the little herd of frightened humanity into the woods. All day long they hurried westward, the captives offered nothing to eat or drink. "Whenever the little children cried for water, the Indians would make them drink urine or go thirsty." That night they slept, hungry, exhausted, and afraid, on the ground, and before dawn were forced to march on. They were given some breakfast at dawn, and some supper that night when they camped in a swamp.

After supper the Shawnees tore the shoes from Mary's feet and replaced them with moccasins, and did the same for one of the neighbor boys. Mary's mother knew what that meant and hugged her, urging her to be brave and careful, to remember her English and her prayers. Her father could not speak; he had been "sunk in silent despair" since the attack. The Shawnees led the two children away from the rest of the captives, whom they then tomahawked, scalped, and dismembered. Mary was spared the sights and sounds of the killings, but was forced to watch as the warriors stretched, cleaned, and cured the scalps. "My mother's hair was red, and I could easily distinguish my father's and the children's from each other."

Mary was adopted by a Seneca family at Logstown, married to a Delaware warrior, widowed in a Cherokee raid, and later moved to western New York's Genesee River country, where she chose to spend the rest of her eight decades of life as an Iroquois wife, mother of eight, and matron.

As horrifying as such raids were to the victims, and to the neighbors and relatives who repeated the awful stories to each other, the outrages were barely significant in traditional military terms—the numbers of combatants engaged, casualties suffered, and acres of ground gained by the enemy. In Augusta County, which was arguably the hardest hit of any on the frontier, Colonel William Preston counted a total of 298 casualties—killed, wounded, and captured—in four years of raids, fewer than half the casualties suffered by the British at Braddock's defeat. Nevertheless, the raids were psychologically devastating, and not only to the relative few who suffered them directly. During the next two years, the outrages would drive much of the European population from the western frontier, Washington to distraction, and Dinwiddie into retirement.

During that time neither the commander nor the governor (much less their superiors in London) would grasp either the military nature of the threat or an appropriate strategy for dealing with it. While each man would maintain that nothing was more important than defending the domain of his King and relieving the suffering of the victims, each would pursue a secret, personal agenda of higher priorities. For Washington these priorities would continue to be personal advancement and public acclaim; for Dinwiddie they would continue to be enlargement of his domain, Virginia, and of his equity in the Ohio Company.

This is not to say that either man shirked the duties that devolved upon him during this trying time. For his part, Washington labored mightily, applying the hard lessons he had learned during the two previous, disastrous expeditions to the Ohio country. In September 1755, immediately after rejoining the Virginia Regiment as its commander, he promoted his most trusted subordinates—Adam Stephen to lieutenant colonel and Andrew Lewis to major—to help him administer the Virginia regiment. Then, with unprecedented vigor and attention to detail, he generated a blizzard of orders specifying recruiting methods and quotas; the times and places for musters and drills; the required amount of target practice; the specific kinds, quality, and sources of supplies, shoes, uniforms, arms, ammunition, and equipment to be procured; and exactly how the goods were to be stockpiled and issued. After sending instructions to his officers, he went to see them—in Fredericksburg, Alexandria, Winchester, and all along the 120-mile frontier from Fort Cumberland in the north to Fort Dinwiddie in the south (on Jackson's River in Augusta County). No longer a novice at military administration, Washington had made careful note of those things that contributed to success and those that bred failure, and he wanted nothing more to do with failure.

After a month of intensive organizational work and extensive travel, Washington was on his way to Williamsburg for a conference with Dinwiddie when Stephen's fearful report reached him near Fredericksburg on October 8, 1755. Washington decided to return to his command, contenting himself with a letter to the governor detailing the things that were still frustrating his attempts to defend the frontier.

The letter raised the two problems that would preoccupy both men for the next two years: the lack of discipline among the defenders of the colony and the lack of supplies and equipment for them. Washington complained that the members of the regiment, the militia, and the general public were uncooperative and insolent; that there were no laws permitting him to use what he regarded as sufficient brutality to impose order; that there was not enough money for the regiment's payroll and expenses; and that even when money was available, he could find no "tents, kettles, arms, ammunition, cartridge paper, etc. etc."

Despite all that Washington had learned on his expeditions, and despite the detailed attention he was now giving to logistics, he still had a simplistic view of the military situation. He made no distinction between strategy and tactics, and seemed to think the gravity of the crisis would somehow mitigate his logistical problems. His mission, as he defined it for Dinwiddie, was simply to "repulse the enemy if they are still committing their outrages," and to "repel those barbarous and insolent invaders of our country." Dinwiddie's view was no more complex or thoughtful. He expressed some dismay at the enemy onslaughts, but seemed to take heart from Washington's air of assurance. In the manner of cheering on a rider to hounds, he exhorted Washington to "drive those banditti from our frontiers" and "send down a number of their scalps."

Both men must have believed that with the crisis at hand and the frontiers of Virginia under attack, supplies and transport would appear where they had been unavailable, money would be spent willingly by the once-miserly House of Burgesses, the men under arms would become obedient instead of unruly, and the population would become supportive instead of indifferent. Washington envisioned not only a united colony, but a cooperative enemy that would present itself for military engagement. He declared that he would be "proceeding immediately at the head of some militia to put a stop to the ravages of the enemy."

Washington was dumbfounded to be told that despite the emergency, all but two dozen of the able-bodied men in Frederick County "absolutely refused to stir, choosing as they say to die with their wives and families." Once again the ungrateful wretches let him down, placing a higher value on their homes and families than on service to their governor. Nor would these Westerners defer to a man who was obviously of high station. "In all things I meet with the greatest opposition," he fumed. "No orders are obeyed but what a party of soldiers, or my own drawn sword, enforces." He had even heard that townspeople were muttering threats "to blow out my brains."

One Sunday, a local man rushed to Washington's headquarters to report an attack within four miles of Winchester, that he "had heard constant firing and the shrieks of the unhappy murdered." Washington grabbed about forty men and marched for the scene. He ordered a captain of the county militia to deploy his men in the town as a reserve force but, Washington later reported to Dinwiddie, "this great captain answered that his wife, family and corn were at stake, so were those of his soldiers, therefore it was not possible for him to come. Such is the example of the officers! Such the behavior of the men! And such the unhappy circumstances on which our country depends!" Fortunately, the threat in this case turned out to be posed by three drunken Virginia rangers howling and shooting into the air.

In fact, Washington's own men were as intractable as the townspeople and the militia. "I see the growing insolence of the soldiers, the indolence and inactivity of the officers," he griped to Dinwiddie, blaming it all on his limited powers to punish. "If these practices are allowed, we may as well quit altogether. Unless the Assembly will enact a law to enforce the military law in all its parts, I must with great regret decline the honor that has been so generously attended me." It was the first time since his return to service forty-one days earlier that he threatened to resign; it would not be the last.

Word came from the South Branch of the Potomac, thirty miles westward, that the invasion was not quite as awesome as first reported. Scouts reported that about 150 marauders had passed through the valley, that "70, or near it, of our people are killed or missing, and that several houses and plantations are destroyed—but not so great havoc made as was at first represented." But those first reports, laced with all the terror of a nightmare confirmed, had raced from farm to farm along the frontier, no doubt redecorated during each retelling with the ghastly paraphernalia of long torture and slow death.

Just as Braddock's troops had done on the long march west, the settlers were convincing each other that murder lurked behind every wilderness tree; there was no use in trying to tell them that things were not as bad as they seemed. Captain Thomas Waggener, on the march from Alexandria with thirty recruits for the regiment, said his westward progress was slowed on the Blue Ridge by "crowds of people who were flying as if every moment was death," leaving their life's work and best chance behind and running for their lives, "firmly believing that Winchester was taken and in flames."

Washington tried to stem the migration with a proclamation published in Winchester on October 13, "to give notice to all people that I have great reason to believe that the Indians who committed the late cruelties are returned home, as I have certain accounts that they have not been seen nor heard of these ten days past." People should stop listening to "false reports" spread by "timorous people," and should "keep to their homes, and take care of their crops." Three days later, twenty-five settlers were killed in a raid near Harris's Ferry (later Harrisburg), Pennsylvania. But in Adam Stephen's opinion, "the inhabitants of Pennsylvania are more scared than hurt. I can hear of no person that has seen this large body of French and Indians, and am of the opinion that the intelligence is not to be depended on."

This military optimism was as unrealistic as some of the fearful exaggerations by the settlers. The reality was that small bands of warriors, usually accompanied by a handful of French officers, were roaming the back country at will, looking for targets of opportunity, easily avoiding the clumsy defenders while they sowed terror among the civilian population. As Adam Stephen had so pungently observed after Braddock's defeat, "you might as well send a cow in pursuit of a hare as an English soldier, loaded in their way with a coat, jacket, etc., etc., etc., after Canadians in their shirts, who can run well, or naked Indians accustomed to the woods." The provincial troops had learned to take cover when attacked, and were learning to travel lighter and faster, but they were a long way from being a match for the fleet-footed bands abroad in the dark expanses of forest. Having determined that there was, in fact, nothing for him to do in the Winchester area, Washington decided to leave for Fort Cumberland "with about 100 men" on October 17. But virtually none of his troops were ready to march at the appointed time, and he had to issue new orders with a different timetable. Then he had to postpone again, even though the men were finally ready to go, because he lacked enough wagons to carry their supplies. He did not get to Fort Cumberland until October 25.

He encountered there a situation that galled him beyond endurance. He had been warned by Stephen, in his letter of October 4, to expect trouble from a captain of Maryland militia, one John Dagworthy. Nine years before, Dagworthy had left his New Jersey shop to join a planned expedition against French Canada. In a precedent that Washington must have found enviable, its officers had been commissioned by the King. The expedition had been aborted, and Dagworthy, after trying for a time to continue his military career, had mustered out, accepting a lump-sum settlement of his lifetime officer's pension. But now, in the service of Maryland, he could not forget that he had once held that King's commission.

Colonel James Innes, who had been appointed governor of Fort Cumberland by General Braddock, had gone to North Carolina on personal business in September. Innes had turned over the command of the fort to Adam Stephen, the senior Virginia officer in a fort that had been built, supplied, and for the most part manned by Virginians. But Dagworthy noted that the fort was in Maryland, and that he was the senior Maryland officer present. Moreover, he took the position that by virtue of his brief possession of a King's commission, he was forever senior to any provincial officer of any rank. He stopped short of trying to command the Virginia troops, but he assumed the status of garrison commander. Stephen had written to Washington, "I have reason to believe that Captain Dogworthy [the misspelling may not have been accidental] will look upon himself as commanding officer after you have joined the troops."

This was even worse than the problem with Captain Mackay the previous year. In Washington's view, Dagworthy's pretensions were ridiculous, yet the situation was complex. General Braddock himself had calculated during the march to Fort Duquesne that the date of Dagworthy's former commission made him senior not only to all provincial officers, but to all but two of Braddock's regular captains. Thus Washington had reason to think that if he pressed the issue, he could lose. To his person and his office, submitting to Dagworthy would be utterly intolerable.

Washington dealt with this difficult situation in a surprising and uncharacteristic way. He ducked it. With Mackay, in the face of the enemy, he had found a way to function. But now there was no enemy in sight, and he was dealing with a man for whom he had no respect. Somehow, he got to Cumberland, made his inspections, gave a series of orders, and got out—all without confronting Dagworthy. Three days later, Washington was back in Winchester, and before another week was out, by November 3, he was in Williamsburg.

Dinwiddie had summoned him there to help persuade the Burgesses to authorize harsher discipline of the Virginia Regiment. But Washington was preoccupied by the Dagworthy matter, and as a first order of business he prevailed on Dinwiddie to appeal to Governor Shirley of Massachusetts, the acting British commander in America. Washington remembered his favorable impression of Shirley at Braddock's April conference in Alexandria, and now more than ever he hoped the respect had been mutual. Dinwiddie asked Shirley to resolve the situation by conferring brevet, or honorary, rank in the regular establishment on Washington and his two field-grade officers, Stephen and Lewis.

With that request dispatched, Washington and Dinwiddie turned to their lobbying duties, with complete success. The Burgesses passed the measure for which Washington had been clamoring, authorizing courts-martial of the Virginia Regiment to impose the death penalty for mutiny, desertion, and disobedience. Moreover, they met another longstanding demand by granting him a commander's purse of £10,000.

Washington reported all this in an expansive and optimistic missive to Stephen. He looked forward to the new order among his soldiers, based on his ability to hang them; "We now have it in our power to enforce obedience, the men being subject to death." He looked forward to a regular commission, either from Shirley in response to Dinwiddie's request or, less likely but rumored to be in the works, directly from the King in appreciation for past services. He was especially buoyed to learn that his reputation, and that of his command, had not been tarred with the brush of Braddock's defeat, but to the contrary, "the behavior of the Virginia troops is greatly extolled, and meets with public praises in all the coffee houses in London. Yea, they exceed the bound of probability, by saying in the London Magazine for August that 800 Virginians maintained an unequal fight against 1600 French and Indians for three hours after the Regulars fled." Back in Winchester, Stephen was unaffected by the euphoria sometimes produced by immersion in Williamsburg society. "The accounts of our behavior," he replied in a sardonic bookkeeper's pun, were "much exaggerated. We must give them credit and pay the public the balance next campaign."

Although there had been no news of further outrages since October, the continuing problems of recruitment, training, discipline, and supply might have led Stephen to expect his commander's immediate return to headquarters on adjournment of the House of Burgesses. Instead, Washington headed for Alexandria, assuring Stephen that it was "only for a few days." A week later, Washington was still there, offering various reasons for his delay in returning—he needed to find more salt for the regiment, he should check on recruiting, there was a vessel expected with supplies and he really ought to meet it. In fact, he was waiting to hear from Shirley that the royal commissions had been granted and the Dagworthy matter was settled. He hoped "the delays may not prove ominous," he wrote Dinwiddie. "In that case, I shall not know how to act; for I can never submit to the command of Captain Dagworthy." While

Washington waited, Stephen struggled with the bickering and rebelliousness of 513 men and officers, writing plaintively to a preoccupied Washington that everyone present "would receive a great pleasure at seeing you at Fort Cumberland."

But it was becoming obvious that Washington had no intention of setting foot in Fort Cumberland so long as that meant the possibility of yielding to Dagworthy. Dinwiddie, whose letters were showing more frequent flashes of irritation with his prickly young commander, grumpily acceded to what Washington was doing: "If you find it for the good of the service to remain below"—that is, away from Cumberland—"I have no objection to it; but I hope the men are duly exercised and taught the Indian method of fighting."

January came, but no royal commissions and no resolution of the Dagworthy matter. Many other issues remained unresolved as well. The regiment remained below strength because of failed recruiting efforts; discipline was still lax because, in Washington's view, the legislation permitting him to hang miscreants proved to be too unwieldy, requiring as it did exchanges of commissions and death warrants with the governor; supplies were still unsatisfactory; no one knew what the enemy was doing, or where the next blow would fall (twenty-two settlers at Gnadenhutten, Pennsylvania, were killed in December). But it was the Dagworthy matter that preoccupied Washington, who eventually had to return to Winchester without learning how Shirley had responded to the frontier crisis. Shortly thereafter, Dinwiddie reported that Governor Sharpe of Maryland, instructed by Governor Shirley to straighten the matter out, had forbade Dagworthy to assume any authority over members of the Virginia Regiment.

That was not good enough for Washington. In his view, Governor Sharpe was backing his fellow Marylander, Dagworthy. Only Shirley could resolve the matter, and only by conferring a King's commission on Washington, who now proposed to confront him and request it. This was not his idea, Washington wrote disingenuously to Dinwiddie, it was his officers who were clamoring to be taken into the British military establishment. As he made his case, the intensity of his desire was revealed, as usual, by his dishevelled syntax: "This would at once put an end to contention which is the root of evil and destruction to the best of operations, and turn all our movements into a free easy channel—They have urged it in the warmest manner to me to appear personally before the General for this end—which I would at this disagreeable season gladly do things being thus circumstanced if I have your permission which I more freely ask since I have determined to resign a commission which you were generously pleased to offer me (and for which I shall always retain a grateful sense of the favor) rather than submit to the command of a person who I think has not such superlative merit to balance the inequality of rank." In other words, let me go to Shirley or I quit.

The week before sending this ultimatum to Dinwiddie, Washington had lectured all of his subordinate officers on the proper regard for their duty. "Remember that it is the actions, not the commission, that make the officer," he told them, "and that there is more expected of him than the title."

Robert Dinwiddie was getting tired. By January of 1756 he was merely batting away Washington's complaints as a weary man waves off flies, without expecting to be rid of them. Dinwiddie was no longer the formulator of plans, the cheerleader, the inciter. Unlike Washington, he seemed to have been deeply affected, in fact virtually broken in spirit, by Braddock's disaster. Where once he would have been jealous of Washington's dealing with other governors, such as Shirley or Robert Hunter Morris of Pennsylvania, Dinwiddie no longer seemed to see the point of anything. "I have lately wrote to all the governors, and now I have no time, or have I any thing now to write them," he wrote listlessly to Washington, approving his request to see Shirley. "In your return see Governor Morris and make yourself master of what plan that gentleman proposes for the next campaign, which will in some measure make me able to concert a proper plan for our forces."

Morris, on the other hand, had become energized by his legislature's appropriation of £60,000 for defense (Benjamin Franklin and his political allies were in the process of breaking the stranglehold of the pacifist Quakers on the Assembly). Morris spent the month of January on the Pennsylvania frontier, overseeing the construction of a line of "forts and block houses," as he wrote Washington, "from Delaware along the Kittatinny hills as far as the new road that leads to the Allegheny hills." Each fort was garrisoned by seventy-five men ordered to range the woods in all directions to detect and pursue any hostile parties. Morris worried that his province was not prepared for the financial burden of maintaining the forts, but thought the crushing expense might be the very thing to convince them that the French must be dislodged from the Ohio country, "for while they continue there we have no reason to expect the Indians will return to their dependence on us."

The activity in Pennsylvania made clear by contrast what Virginia was not doing. Remarkably, six months after Braddock's defeat and the launching of a campaign of terror against the frontier, Virginia's leaders had not decided on a strategy for dealing with the threat. There had been lengthy struggles over supplies, clothing, pay, rank, and prestige, but all that served merely to maintain the status quo. There was as yet no plan of operations beyond driving "those banditti from our frontiers." Finally, in a January letter to Dinwiddie, Washington asked the central question: "I should be glad to have your honor's express commands either to prepare for taking the field, or guarding our frontiers, in the spring."

What Washington presented was a horned dilemma. Offensive operations seemed out of the question. "Without a much greater number of men than we have a visible prospect of getting I don't see how it's possible to think of passing the mountains." Then, too, there was the matter of "wagons, horses, forage, pack saddles, etc., etc." It had been hard enough to round them up for Braddock's expedition, and most of the people who had supplied them, in response to Franklin's promises of compensation, had never been paid. "It will be impossible to get wagons or horses sufficient without the old score is paid off," said Washington, "the people are really ruined for want of their money and complain justly of their grievances."

If, on the other hand, the plan was to defend the frontiers, Washington saw a different, equally critical problem. A new, major fort should be built in Virginia to replace Fort Cumberland, which should be abandoned, "since it will ever be an eye sore to this colony." He had already sent Colonel Stephen out looking for a site for the new fort, specifying only that it be on the Virginia side of the Potomac. The Wills Creek site had been a favorite location of tribes, traders, settlers, and soldiers alike for years, but now Washington declared it to be "attended with more inconveniences than it's possible to enumerate." The fort there commanded the river, the creek, and a major gap in Big Savage Mountain to the west, and seemed a logical anchor for the existing line of forts along Patterson Creek. Washington's desire to abandon Cumberland startled Dinwiddie, but for the moment the matter receded into the background.

On the second day of February 1756, with spring and the likely resumption of fierce attacks a matter of weeks away, Washington again left his headquarters to do several things he enjoyed above all others: bask in the approval of his fellow men, curry favor with a superior, and seek personal advancement. Escorted by two of his favorite staff officers, George Mercer and Robert Stewart, along with two menservants, Washington made a progress northeastward to Boston to see Shirley and plead for King's commissions. He took the position that his cause was not personal ambition, but human rights: "If reason, justice, and every other equitable right can claim attention, we deserve to be heard."

It was an exhilarating time, an inebriating dose of the rewards of his chosen profession. He was the center of attention in Philadelphia, New York, New London, Newport, Providence, and Boston. He was received cordially and respectfully by the governors of Pennsylvania, New York, and Massachusetts, the latter of course also serving as His Majesty's commander in North America. The young colonel was no longer a hanger-on at the court of the Fairfaxes, or an anonymous member of a general's staff, or a slightly down-at-the-heels planter from the fringes of Virginia society. He was the commander-in-chief of the forces of the largest colony in British North America, and the hero of the Monongahela.

It was hardly surprising that a brief dalliance should have been part of the holiday. Nor was it surprising that the subject of the dalliance should have been a lady of impeccable credentials and substantial net worth. Washington's host in New York was Beverly Robinson, brother to the Speaker of the Virginia House of Burgesses. Beverly Robinson had married very well, and had as a member of his household his wife's sister, Mary Eliza Philipse. The lady, later referred to by a mutual acquaintance, with a figurative wink, as "the agreeable Miss Polly," was agreeable on several counts, including the quality of her social connections and the size of her inheritance.

Romance flared brightly in Washington's breast, then as quickly died as he moved on to affairs of state and she to betrothal to someone else.

Governor Shirley listened to Washington's complaint, grilled him thoroughly and repeatedly for several days about conditions on the frontier, and on March 5 called him in and handed him a letter written to resolve the Dagworthy matter. It was Shirley's ruling that Captain Dagworthy carried a provincial, not a King's, commission, "and of course is under the command of all provincial field officers." Specifically, when Dagworthy and Washington were together, "it is my orders that Colonel Washington should take the command."

Yet Colonel Washington was far from satisfied. This is surprising if one thinks he went to Shirley to settle the Dagworthy matter, but of course that was the symptom and not the disease. His motive, as always, was to get for himself the very preferment that Dagworthy had claimed against him, the King's commission. Once again he had failed, achieving only the trivial victory of superiority over Dagworthy. Adam Stephen no doubt reflected Washington's attitude when he wrote sarcastically, "I have learned that you have been a long journey, purely to pay your compliments, and hear some handsome things, which one is always to expect from persons conversant at the courts of princes." Washington set out on his return journey "fully resolved to resign my commission," he declared, "but was dissuaded from it, at least for a time."

Returning leisurely by way of New York and Philadelphia, Washington did not get back to Williamsburg until March 30, the very eve of campaigning weather, and almost time for the outrages to begin again on the frontier. The seasonality of this conflict was the result of several factors. Armies dependent on supply lines and artillery needed campaigning weather to be able to move their men and wagons and camp in comfort. The warriors, on the other hand, could travel and live off the land at any time, yet they found their raiding restricted to the same season for different reasons.

The logistics of the raids were a mystery to no one. The French had made a straightforward deal with their warriors—who included the traditional French allies from the Great Lakes area, along with the Shawnees, some of the Delawares, and more than a few Mingos from the Ohio country who had been insulted by Braddock, or impressed by his defeat, or both. The French expected the warriors to spend the summer raiding the frontier settlements of Virginia, Maryland, and Pennsylvania in order to halt the westward migration of settlers, sow panic among the population, and occupy the colonial forces. The fact that the strategy was born of desperation—the French did not have enough strength to defend Duquesne, much less mount an offensive—did not lessen its effectiveness. The raids succeeded in paralyzing the English to a degree unrelated to the numbers of fighting men involved.

But the warriors thus occupied did not have the time to clear new cornfields, build fish traps, prepare for the fall hunt, and assemble the food supplies they would need to survive the winter, so the French took responsibility for feeding the tribes. Thus the seasonality of the years of the outrages quickly became apparent. The raids would begin when spring refreshed the water supply, provided leafy cover for espionage and ambushes, and made it possible to travel light, unencumbered by blankets and shelter. With the onset of harsh weather in late October or early November, the warriors crossed the Alleghenies to rejoin their tribes in the comfort of winter camps near French supply depots.

Once observed, this pattern led several settlers into fatal errors. Assuming with the first hard freezes and snowfall that the warriors had departed, settlers often left the security of villages and forts to return to their isolated farms to gather in what crops they could and make repairs to their buildings. Frequently they were butchered there by warriors who, from their longer experience of the weather patterns, knew that the first onset of winter weather was almost always followed by a stretch of warm dry weather. It came to be known as Indian summer.

But in April of 1756, with hostilities no doubt imminent as usual, Washington had urgent business to keep him from the frontier. He had learned that the commander-in-chief, whom he had worked so diligently to charm, had been replaced. Another Scot, John Campbell, Earl of Loudoun, had been named not only commander of all forces in North America, but titular governor of Virginia as well. Unlike Braddock, Loudoun was an experienced commander. He had led troops in many battles, and had been a lieutenant of Cumberland's at the time of the Battle of Culloden.

Unfortunately, Loudoun had lost every battle for which he had been responsible, and exceeded even Braddock in haughty arrogance. Nevertheless, he had been assigned to unite the British colonies and conquer the French in America.

As part of the reorganization, Washington soon learned, Governor Sharpe of Maryland was to command the forces in the southern colonies and any expedition against Fort Duquesne. In January, Washington had been convinced that Sharpe was conniving in support of Captain Dagworthy; now Washington did not hesitate to ask the governor for help in a last-ditch attempt to get a King's commission from Shirley before Loudoun arrived. It was certainly worth a try. Shirley was famous for rewarding his friends with contracts and appointments, and was redoubling his generosity during the few weeks of power remaining to him. Even after Loudoun arrived, Shirley would hand out fifty-nine civil appointments in two months, before his exasperated superiors recalled him to London to face investigation and a genteel retirement.

"The inclosed letter I am desired to forward to your Excellency from Colonel Washington," Sharpe obligingly wrote to Shirley on April 10, 1756, "and to request you to commissionate and appoint him second in command" of any expedition "to westward this summer." It was a long shot, and no one should have been surprised that Shirley declined to preempt Loudoun in quite so bold a way. Once again, Washington had to content himself with the handsome words in which Shirley's refusal was couched: "I know no provincial officer upon this continent to whom I should so readily give it."

After setting these things in motion, Washington at long last returned to Winchester, where he found as he might have expected that the hatchet restrained by the inhospitable months of winter had once again fallen on the frontier. "The enemy have returned in greater numbers, committed several murders not far from Winchester, and even are so daring as to attack our forts in open day," he wrote to Dinwiddie on April 7. "Many of the inhabitants are in a miserable situation by their losses, and so apprehensive of danger that, I believe, unless a stop is put to the depredations of the Indians, the Blue Ridge will soon become our frontier."

He circulated what he called "an exhortation (for orders are no longer regarded in this county)" to be read at musters of the militia, urging the men to turn out in force on April 15. They would then, Washington announced, "march out and scour the country." As it turned out, the county had no more regard for exhortations than for orders—a mere fifteen men appeared at the appointed hour.

Disgusted with the lack of response, Washington called on Dinwiddie to draft the needed men from "the lower counties," suggesting that to ease resistance they be drafted for a limited period, of perhaps eighteen to twenty months, time for "two full campaigns." He thought the legislature should compel the frontier settlers to move into towns, and to herd their cattle into the more thickly populated interior for protection. Then they could visit their outlying farms in armed bands.

Washington casually acknowledged that savagery was begetting savagery when he reported that a detachment out of Winchester had encountered a "small body of Indians" which they chased away after a half-hour fight. The French leader of the enemy party, Washington cheerfully reported, "was killed and scalped." The trophy was being sent to the governor for his admiration, and Washington hoped that "although it is not an Indian's," the men who lifted it "will meet with an adequate reward, as the Monsieur's is of much more consequence." Later, the House of Burgesses dutifully awarded a bounty of £25.

It was a rare encounter. In the spring of 1756, as would prove true throughout the summers of the outrages, white men under arms seldom saw their savage foe. The attacks would come at random, two or three of them a month from April to September, usually falling upon isolated farm families. Occasionally there would be some taunting or harassing of a fort or armed force, but almost never an armed confrontation. Typically, a detachment would hear a report of an atrocity, hasten to the location, and find nothing but scalped and mutilated bodies to bury. Then, seething with frustration, the men would return to their garrison to endure the boredom and fear for more long weeks.

The conditions of their service would have caused difficulty had the men been superbly led, and they were not. Adam Stephen had begun complaining about the company-grade officers at the end of March, writing Washington that "we have several who do little honor to the regiment, and seem to me to have entered the service out of mercenary rather than honorable views. If they can comply with their duty as far as to keep their commission, they have no anxiety about the desolation of the frontiers or interest of their country." Something needed to be done, wrote Stephen. "We stand in need of a purgation."

Thus it could not have been a total surprise to Washington to learn that unflattering accounts of his officers' behavior had reached Williamsburg. "The assembly were greatly inflamed," Dinwiddie reported, "being told that the greatest immoralities and drunkenness have been much countenanced and proper discipline neglected." Speaker John Robinson referred vaguely to certain "terrible reports" in circulation in the capital. Perhaps as a result, the committee overseeing the payment of accounts for the regiment was turning waspish. According to William Fairfax, "your appointment of an aide de camp and secretary is thought extraordinary," and the committee was not inclined to pay for them.

Washington immediately wrote to Dinwiddie and Robinson passionate and detailed letters of defense: not of his slandered subordinates, but of himself. As to whether the officers deserved the slander, "I will not take upon me to determine." In fact, "there are some who have the seeds of idleness too strongly instilled into their constitution either to be serviceable to themselves or beneficial to the country." But, he insisted, there had been no countenancing or neglect on his part. "I have, both by threats and persuasive means, endeavored to discountenance gaming, drinking, swearing and irregularities of every kind." He now admitted that he had been avoiding Fort Cumberland because of "the unhappy difference about the command," and that he had consequently been prevented "from *enforcing* the orders which I never failed to *send*."

He was crisp and almost dismissive in his letter to Dinwiddie, but went on at greater and more emotional length to Speaker Robinson, adding specific permission "that the contents, if you think proper, may be communicated to the whole" of the general assembly. The argument he wanted communicated was that whatever his officers did wrong, they did at Fort Cumberland; that Fort Cumberland was in Maryland and commanded by Captain Dagworthy (a claim he had everywhere else denied); that he, on the other hand, had made "unwearied endeavors" all the while "to serve my country with the highest integrity"; and that if the criticism did not stop he would quit. "It will give me the greatest pleasure to resign a command which I solemnly declare I accepted against my will."

He gave wide distribution among his influential friends to this, his fifth resignation threat in seven months. Landon Carter, a Richmond County planter and burgess, thought Washington's reaction was disproportionate to "some reflections that at most were only hinted at," concerning "some few of the officers who perhaps may have behaved like disorderly young men." Later, Carter protested a deluge of defensive letters from regimental officers "as if all were affected with the poison of one babbling tongue. Some are very daring, charging the country with ingratitude, boasting of their great toil and willingness to serve her when they had ease and plenty at home. Surely, sir, these fellows write letters with the points of their swords and seal them with pistol bullets." They were having a bad effect, Carter warned Washington, making "many friends to your corps ashamed" in the midst of efforts to enlarge the regiment and have it taken into the regular British army. "There is some atonement due for this." Charles Carter, a neighbor of Washington's Fredericksburg farm and a burgess from King George County, agreed. "You are too much affected. I hope you will have a better opinion of your country and not condemn us upon a misrepresentation." He advised Washington to "arm yourself with patience and despise such reflections as may be cast by any malevolent enemies to you and every upright member of society." William Fairfax wrote to report that Dinwiddie was irritated by the whole thing, that the assembly was not taking the allegations against the officers seriously, and that Washington should let matters settle.

Immediately after the perceived slur on his conduct of the command and the threat to withhold money for his servants, Washington made a dramatic change in the way he referred to the people of the frontier. He had been unremitting in expressing his contempt for Winchester ("this vile hole"), Frederick County, and all who lived there. "The timidity of the inhabitants of this county is to be equalled by nothing but their perverseness," he raged on one occasion. His aristocratic correspondents agreed with his assessments, Speaker Robinson concurring that the "unhappy situation our back inhabitants are in" was due in large measure to "the obstantcy and dasturdlyness of the people themselves."

But two days after receiving word of the problems in Williamsburg, Washington referred to the area's "poor, distressed people." And two days after that he was even more deeply moved by their plight: "I am too little acquainted, sir, with pathetic language to attempt a description of the people's distresses, though I have a generous soul, sensible of wrongs and swelling for redress. But what can I do? If bleeding, dying! would glut their insatiate revenge, I would be a willing offering to savage fury, and die by inches to save a people. I *see* their situation, ***know*** their danger, and participate in their *sufferings*." Two days later, he took up the theme again: "The supplicating tears of the women and moving petitions from the men melt me into such deadly sorrow that I solemnly declare, if I know my own mind, I could offer myself a willing sacrifice to the butchering enemy provided that would contribute to the people's ease."

"Not an hour, nay, scarcely a minute passes that does not produce fresh alarms and melancholy accounts," Washington began his April 24 letter to Dinwiddie, adding, "I am distracted what to do!" Indeed, it had been an active week. On April 18, there was a skirmish at Edwards's Fort on the Cacapon River, twenty miles west of Winchester. Captain John Mercer, Lieutenant Thomas Carter, and sixty men went out to drive off a band of enemy marauders seen in the area. About a mile from the fort they were attacked, and after half an hour or so of heavy fighting had to retreat to the fort. The two officers were killed, and fifteen of the men were dead or missing. The messenger who brought word of the fight to Winchester said the fort was surrounded by a hundred or more men, including French, most of them mounted.

Washington, who still did not comprehend what his enemy was doing, saw in this skirmish confirmation of his worst fear—that a large invasion force was moving against him, en route to the conquest of Virginia. He called for reinforcements from the militia, ordered the townspeople to muster with the troops, directed that the brush be cleared from the approaches to the town, and in every way possible braced for an onslaught. Meanwhile, small parties of warriors wandered about the South Branch valley as usual, descending on isolated families or detachments while deftly avoiding standup fights. "Three families were murdered the night before last at a distance of less than 12 miles from this place," Washington reported, "and every day we have accounts of such cruelties and barbarities as are shocking to human nature. Nor is it possible to conceive the situation and danger of this miserable county: such numbers of French and Indians all around; no road is safe to travel; and here we know not the hour how soon we may be attacked!"

Dinwiddie responded by expressing mild irritation at what he described as "mischievous miscreants." His advice to Washington was to "keep up your spirits and in time I hope we shall be able to vanquish them." However, he did call up half the militia of ten counties and ordered them to Winchester to help.

Then, on May 3, Washington had a sudden change of heart. The invaders, he informed Dinwiddie, may have returned to Duquesne, for which suggestion he offered a curious piece of evidence: "The roads over the Allegheny Mountains are as much beaten as they were last year by General Braddock's army." Three weeks later he repeated his opinion in an advertisement, similar to the one he had published the previous October, announcing that the dangers were now "pretty much over," and the unfortunate people who had been driven from their "plantations" could and should now return. They could now expect to live "in the greatest security and peace," because the militia was "so posted and dispersed around the frontiers—building forts, scouting, scouring and patrolling the woods—that the least appearance of the enemy will soon be discovered and every necessary measure taken to repel them and defend the inhabitants from any danger or trouble."

In fact, it was to be one of the worst summers of all the years of the outrages.

CHAPTER 12

Indian Summers

"No troops in the universe can guard against the cunning and wiles of Indians."

OCTOBER 25, 1757

On the very day of Washington's bright announcement to Dinwiddie that all was well—May 3, 1756—a detachment went out from Fort Cumberland in vain pursuit of an enemy party that had killed Thomas Cresap's son. From May through September the pattern of the outrages remained the same; a family killed here, a straggler caught there, every few weeks another incident, now a few from Augusta County, then a cluster of reports from the South Branch Valley, now some activity near Conococheague. There were not any more attacks in this period than had occurred when Washington had been talking about offering himself as a sacrifice to the implacable foe, but neither were there any fewer. From early May onward, however, his sympathy for the suffering population was no more to be found. "People here in general are very selfish; every person expects forces at his own door, and is angry to see them at his neighbor's," he would observe in September. "The timorous disposition of the inhabitants occasions much confusion and trouble; and constantly are for flying off at the least noise or report of danger."

Dinwiddie could not agree more: "I am really ashamed of the dastardly, pusillanimous spirit of the people in general at this time of danger."

With the crisis apparently over, Washington returned in early May to the familiar problems of supply, discipline, and above all direction. "I must again beg leave to desire your particular instructions and information of what is to be done; as being in a state of uncertainty, without knowing the plan of operations, or what scheme to go upon, reduces me to the greatest straits, and leaves me to guess at every thing." Again the question: offense or defense? Washington had answered that to his own satisfaction on April 24, when he wrote at great length to John Robinson, outlining a proposed new strategy. He explained why offensive operations were impossible: "We have neither strength nor abilities, of ourselves, to conduct an expedition. We have neither a train of artillery, artillery men, engineers, etc., to execute any scheme beyond the mountains against a regular fortress. Again, we have not, that I can see, either stores or provisions, arms or ammunition, wagons or horses in any degree proportioned to the service."

Then it must be defense, he reasoned, and he defined the requirements of defense: a chain of forts within a day's march of each other, which is to say fifteen to eighteen miles, and in each fort a garrison of at least eighty to one hundred men to conduct patrols. He explained how this arrangement would enable mutual support, interlocking patrols, and accessible refuge for the inhabitants. It would do no good to locate the forts at the outer edges of settlement, he argued, "for the people, so soon as they are alarmed, fly inwards." If one placed the line of refuges east of them, he thought, they would be less likely to flee. Hence the forts should be located no farther west than North Mountain, the first range of mountains west of the Shenandoah Valley. The base for this system, the largest fortress and storehouse, should be at Winchester, which, "though a place trifling in itself, is yet of the utmost importance." Not until three days later did Washington send an abbreviated version of his arguments to Dinwiddie. Although he received no clear direction from the governor, he did get an appropriation of £1,000 from the burgesses to pay for his proposed fort at Winchester.

In mid-May, Winchester and Washington were inundated with a flood of militiamen responding to Washington's month-old cries for help. When Washington had changed his mind at the first of the month, he had joked that Dinwiddie would have plenty of time to recall the militia, since they never appeared when called anyway. But this time they did. In one three-day period, 670 militiamen from Fairfax, Culpeper, Caroline, and Spotsylvania counties arrived, followed a few days later by 230 more from Orange and Louisa.

Even George Fairfax had been so moved by the danger and the general alarm that he had almost decided to serve his country. Nor was it the first time. The previous September, immediately after Washington took command of the regiment, Fairfax had notified Dinwiddie that he was willing to serve "if you are at a loss for officers." However, should Dinwiddie be inclined to take this offer seriously, he should not do so quickly, Fairfax had added, but "postpone any office you may incline to favor me with until I consult my good and indulgent Parent, and my worthy patron Lord Fairfax who I am in hopes will spare me from his office. Wives, good sir, are not to be consulted upon these occasions, but I make no doubt but mine would consent upon so laudable a call."

Having been spared the agony of a decision on that occasion, Fairfax now confided to Washington that on learning of the prospective invasion of his homeland he had sort of hurried home from Williamsburg, only to find that the Fairfax militia already had marched for Winchester, "otherwise I believe I should have accompanied them." He was glad to hear that the invasion was over, but "if those cruel savages should hereafter return," Washington should "freely command me, being willing and always desirous of serving my country."

Thus informed of the loyalty and courage of his boyhood friend, Washington turned to the crisis caused by the people who had come to help him. There was in Winchester a great floundering about, a loud and unending chorus of complaints about food, cries to go home, and arguments about rank and command. Laboriously, Washington worked out assignments for nine hundred men when he had use for no more than five hundred. That problem was solved on the eve of the troops' departure to their assigned stations when a false report reached Winchester of what was described as "a considerable body of Indians" on the South Branch. By the hundreds, the militia vanished.

Washington was not unhappy to see them go, but was worried about the effect of the mass desertions on his regiment. He looked forward to the scheduled execution of two deserters who had been sentenced to death; it would, he thought, be a "proper encouragement for good behavior." However, he could not yet bring himself to go through with the hanging.

Through all these alarms and difficulties, Washington never lost sight of the fact that a new commander-in-chief, which was to say a new source of a King's commission, was on the way. Although things were becoming ever more strained between the colonel and his governor (the latter, sixty-three years of age, was unwell and was talking about returning to England if he did not soon recover), Dinwiddie was still a willing accomplice in the art of buttering superiors. "You need not have wrote me to recommend you to the Earl of Loudoun," Dinwiddie wrote on May 27th; he had already begun the campaign by writing "fully to General Abercrombie, who is second in command and my particular friend, which I think much better than writing directly to his Lordship." During the summer, Washington and Stephen spent considerable time drafting a proper introductory letter to present to his lordship on his arrival. Loudoun stepped ashore at New York on July 23, and two days later Washington dispatched his missive: "We, the officers of the Virginia Regiment, beg leave to congratulate your lordship on your safe arrival in America: and to express the deep sense we have of His Majesty's great wisdom and paternal care for his colonies in sending your lordship to their protection at this critical juncture." There was more in this vein, but the letter elicited merely a resounding silence. Adam Stephen worried that they might not have used the proper salutation. William Fairfax contributed detailed advice on further measures: "A kind and favorable letter from Lord Fairfax may give you a successful introduction; and perhaps Colonel Gage at your request may mention you in a genteel manner."

Meanwhile the outrages continued. During July, ten people were killed and many of them scalped near Maidstone, at the mouth of the Conococheague, and six more were killed in two separate attacks near Fort Cumberland. Against these depredations the Virginia Regiment continued to be completely ineffective. A captain of the regiment, Thomas Waggener, sent a report of a typical incident from Fort Pleasant on the South Branch: "An old man and his wife were killed and scalped about sunset this evening within a mile of this place. A command went out immediately upon hearing the guns fire but could not come up with the enemy, which we have always found impossible to do, their parties I believe are but small, which favors their escape."

Washington meanwhile remained mired in logistical difficulties. His preferred correspondent in Williamsburg was now John Robinson, speaker of the House of Burgesses and treasurer of the colony. "I hope you will not be surprised by my sudden demands for money," began one enormous catalog of problems, written on August 5. Washington reported that a £5,000 appropriation grudgingly given by the committee had been spent, mostly for back pay for the men, and that he was being besieged by demands for payment for supplies, transportation, clothing, medical care, medicines, ammunition, on and on. He was, he complained, "under such uncertain regulations, and subject to so much inconvenience, that I am wandering in a wilderness of difficulties, and am ignorant of the ways to extricate myself." Washington now felt it necessary not only to curry favor with Robinson, but to disparage Dinwiddie while doing so. After reviewing his case for abandoning Fort Cumberland, Washington wrote that he "applied to the Governor for his particular and positive directions in this affair. The following is an exact copy of his answer. 'Fort Cumberland is a king's fort, and built chiefly at the charge of the colony, therefore properly under our direction until a governor is appointed.'" Washington professed to be unable to understand this response to "the plain, simple question asked, is the fort to be continued or removed? But in all important matters I am directed in this ambiguous and uncertain way."

This was an outrageous misrepresentation. In the two-month-old letter Washington quoted, Dinwiddie had been responding to a question from Washington about his legal authority to command Virginia forces outside of the colony, for example at Fort Cumberland, in Maryland. Dinwiddie's response was that, legally, the forces were not Virginia's, but the King's; "Ordering them to the

Allegheny Mountains as king's forces is proper, and may be necessary on occasion as I conceive the mountains are in the limits of the government, though not settled." Similarly, Fort Cumberland should be viewed not as a Maryland facility, but as "a king's fort, and built chiefly at the charge of the colony [of Virginia], therefore properly under our direction until a governor [that is to say, a British military commander of the fort] is appointed." To represent to Speaker Robinson that this was Dinwiddie's answer to a question about abandoning Fort Cumberland was as disreputable a thing as Washington ever did.

In May of 1756, England and Prussia had formally declared war on France and Austria, commencing what could be called the first world war, involving as it eventually did hostilities in Europe, India, America, and on the high seas. On August 7, the war was formally proclaimed in Williamsburg, and on August 15, Washington performed that ceremony in Winchester. "You see, gentlemen soldiers, that it hath pleased our most gracious sovereign to declare war," he announced to the assembled troops and citizens, in a proclamation that hewed to the florid, imperial form for these occasions until it came to the last sentence. "Let us shew our willing obedience to the best of kings, and by a strict attachment to his royal commands demonstrate the love and loyalty we bear to his sacred person; let us by rules of unerring bravery strive to merit his royal favor, ***and a better establishment as a reward for our services.***" Having heard it declared that they were at war, and why, Washington's men for the rest of the day marched about the streets of Winchester cheering, discharging their weapons and drinking, according to the *Virginia Gazette*, "his majesty's, and many other loyal healths."

It was no doubt the best day of Washington's summer, and although he did not know it until later, it coincided with one of the low points for British fortunes in the Seven Years' War. On the previous day, August 14, 1756, the British outpost on the Great Lakes—Fort Oswego, at the mouth of the Onandaga River on Lake Ontario—had surrendered to a French force under the recently arrived French commander in North America, the Marquis de Montcalm. Warriors allied with the French had massacred dozens of people in the aftermath of the surrender. Washington's New York friend, Beverly Robinson, described the loss as a "fatal stroke," and Lord

Loudoun as "greatly perplexed, finding our affairs in so bad and confused condition." The forces available to the colonies had been reduced at one stroke from seven thousand to four thousand effectives, and were "declining every day by sickness and desertion."

Despite the temporary distraction of celebrating the new state of war, things were no better at Winchester. Enemy marauders were at work again in western Pennsylvania, and according to Washington "the whole settlement of Conococheague is fled and there now remain only two families from thence to Frederick-Town." He had a report from Monocacy that "350 wagons had passed that place, to avoid the enemy, within the space of three days." Once again he pleaded for help from the militia, with little hope of getting any. "When Hampshire [county] was invaded, and called upon Frederick [county] for assistance," he reflected, "the people of the latter refused them aid, answering, 'let them defend themselves, as we shall do if they come to us.' Now the enemy have forced through that county, and begin to infest this; those a little removed from danger are equally infatuated, and will be I fear, until all in turn fall sacrifice to an insulting and merciless enemy."

Throughout the month of August, Washington complained bitterly and frequently about, among other things, his men and his officers. The officers seemed unable to count, reporting to Washington that they had mustered 926 men, but at the same time claiming pay for 1080. It was, suggested Washington, "unhappy for the country to have officers so little acquainted with the management of their companies." He gave angry orders to combat the "paltry tippling houses and gin-shops" of Winchester, the wasting of ammunition, and, contrary to his specific orders to the contrary, the sporting of short haircuts. Desertion remained a constant problem, as well as malingering and misbehavior by those who remained. Some of the troops were actually trading in horses gathered in from deserted settlements, whose owners later complained to Washington, as he put it, "that they are more oppressed by their own people than by the enemy."

Washington continued to believe that only the execution of some selected offenders would bring an end to the more serious crimes of desertion and cowardice. But he was not about to take anyone's life without being on solid legal ground, and he remained unsatisfied with the legislation on capital punishment. Meanwhile, he favored the administration of the lash for any and all offenses. Adam Stephen reported enthusiastically from Fort Cumberland that "we catched two in the very act of desertion and have whaled them till they pissed themselves and the spectators shed tears for them—which will, I hope, answer the end of punishment."

But nothing his men could do had the power to enrage Washington as did public criticism of them—which, of course, implicated him. On September 3, 1756, there appeared in the *Virginia Gazette* one of a series of articles by a correspondent known only as Centinel. In language that Washington might well have used while fuming over his subordinates' inability to count their men, Centinel described the Regiment's officers as "rakes, spendthrifts and bankrupts, who have never been used to command, or who have been found insufficient for the management of their own affairs." Centinel reported, quite accurately, that most of the regiment was spending most of its time inside various forts. "Instead of searching out the enemy, waylaying and surprising them, obstructing their marches and preventing their incursions, they tempt them by their security and laziness to come in quest of them and attack them in their fortifications." The officers were, Centinel declared in his most pungent alliteration, a bunch of "dastardly débauchées."

For the sixth time in less than a year, Washington threatened to resign. He did not do so directly to Dinwiddie, but once again broadcast his intention among the influential men of the colony. While awaiting their reaction, he toured the southern frontier, down through Augusta County toward North Carolina. He sent back a scathing assessment of the militia serving there: "They are obstinate, self-willed, perverse; of little or no service to the people and very burdensome to the country. They keep no guard but just when the enemy is about, and are under fearful apprehension of them. Nor ever stir out of their forts from the time they reach them 'till relieved." It must have occurred to him that Centinel could scarcely have been more acidic, for he prefaced his invective by writing, "I scorn to make unjust remarks on the behavior of the militia as much as I despise and condemn the persons who detract from mine and the character of the regiment."

When the officers of the Virginia Regiment at Fort Cumberland saw the Centinel article, on October 5, their reaction was more direct than Washington's. They assumed that the *Gazette* would not have dared to publish such an article without the governor's approval (and in a country whose experiments with a free press had been few and hesitant, that was hardly an unwarranted assumption). They would remain in the service of the colony no longer than November 20, the officers vowed, "unless we have as public satisfaction as the injury received." Failing that, they invited Dinwiddie to procure "gentlemen to do that duty, a denomination point blank contrary to that which the Centinel has given *us*."

The ultimatum required Washington, immediately after his return from the southern outposts, to make one of his rare, and typically brief, visits to Fort Cumberland. While there, he placated his officers, recalled them to their duty, and won a promise from them to give him time to assess the damage to their reputations. Then he made a careful assessment of the reactions to his own threat of resignation. His brother Augustine's report from Williamsburg was typical in making two points. First, the effect of the Centinel article on influential people was minimal: "Your character does not in the least suffer here," he wrote, "you are in as great esteem as ever with the Governor here and especially the House of Burgesses." And second, Washington had a duty that transcended personal pique: "Your country never stood more in need of your assistance." John Robinson was less gentle. It was all right to resent the aspersions of "a vile and ignorant scribbler," he wrote, "but my dear sir, consider of what fatal consequence to your country your resigning the command at this time may be."

As he had the previous November, Washington left Fort Cumberland after a stay of little more than twenty-four hours and headed east, to attend the deliberations of the House of Burgesses. His immediate purpose was to attend a meeting to settle some lingering and unpleasant disagreements over Lawrence Washington's tangled estate. If he had any thought of repeating the previous year's all-winter stay, he was to be disappointed. His relations with Robert Dinwiddie took a sudden and dramatic turn for the worse.

Feelings on both sides had been souring for some time, principally over the continuing lack of a strategy for dealing with the incursions of the enemy. Should Virginia attack the French, or should Virginia defend her frontiers? Washington continued to argue both for and against both propositions. Mounting an expedition to the Ohio country to attack Fort Duquesne, he wrote in August, would be "the best and *only* method to put a stop to the incursions of the enemy; as they would then be obliged to stay at home, to defend their own possessions. But we are quite unprepared for such an undertaking." From time to time he toyed with, but never completely embraced, an unorthodox but highly practical strategy of an offensive defense. Perhaps, he wrote on one occasion, it would be best to "deal with the French in their own way, and by visiting their country, keep their Indians at home."

In fact, that very approach was tried a few times, with varying results. In February, Dinwiddie had ordered Andrew Lewis to strike westward from Augusta County with a force of soldiers and Cherokees to attack Shawnee villages on the Ohio River. "I am apprehensive [this scheme] will prove abortive," Washington told the governor, "as we are told that those Indians are removed up the river into the neighborhood of Duquesne." He proved right. The so-called Sandy Creek expedition was a dismal failure, and the men very nearly starved to death in the sterile winter woods before staggering back to Augusta.

On the other hand, on September 8, a Colonel John Armstrong with a Pennsylvania force attacked a Delaware village twenty-five miles above Fort Duquesne with overwhelming surprise and force. The defenders, led by a war chief and friend of Shingas called by the British Captain Jacobs, made their last stand in their chief's bark hut. Armstrong's men set it afire and called on Jacobs to surrender. Captain Jacobs preferred to die, and just before doing so shouted his last defiant words: "I eat fire."

The *Pennsylvania Gazette* called Armstrong's success "the greatest blow the Indians have received since the war began." But no one embraced this manner of counterattack with any enthusiasm or tenacity. In Washington's view, if there were not resources for an all-out expedition against Fort Duquesne, then the only alternative was defense from a chain of forts. But he frequently pointed out that he did not have enough men or materials to build the forts, nor did he have enough troops to garrison and patrol them once built, nor supplies to sustain them. It was, he reflected, a case of "neglect the inhabitants and build the forts, or neglect the forts and mind the inhabitants." What, he asked Dinwiddie over and over again, should he do? Washington complained frequently that Dinwiddie gave him no clear answer.

In fact, the answer was not Dinwiddie's to give. Whether and when to mount an expedition against Fort Duquesne was a matter only Lord Loudoun could decide, and for the moment he was uninterested in the Ohio country, convinced that the war had to be fought on its northern front.

However, Dinwiddie could decide whether to maintain Virginia troops at Fort Cumberland, and around that particular thorn the unease between the two men had been festering all year. Washington seldom let an opportunity pass to remark on the difficulties posed by the outpost where the largest contingent of his regiment was posted, and where he spent as little of his time as possible. The fort was too distant, he said, too exposed, it required too many men to garrison and supply it, and so on. For a year, Dinwiddie remained virtually silent on the question, but as events would soon show, he was increasingly vexed by Washington's insistence.

The arguments used by each man failed to explain fully his doggedness in this matter. Washington simply refused to deal with Fort Cumberland, even after the Dagworthy matter was settled, leaving to Adam Stephen the unpleasant daily details of administering the outpost and facing the constant danger of attack. Dinwiddie remained puzzled at Washington's vehemence in recommending abandonment of a fort that appeared from the map to be an ideal position astride a main route from Fort Duquesne to Virginia.

One likely reason for Dinwiddie's equally vehement insistence that Cumberland be retained was never stated by him and was apparently forgotten by Washington. Fort Cumberland, previously familiar as Wills Creek, might be dispensable to the defense of Virginia, but not to the future profits of the Ohio Company. The Company and its grand schemes were almost never mentioned during the years of the outrages, but that does not mean they had diminished in importance to a governor who was facing illness and retirement. It is small wonder that when Dinwiddie realized that he would have to deal officially with Washington's harping about Fort Cumberland, he exploded.

In August, he had tried again to brush away any decision by saying that since it was "a King's Fort and a magazine for stores, it's not in my power to order it to be deserted, and if we did it would encourage the enemy to be more audacious." Washington could take the matter up with Lord Loudoun, Dinwiddie said, when the commander-in-chief came to Virginia. Of course, if Loudoun came to Virginia, it would in all likelihood be to prepare an expedition to the Ohio, to which Fort Cumberland would be essential. But a month later, Loudoun had shown no interest either in Virginia or Duquesne, and Washington was still harping about Cumberland.

Testily, Dinwiddie told Washington to call a council of officers and decide whether "to keep it, or demolish it." In doing so, he restated his own strong feelings in the matter ("I have wrote you how disagreeable it was to me to give up any place of strength") and added a heavy-handed reminder: "Be very explicit in your arguments as they must be laid before Lord Loudoun." Not surprisingly, the council of officers decided the issue was too large for them to decide and bucked the matter back up to the governor's council.

There Dinwiddie's influence was of course absolute, and the council's decision was almost unanimous. Speaker Robinson, who of course had been fully briefed on Washington's arguments by increasingly numerous and lengthy letters (and who was an investor in the Greenbrier Company, competitor to the Ohio Company), argued at length for abandoning the troublesome and distant fort. "Yet notwithstanding all I could say," he reported to Washington later, "they persisted in their resolution without alleging any other reason for it than that it was in pursuance of Lord Loudoun's desire. It can't be any difficult matter to guess who was the author and promoter of this advice and resolution, or by whom my lord Loudoun has been persuaded that the place is of such importance."

Given the decision he wanted, Dinwiddie communicated it in a sulphurous November 16 letter that reached Washington in Alexandria. In a preliminary way, Dinwiddie accused Washington of having made a "vague" report, an "unmannerly" inference, and "irregular" appointments of a commissary and chaplain. Then Dinwiddie dealt with the main subject in brutally direct language: "I hereby order you immediately to march one hundred men to Fort Cumberland from the forces you have at Winchester, which Captain Mercer says are 160 listed men; you are to remain at Fort Cumberland and make the place as strong as you can in case of an attack. You are to send out parties from the fort to observe the motions of the enemy if they should march over the Allegheny Mountains. You are to order one of your subaltern officers to command at Winchester and to oversee the finishing of the fort building at that place. These orders I expect you will give due obedience to."

This letter was received by a man who had been smarting for two months over being insulted in the press; had been threatening regularly to resign; had failed in all his attempts to curry the favor of (and obtain a commission from) his commander-in-chief; and had experienced nothing but frustration in more than a year of constant setbacks. At the moment, he had made a long journey for the unpleasant purpose of dealing with familial squabbling over Lawrence's will, only to find the meeting could not be held because the General Assembly had been called into session and some of the principals were not available. This was his situation when he took up a pen to respond to Dinwiddie's broadside.

He did so with an air of steely, wounded resignation. He was sorry to be thought unmannerly: "I never intended insults to any." He had not meant to be vague, but to explain matters on the frontier, "and am sorry to find that this and my best endeavors of late meet with unfavorable constructions." He had had specific authority to appoint the commissary and chaplain. But where unjust criticism in the newspaper had had him talking about resigning, unjust criticism from his governor had the opposite effect. "If my open and disinterested way of writing and speaking has the air of pertness and freedom, I shall redress my error by acting reservedly, and shall take care to obey my orders without offering more."

Then, of course, he offered more. He would obey his orders, but Dinwiddie had ordered him to take more men with him to Cumberland than would be present at Winchester when the current draft expired on December 1, a week hence. He would obey his orders, he said, even though to do so would leave Winchester "entirely destitute of all protection, notwithstanding it now contains all the public stores of any importance." He would obey, and offer nothing more, except to note that "the works which have been constructed and conducted with infinite pains and labor will be unfinished and exposed; and the materials for completing the building, which have been collected with unspeakable difficulty and expense, left to be pillaged and destroyed by the inhabitants of the town." But, of course, he would comply.

Washington continued this passive resistance in the form of compliance after he returned to Winchester, reporting dutifully that he was preparing to obey orders, but that there were in Winchester only eighty-one members of the regiment, "including the sick, and young drummers who were sent here to learn"; that he intended to leave soon for Cumberland, but there was no flour to take along with which to feed the men, and no wagons to transport the flour if he had it; that "your Honor's late and unexpected order has caused the utmost terror and consternation in the people," who were, he thought, "in the greatest dread for the consequences." But "no delays or protracting of orders proceeds from me." In fact, he would now prefer to move to Fort Cumberland, "for I am tired of the place, the inhabitants and the life I lead here."

On December 10, Governor Dinwiddie, with a figurative clearing of the throat, allowed that he had been misinformed about the number of soldiers at Winchester, and about the amount of stores deposited there, and had discussed the matter anew with his council. Washington was still ordered to Fort Cumberland with a hundred men, but should also reinforce Winchester with another hundred men gathered in from the small outlying forts. Dinwiddie might have heard much more from Washington about the difficulties of obeying orders had he not included in his letter a quote from Lord Loudoun: "I cannot agree with Colonel Washington in not drawing into him the posts from the stockade forts in order to defend that advanced one. If he leaves any of the great quantity of stores behind, it will be very unfortunate, and he ought to consider that it must lie at his own door. This proceeding, I am afraid, will have a bad effect as to the Dominion and will not have a good appearance at home." Enough said. Ten days later Washington left for Fort Cumberland.

But not before requesting permission to leave Cumberland immediately on his arrival there. Dinwiddie had already said that Washington could meet with Loudoun when the latter visited the colony, and the colonel now wished to confirm that "nothing has intervened to alter that indulgence." It was urgent, Washington explained, because he had "read over that paragraph in Lord Loudoun's letter, which your Honor was pleased to send me, over and over again, but am unable to comprehend the meaning of it."

It was small wonder, for just as Washington had quoted Dinwiddie out of context for his own purpose, so had Dinwiddie misrepresented Loudoun. Loudoun's comments had been made in response to Dinwiddie's description of a situation in October, when Washington had seemed ready to abandon Fort Cumberland in the face of an imminent attack. Thus while Loudoun's statements seemed to oppose the abandonment of Cumberland in general, their particular references made no sense to Washington. Loudoun, he complained to Dinwiddie, "seems to have prejudged my proceedings without being thoroughly informed." In Washington's view, this was simply a matter of Loudoun's not knowing him well enough, for "no man ever intended better, nor studied the interest of his country with more affectionate zeal than I have done; and nothing gives me greater uneasiness and concern than that His Lordship should have imbibed prejudices so unfavorable to my character." As 1757 began, Washington was treating Dinwiddie with exaggerated courtesy and the promised reserve, while conducting a vigorous campaign against the governor on all fronts. Whether entirely or only partly because of Washington's continual criticisms, John Robinson became pessimistic, and hinted that Dinwiddie would have to go: "The present unhappy state of our country must fill the minds of every well wisher to it with dismal and gloomy apprehensions, and without some speedy alteration in our counsels, which God sends, the fate of it must soon be determined."

As fate would have it, Loudoun decided yet again not to travel to Virginia, and Washington resorted to a long letter to him, recounting the events of his entire military career and the errors of Robert Dinwiddie. The governor, according to Washington, had been too slow in reacting to the French, had procured too few provisions for the first expedition to Fort Duquesne, had interfered with recruitment, and had bungled the necessary drafting of troops.

As a result, Washington concluded, it should be no surprise that "under all these concomitant evils I should be sickened in a service that promises so little of a soldier's reward." He had not wanted the command, "but the solicitations of the country overcame my objections." He had not wanted to remain in command, until "the dawn of hope that arose in my breast when I heard your Lordship was distinguished by His Majesty with the important command of his armies in America, and appointed to the government of his dominion of Virginia." Yet after all he had been through, Washington still had not lost his taste for pandering. "Although I have not the honor to be known to your Lordship, yet your lordship's name was familiar to my ear on account of the important services performed to his majesty in other parts of the world—don't think, my lord, I am going to flatter. My nature is honest, and free from guile."

Then Washington got to the matter of the commission. The regiment had been waiting "in tedious expectation" of being taken into the British regular army, but it had not yet happened. As for Washington, General Braddock had promised "preferment equal to my wishes," but Braddock was dead. General Shirley had been "not unkind in his promises," but General Shirley was gone.

Washington concluded with two remarkable statements. Virginia, he said, was "a country young in war," which "until the breaking out of these disturbances has lived in the most profound and tranquil peace," and could not be expected to know how to defend itself. While this was a valid observation of his personal experience, as a historical perspective—and that is the way in which it was offered—it was a surprising misstatement of fact. The hundred-year history of the colony of Virginia had been a story of continual warfare with the native tribes. At every stage of westward progression, from the Atlantic beaches to the Tidewater to the Piedmont—as now in the Shenandoah Valley—Virginia's frontier had been subjected to precisely the kind of assault it was suffering now. That Washington and his colleagues were apparently ignorant of the lessons of that history explains much.

His corollary point was even more surprising. The man who had spent the past year in uninterrupted complaint about his treatment at the hands of the colonial government now wrote that when it came to "the sinews of war," the colony was doing its best: "All that can be expected at her hands she cheerfully gives." The only thing needed now to attain success was "a person of your Lordship's ability and experience to direct the application."

Loudoun was simply not interested. He offered no commission, no role for Washington in the grand scheme of continental war, nothing. Still Washington would not give up. On learning that there would be a conference of Loudoun and the southern governors in Philadelphia in February, Washington asked for permission to attend, which Dinwiddie grumpily gave, even though "I cannot conceive what service you can be of in going there."

Washington rode into Philadelphia on February 21, only to spend the next two weeks waiting for the great man to arrive. On March 10, he asked Dinwiddie for help in preparing his case, offering a summary for the governor's comments.

This statement offered an early glimpse of the Washington that was to be. With Dinwiddie, Washington had dropped altogether the verbal tugging at the forelock, the mannerly bowing and scraping, that he was still using on Loudoun and other superiors. Now there was no wistful appeal to what Braddock might have done, or to how grateful a loyal subject would be for a crumb from his lordship's table. With a hard and unadorned eloquence that was to become his style, with an appeal to unequivocal and unemotional facts organized in martial ranks and files, Washington defined his situation and stated his need.

"The Virginia regiment was the first in arms of any troops upon the continent in the present war." The men had been under arms for three long years, "continuing in a service precarious and uncertain, hazarding life, fortune and health to the chances of war and a bare subsistence." Their condition was a "matter for serious and melancholy reflection." For three years Washington had been whining after a King's commission for himself. Now he argued that his entire regiment deserved to be taken into the regular British army.

Now Washington leaned his case on a proposition that was as yet a sapling, but that had taken root in hard western soils: that Americans of high achievement were as deserving as Englishmen of high station. "We cannot conceive that being Americans should deprive us of the benefits of British subjects," he wrote. "I apprehend it is the service done, not the service engaged in, that merits reward; and that there is as equitable a right to expect something for three years hard and bloody service as for ten spent at St. James, etcetera, where real service or a field of battle never was seen."

With the confidence of a man whose cause was just, Washington charged Dinwiddie on behalf of his fellow officers to "give them reason, by your earnest endeavors with his Lordship, to hope for a soldier's reward."

The emergence of the new Washington was as fruitless as it was brief. Loudoun arrived on March 14, let Washington make his case, and rejected it out of hand. He directed Washington to continue as a provincial officer, to hand over Cumberland to Captain Dagworthy and the Maryland troops (a mixed blessing), to deploy six hundred of his men along the Virginia frontier and dispatch four hundred to the aid of South Carolina. Having thus disposed of 345 more troops than Washington commanded, Loudoun returned to his plans for winning the war. Loudoun was secretive about whatever it was he planned to do, but clearly there was to be no offensive to the Ohio country.

The year 1757 was becoming a bitter echo of the previous one. As before, Washington returned from an unsuccessful conference with his superiors, stopped briefly at Winchester, and went on to Fort Cumberland to face the resumption of the outrages. He did not have a long wait. On April 16, two friendly Catawbas were killed in an ambush 150 yards from the fort. The enemy raiders escaped easily from the two hundred men who boiled out of the fort in hot but fruitless pursuit. Shortly thereafter, two soldiers of the regiment were killed and one captured from a party on its way to the fort. But Washington seemed as put upon by the Catawbas within the fort as the bushwhackers outside: "The Indians are all around, teasing and perplexing me for one thing or another, so that I scarce know what I write."

As before, he tried to find out what Dinwiddie wanted him to do, asking courteously but doggedly how he was supposed to deal with the unexpected arrival of a party of Catawba allies, how and when to pull out of Fort Cumberland, and how to send to North Carolina troops he did not have. Dinwiddie responded with curt instructions to detach two hundred men, not four hundred, for South Carolina, to entertain the Catawbas "with great civility," and send them out "with some of your men a-scalping etcetera." Moreover, said Dinwiddie of his vague imperatives, "I expect an exact obedience."

Maintaining civility with apparent effort, Washington reported to Dinwiddie that he had convened a formal council of war during which he and his officers had tried to make sense of the governor's "altogether inexplicable" instructions. They agreed that Dinwiddie could not have meant, as he seemed to direct, that the Virginia troops should leave Fort Cumberland before any Maryland troops arrived to take it over; that he could not have meant, as he at one point said, that all the troops of the regiment should gather in Winchester, abandoning the entire frontier just as the enemy raids were resuming. Dinwiddie responded with rising annoyance, giving precise instructions where he lacked particular knowledge, remaining enigmatic about the issues Washington most needed resolved, and insisting peevishly on "exact obedience."

Washington obeyed to the extent that he could, and simmered. The frustrations of day-to-day administration were bad enough, but the lack of strategy made everything worse. "We must bid adieu to peace and safety while the French are allowed to possess the Ohio," he wrote to his relative, the London merchant Richard Washington. "Yet, from what strange causes I know not, no attempt this season will be made, I fear, to destroy this hold of barbarians."

As in the previous year, Washington was summoned to Williamsburg to attend the House of Burgesses. On April 29, lodged in the capital, he wrote his customary bill of particulars: he needed improvements in martial law; help with the natives, in the form of a "judicious person acquainted with their customs" to take over relations with the tribes; more men, more money, a better militia, and so on. But in this respect, 1757 was quite a different year. Where in previous years both governor and assembly had at least tried to respond to Washington's problems, this year they were inclined to dismiss them. Whether they were reacting to Loudoun's lack of interest in their theater of operations, or acted simply out of weariness, Dinwiddie and the burgesses reorganized the Virginia Regiment, decreased Washington's authority over it, demoted his officers, and cut his pay.

Weariness may have accounted for the burgesses' turning over to the governor the financial administration of the Regiment, a power they had jealously defended in August of 1755, now a burden they were glad to give up. Efficiency probably justified the reduction of the number of companies in the regiment to ten—many of the companies were not fully manned, and there were too many officers for too few men. Habitual frugality was no doubt the main reason Dinwiddie balked at the sight of Washington's 2 percent commission on all the public money he handled. And it was in concert with Washington's specific recommendation that he was divested of all authority for dealing with the tribes and told to defer all related questions to the new, crown-appointed Indian Agent for the Southern Department, Edmond Atkin.

But there was vindictiveness in the brusque manner with which Dinwiddie ordered the demotion to lieutenant of all captains but seven he named; dictated the deployment of garrison troops to the "following posts in the following manner"; told Washington where to make his headquarters; and swept away the 2 percent commission, despite Washington's plea that it was "the only perquisite I have."

Washington arrived back in Winchester by May 24. He found there nearly four hundred Catawbas, Cherokees, and Tuscaroras, some returned from raiding parties to the west against the French, some arriving from far southern Virginia and the Carolinas in response to vigorous recruiting efforts by Virginians. (The previous year, William Byrd III and Peter Randolph of the governor's council had negotiated a mutual-aid treaty with the Cherokees and Catawbas.)

Washington had no use for all these warriors. There would have been too many of them to supervise and deploy if they had been pliable, and they were anything but. Not only were they by nature highly individualistic and proud, but by the time Washington saw them most were deeply angry, because they had been promised that they would be given everything they needed if they would make the long journey to Winchester and go to war for the English. Washington had nothing to give them.

Once again Washington demonstrated how little he had learned about the tribes during three years of close contact. He was contemptuous of what he took to be their greedy insistence on being given presents, and of their unhappiness when the Virginians had nothing to give them. "An Indian will never forget a promise made to him," he complained to Dinwiddie, as though this were a great failing. "They are naturally suspicious, and, if they meet with delays or disappointments in their expectations, will scarcely ever be reconciled. They are the most insolent, most avaricious and most dissatisfied wretches I have ever had to deal with."

Washington and his fellow Virginians heard the clamor for presents and in their condescension failed to grasp the imperative need being expressed. It had been explained to them several times, for example by a Cherokee in Augusta County whose words were relayed to Washington, but made little impression: the Cherokees expected to be supplied because "if they had stayed at home and hunted they could buy as much goods as they wanted with their skins."

One of the Cherokee war chiefs who came to Winchester that spring, known to the English as the Swallow, explained that he did not want presents for himself, but had promised them to his young men as a reward for the long march and the support of the Virginians. By failing to provide them as agreed, he said, Governor Dinwiddie had made the Swallow seem a liar to his warriors: "It looks to me, the governor has little regard for you that are in the back settlements." Other warriors were far less diplomatic than the Swallow, declaring that as they saw it, "from every action, the great men of Virginia were liars."

At the end of May, Washington was not only chafing at the delay in Edmond Atkin's arrival, but was pleading for the appointment of a colonial director of tribal affairs to assist Atkin in his departmental duties. Washington still thought the solution was to assign the problem to "some person of good sense and probity, with a tolerable share of the knowledge of their customs." His candidate for the post was Christopher Gist. "He knows but little of their language it is true, but is well acquainted with their manners and customs."

Edmond Atkin finally appeared in Winchester on June 3. Whether or not as a result of Washington's recommendation, one of Atkin's first actions was to hire Gist as his assistant. Another was to have a falling out with the more knowledgeable Pennsylvanian, George Croghan. Although Atkin was the counterpart of the Northern Department's Sir William Johnson, Atkin's approach to his charges was nothing like that of the celebrated emissary to the Iroquois. Johnson knew Iroquois ways, spoke their language, wore their clothing, married one of their women, hunted and often lived with them, studied and shared their values. Atkin, on the other hand, knew little about the tribes and cared less. He was going to issue them passports and certificates, approved routes of travel, timetables, postings and schedules. His highest priority was to organize the comings and goings of these savages in the manner of a British harbormaster.

Washington soon realized that Atkin was hardly the "judicious person acquainted with their customs" that he had envisioned as his savior where tribal affairs were concerned. When the Cherokee war chief Outacite arrived at Winchester in late June and announced that he had many more warriors coming to help, Washington wondered sarcastically whether they would "wait for Mr. Atkin's passport, or will come on with their own." When a group of warriors arrived and declared their willingness to fight the French, Atkin declared that they "spoke to me in the Mingo tongue by an interpreter." Whatever Atkin thought the Mingo tongue was (that being merely the term for the western Iroquois tribes), he decided it was highly suspicious. Even worse, he thought their "captain" behaved "rudely." Atkin ordered the lot of them locked up as spies, discovering only later that they were in fact Cherokee allies.

It is remarkable that any of the southern tribes continued to serve the English, and yet they did. On June 10, the Swallow was killed in a skirmish with French raiders. Other Cherokees and Catawbas continued to go west from time to time, but many more returned home instead, enraged at the arrogant indifference of their would-be allies. "I am sorry the Indians are so refractory," pronounced Governor Dinwiddie, "which I conceive is entirely owing to Captain Mercer's promising them presents." He had learned his lesson: "It is a very great error to make them any promises whatever."

The dreary repetitiveness of the year continued. As had happened in April 1756, there was a massive invasion scare in June 1757. Captain Dagworthy at Fort Cumberland relayed rumors of a large French force, accompanied by artillery, headed eastward from Fort Duquesne. Once again Washington alerted, mustered, and entrenched his men at Winchester, Dinwiddie flogged the militia into resentful motion, and the Western population flinched for the long-awaited blow. Then Dagworthy sent word that his report had overestimated the danger. Washington was understanding about the embarrassment of his former nemesis, and made sure all his correspondents knew about it: "Captain Dagworthy might easily have misunderstood these people for want of a good interpreter," he wrote on one occasion, and on another a month later, "It was a surprising mistake for an officer in the least acquainted with the service to make." Nearly simultaneous attacks at three widely separated locations on North Mountain, near Conococheague and in South Branch Valley, made it apparent that the large force reported heading east from Duquesne had followed the usual pattern, diverging in small raiding parties.

Desertions from the regiment continued to plague Washington. Of one group of four hundred draftees sent to him that summer, 114 disappeared. Efforts to recapture the runaways met with passive resistance from sympathetic civilians and active resistance, sometimes involving casualties, from the deserters themselves. Washington declared in July, "I have a gallows near 40 foot high erected (which has terrified the rest exceedingly) and I am determined, if I can be justified in the proceeding, to hang two or three on it as an example to others."

The justification arrived on July 18, in the form of the new "Act for Preventing Mutiny and Desertion," passed April 14, providing for the death penalty in a form that at last satisfied Washington. He did not delay. The first court-martial under the new act was held within the week, and three days later the first two men died as punishment for deserting from the Virginia Regiment. "Your Honor will, I hope, excuse my hanging, instead of shooting them: It conveyed much more terror to others, and it was for example's sake we did it."

But within two months he had lost all enthusiasm for his hard-won power over life and death. His intractable charges were intimidated no more by the noose than they had been by the lash, when the alternative was hard and dangerous service away from their families. "One of those who were condemned to be hanged, deserted immediately on receiving his pardon," Washington fumed in September. "In short, they tire my patience and almost weary me to death!"

Another summer of frustration, of fitful alarms and fruitless responses, plodded toward fall. In mid-September an unusually ferocious raid on Cedar Creek, within twelve miles of Winchester, killed a reported thirty-four people, and another struck a settlement on

Stony Creek south of Woodstock. Although the casualty count was later revised downward as missing people reappeared after the raiders had gone, the settlers were terrified anew, and the response of the Virginia Regiment had the usual results: "It is next to impossibility that any of our parties should ever see the enemy," fumed Washington, going on to insist again to Dinwiddie that defensive tactics were pointless, that the only hope was to carry the war into the enemy's country. "Unless an expedition is carried on against the Ohio next spring, this country will not be another year in our possession."

Washington endured a bout with dysentery in August and exchanged letters of polite acrimony with Dinwiddie over allowances for batmen and other trivia, even including critiques of literary style: "You must allow this is a loose way of writing," Dinwiddie griped at one point, "and you must be more particular to me." Their letters consisted mainly of point-by-point rebuttals of each other's previous letter. Then September brought another replay of the previous fall's scandal-mongering.

In late August, a member of the regiment informed Washington of a rumor, then enjoying some currency in Williamsburg, that the panic of the spring of 1756 had been invented, "to cause the assembly to levy largely in both money and men, and that there was not an Indian in that neighborhood." Once again Washington took extravagant umbrage, defending himself against the charge with zeal, using lavish detail about the horrors of the enemy onslaught and the terrors of the hapless civilians. His letter rang with oratory about his honor, his nobility, his innocence, the whole seasoned with a becoming touch of humility: "I should esteem myself, as the world also would, vain and empty, were I to arrogate perfection."

Washington asked Dinwiddie whether this "stupid scandal" was responsible for "the change in your honor's conduct toward me." Dinwiddie gave the whole matter short shrift. As to the supposed rumor, he "never heard of it before," and advised Washington "not to give credit to every idle story you hear." As to their relationship, Dinwiddie was obviously tired of it, prepared to sum it up and let it go: "My conduct to you from the beginning was always friendly, but you know I had great reason to suspect you of ingratitude." On reflection, it seemed a bit more than ingratitude. "I had reason to be angry. However as I've his Majesty's leave to go for England I propose leaving this in November and I wish my successor may show you as much friendship as I've done."

Washington could not bear to be thought ill of, even by someone whom he had been criticizing at every turn for months. He denied the charge of ingratitude, characterizing his behavior as "open, disinterested," while the reports of his actions given to Dinwiddie had somehow been "maliciously aggravated." This must all be set right, and he would need leave to go to Williamsburg to "settle some accounts with your Honor" before the governor departed for England. But Dinwiddie was done now. He denied Washington's request for leave: "You have been frequently indulged with leave of absence." And indeed, this exchange took place just a few weeks after Washington's return to duty from a trip east to attend the funeral of Colonel William Fairfax, who had died on September 3. But, complained Washington, "It was not to enjoy a party of pleasure I wanted leave of absence: I have been indulged with few of those, winter or summer!"

September and October passed with no relief from continuous frustration. Edmond Atkin, having made relations with the Cherokees and Catawbas worse than they had been, moved on to serve other constituencies in his vast department, and Christopher Gist was called elsewhere, leaving Washington to do the best he could with the warriors who, despite everything, kept showing up to help their British friends. By order of the governor he was not supposed to deal with what he called "these warlike, formidable people." But since there was no one else in authority, they came to him, having made their raid, brought in their prisoners, or delivered their scalps, and asked for their compensation. On one occasion he was forced to face such a group, empty-handed as usual, without so much as an interpreter: "I have nobody that can make you understand this." Duly informed, Dinwiddie expressed surprise; Atkin had reported everything in order.

Dinwiddie was now waiting for his passage to England, and Washington's continuing drumbeat of warnings had little effect on him. "Nothing but vigorous offensive measures can save the country," Washington now insisted. If there was not a successful attack on Fort Duquesne in the spring, there would not be "one soul living on this side the Blue Ridge the ensuing autumn." He admitted now that his efforts to protect the frontier had been in vain: "No troops in the universe can guard against the cunning and wiles of Indians. No one can tell where they will fall, 'till the mischief is done, and then 'tis in vain to pursue." He pleaded with John Robinson to do something: "While we pursue defensive measures, we pursue inevitable ruin, the loss of the country being the inevitable and fatal consequence! There will be no end to our trouble while we follow this plan, and every year will increase our expense." Robinson agreed, but said there was nothing anybody could do, because Lord Loudoun had "a plan of operations from home."

It had all settled into a depressing routine when a startling message came to Dinwiddie from Captain Robert Stewart. Washington had been seriously ill for three months, Stewart wrote on November 9, with a "bloody flux," or dysentery. During the previous week his sufferings had increased to include high fevers, "stitches and violent pleuretick pains." His doctor, unable to do anything for him but bleed him repeatedly, eventually told Washington to go home, without awaiting permission from Dinwiddie, or die. Washington had protested, but had obeyed. He had left on that day. Stewart was in command of Fort Loudoun (as Washington had named the Winchester fortification), while Andrew Lewis took charge of the Regiment.

Dinwiddie, immediately contrite, wrote a gracious letter of approval to Stewart. Washington's illness, he said, "was unknown to me or he should have had leave of absence sooner. I sincerely wish him a speedy recovery."

That was not to be. Weak and unutterably weary, Washington arrived at Mount Vernon on November 13 and was unable to leave for four months.

CHAPTER 13

Forbes's Road

"It has long been the luckless fate of poor Virginia to fall a victim to the views of her crafty neighbors."

SEPTEMBER 1, 1758

In his frustration and then his illness, Washington was but dimly aware of the larger events of imperial politics and world war that rumbled and clashed over the horizon, out of his view. In London, on June 29, 1757, an eloquent and popular critic of the conduct of the war thus far—William Pitt—had taken over the government by forming a coalition ministry with the Duke of Newcastle. Assigning himself the role of secretary of state for war and foreign affairs, Pitt proved to be a superb judge of character, manager of logistics and molder of public opinion.

Pitt's talents were badly needed. In the summer of 1757, the formidable Montcalm had marched down the Richelieu River, Lake Champlain, and Lake George toward the highlands of Albany and the headwaters of the Hudson River. With an army of more than six thousand troops and another 1,500 or so native warriors, Montcalm had besieged, and on August 9 had taken the surrender of, Fort William Henry, a key British outpost on the southern end of Lake George.

The affair was a mutual disgrace. The British commander, General Daniel Webb, had fled the fight, leaving a portion of his force to make a token, doomed defense. Then Montcalm had allowed his native allies to get out of control and massacre hundreds of captured and wounded Englishmen, as had happened when he had taken Oswego the previous August. Then Montcalm had burned the fort and returned to Canada, thus squandering the fruits of his victory.

Loudoun, meanwhile, had reacted to the yearlong obvious threat of Montcalm's advance by taking a large part of his army to sea to attack Louisbourg, the so-called French Gibraltar on far-off Cape Breton Island. After two months aboard ship, Loudoun had decided that the fortress was too strongly defended, and had withdrawn.

Word of these blunders had reached Pitt at about the same time as news of the disastrous culmination of a campaign in the German electorate of Hanover by the army's captain-general, the Duke of Cumberland. After six weeks of maneuvering without fighting a battle, Cumberland on September 8 had surrendered his army at Kloster-Zeven (now Zeven), thus ending his career.

The effect of all this was to give Pitt a clean slate. He replaced Cumberland and recalled Webb and Loudoun (who despite the disgrace continued to serve both in the army and as nominal governor of Virginia). This was a change not only of personnel, but of basic policy and attitude. Cumberland and Loudoun had dealt with the colonies as corporate vassals, theirs to command in the name of the King. Loudoun had inflamed all of British America with his attempts during the winter of 1756–57 to force the quartering of regular troops in private homes. In May of 1757, he had surrounded New York City with his troops and then had them scour the city's streets for young men to impress into His Majesty's military service. Pitt thought such methods were counterproductive. He insisted on treating the colonies as respected partners of the crown, by consulting them on strategy and sharing expenses. Such was his guidance to his new commander-in-chief, Sir John Ligonier, his new commander for North America, Major General James Abercromby, and the new commander of the southern district within America, Brigadier General John Forbes.

Forbes was under orders to move immediately against Fort Duquesne. Like Adam Stephen, this fifty-year-old officer was a Scot who had studied medicine before being drawn to the darker arts of war. Forbes was a methodical, intelligent man who had distinguished himself as a quartermaster in the War of Austrian Succession and in the quashing of the Jacobite rising in Scotland.

Thus the year 1758 began with a completely new cast of commanders and an utterly changed official attitude toward the prosecution of the war. Robert Dinwiddie, ill and disheartened, set sail on January 12 for England, never to return. Loudoun had been scheduled to replace Dinwiddie, but in the aftermath of Loudoun's recall the post of lieutenant governor went to Francis Fauquier (as a result, persistent rumor had it, of an influential person's taking pity on Fauquier after cleaning him out in a London card game). Fauquier would not arrive in the colony until June, and in the interim the colony's executive authority was John Blair, president of the governor's council.

Washington saw no reason for encouragement in all these developments. He was distracted by his illness, which even at the approach of spring would not release its grip on him. In March, he wrote Colonel John Stanwix of the Royal American Regiment that he feared the dysentery "returning obstinately upon me" was in fact consumption, the disease that had killed his brother. The thought of a third year of frustration at Winchester did nothing to lift the depression: "As I now see no prospect of preferment in a military life, and as I despair of rendering that immediate service which this colony may require of the person commanding their troops, I have some thoughts of quitting my command and retiring from all public business." On March 5, 1758, he left Mount Vernon for the first time since November, setting out for Williamsburg to seek medical advice and consider his future.

Washington moved slowly, traveling short distances and taking long rests. Eleven days later he gratefully accepted an invitation to dine at the home of William Chamberlayne in New Kent County. There he was introduced to another guest, Chamberlayne's neighbor, whom he may or may not have met before in different circumstances. The lady was short and somewhat plump, retiring in nature, and struck some people as dowdy. But she was of a good and constant soul, once describing herself as "an old-fashioned housekeeper, steady as a clock, busy as a bee, and cheerful as a cricket." At the age of twenty-seven, she had been a widow for eight months, after a marriage of eight years that had produced four children, only two of whom—a four-year-old boy and a two-year-old girl—had survived. She was Martha Dandridge Custis.

No one ever accused her of being as pretty and vivacious as Sally Fairfax, but Martha Custis shared two characteristics with the other women who had turned Washington into a suitor: like Betsy Fauntleroy and Polly Philipse, Martha had brown hair and substantial wealth. She had inherited from her late husband more than seventeen thousand acres of land and more than £20,000 in liquid assets. Washington, utterly captivated, uncharacteristically changed his plans, stayed the night, and lingered until late afternoon the next day.

It was then he might have learned of the lawsuit endangering Martha's inheritance. A complicated affair prosecuted by descendants of illegitimate children of her husband's maternal grandfather, the thirty-year-old case seemed at times a mere nuisance, at other times a threat to everything the young widow owned. As they discussed these things, the two of them must have realized that each had much to offer the other. As he had for most of his life, Washington craved a home and family. Martha needed a partner, too, and Washington's fame as a hero of the frontier would do no harm in influencing the responsible tribunals to dispose of the annoying lawsuit.

When Washington finally did arrive in Williamsburg on March 18, it was to receive the further tonic of hearing Dr. John Amson assure him that he was not descending into his final illness, but was in fact well on the road to recovery. Perhaps just as bracing was the first news of significant changes in the war effort. A letter from William Pitt, read to the governor's council on March 31 by acting governor John Blair, confirmed that General Forbes was under orders to move against Fort Duquesne. This time, Virginia was not going to be required to bear a large proportion of the cost of the expedition; the royal government was going to pay its own way. But Pitt did ask that the colony raise as large a number of men as possible to support the effort. With a will they had not shown under the lash of Cumberland and Loudoun, the Burgesses went to work to do just that.

Within two weeks they authorized the creation of a second Virginia regiment, doubling the size of the colony's armed forces to two thousand men, and approved a £10-per-man recruitment bounty for anyone signing up to serve until December 1. They also authorized the regiments to operate outside of Virginia and provided for the militia to act as garrison troops while the regiments were on the march. William Byrd III of Westover, twenty-nine, was designated to recruit and command the second regiment.

Washington was reenergized by all this activity, and by the prospects of a proper expedition to the Ohio country. On learning that John St. Clair, who had served as General Braddock's chief commissary, and Francis Halkett, Braddock's brigade major (and the son of Colonel Sir Peter Halkett), would serve Forbes in the same capacities, he dispatched letters reestablishing contact with both. The next week, on March 25, Washington rode the thirty-five miles from Williamsburg to Mrs. Custis's home and proposed marriage. She accepted. He ordered a ring and an addition to the house at Mount Vernon; she ordered new clothes, "not to be extravagant and not to be mourning."

With that taken care of, Washington headed back to duty, stopping only briefly at Mount Vernon, all thoughts of resignation evaporated. On April 5, he settled into his Winchester headquarters for the first time in five months and confronted the same intractable frustrations that had been his lot for three years. There were four hundred Cherokees and Catawbas in and around Winchester, with 140 more on their way, despite the fact that it was too early in the year to make use of them, and arrangements had not yet been made to supply them as they expected. Moreover, the regiment was dispersed throughout the frontier country and would have to be recalled to Winchester to organize for the campaign. But Washington did not know when the campaign was to begin, so he could not tell when to summon the detachments. If he gave the order too soon, he would quickly run out of forage and supplies for the concentrated force; if too late, he might embarrass himself by missing a deadline under the eye of the new commander.

As Washington had been unaware of events in London and in other theaters of this war, so he remained remote from events on the frontier, where nothing had changed in three bloody years. In many respects, for the settlers who still clung to their frontier homes, 1758 was the worst year yet. The outrages resumed along Mill Creek, near Woodstock, when fifty Shawnees and four Frenchmen surrounded a congregation of several families seeking refuge in George Painter's large log house. When Painter tried a desperate run for help, they shot him down in the yard. The others surrendered, hoping in vain for mercy.

The warriors fired the house and tossed George Painter's body into the flames. They burned the barn and laughed at the screams of the burning animals trapped inside. They snatched four babies from their mothers' arms, strung them up in trees, and used them for target practice until they dangled, quiet and bloody, before the horrified eyes of the families. Then they drove forty-eight surviving prisoners, men, women, and children, on a hellish, six-day march over the western mountains to their village.

There, after consultation with the matrons, they told Jacob Fisher, a pudgy twelve-year-old, to gather a large pile of dry wood. He burst into tears. "They're going to burn me, father," he sobbed.

"I hope not, son, do as they say," said the helpless father. Jacob, weeping, brought the wood, which the warriors and the women arranged in a circle around a sapling. They tied the howling Jacob to the sapling with a long rope cinched to his wrist and set the wood afire. Then, while Jacob's father and brothers watched, the Shawnees poked him with sharpened sticks, forcing him to run around the sapling, first winding himself tight to it, then spiralling outward, into and out of the flames. It took him hours and hours to die.

In the same spring, on the South Fork of the Shenandoah River, a Mrs. Brewbecker was suddenly seized by terrible apprehension and begged her husband to take her and the children away from their cabin. She could see savages on Massanutten Mountain, she said, cooking supper around a fire, and she knew they would come tomorrow. The mountain was two miles off, and no one else could see anything. The men of the family laughed at Mrs. Brewbacker and told her not to be superstitious. In the morning she ran away with the children anyway, and left Mr. Brewbacker to face his fate alone when the attack came, just as she had predicted.

In western Augusta County (later Hardy County, West Virginia), seven warriors crept up to Samuel Bingaman's cabin before dawn.

Bingaman, his wife and parents, and a hired man were asleep inside. When the raiders were ready, they fired one shot into the cabin, striking Mrs. Bingaman in the left breast, and crowded in at the door. Bingaman leaped from bed, grabbed his musket barrel-first, shattered its stock on the head of one attacker, and laid into the others with the remaining metal. When he had thus killed five of his assailants, the other two ran. He picked up a dropped musket, shot and wounded a sixth warrior, and dispatched him with a tomahawk. Mrs. Bingaman recovered. The lone survivor of the raiding party explained to his village that they mistakenly had attacked a devil.

George Washington was never subjected to the horrors of an outrage. He received the reports, of course, with all their barbarous details, but by 1758 they had become routine. He wrote no more about the suffering of the people, never repeated his offer to be a sacrifice for their safety. His concerns were for the coming expedition, and his role in it.

Automatically, in a manner now polished by frequent repetition, Washington resumed his personal diplomacy. "Mention me in favorable terms to General Forbes," he asked the influential Colonel Stanwix of the Royal Americans, with whom he had been corresponding frequently for almost a year. Washington was not interested in "military preferment," he assured Stanwix, for "I have long conquered all such expectancies," but would like to be recommended to Forbes as "a person who would gladly be distinguished in some measure from the *common run* of provincial officers, as I understand there will be a motley herd of us." He asked Colonel Thomas Gage to intercede for him, using identical words, and then after a brief pause wrote directly to Forbes: "It gives me no small pleasure to find we have an officer of your universal good character and consummate prudence to command in this expedition: and it is with an equal degree of pleasure I congratulate you on the promising prospect of a glorious campaign."

Washington hardly bothered, on the other hand, to conceal his disdain for John Blair, who was not doing well as custodian of the colony pending Fauquier's arrival. In late April, Washington and his officers rejected a long, confusing letter of instructions from Blair, having to do with intermixing members of the 1st and 2nd Virginia Regiments, transposing ranger companies and militia units on the southern frontier, and clearing an unspecified road, all within a few days' time.

Then Blair nearly scuttled the one thing that was going well—recruiting. The high bounty and short service prescribed by the Burgesses were much more attractive than the previous terms of enlistment, and both Virginia regiments quickly approached their authorized strength of one thousand men each. But in May, Blair told Washington that there was no money to pay his recruiting bounties of £10 per man; that rate applied, the governor now said, only to those recruited for the new regiment. Only after bitter protests from Washington did the governor and his council reluctantly tender the money.

When John St. Clair arrived in mid-May to help prepare the Virginia Regiments to march to Fort Cumberland, he was appalled by the conditions he found there. In his view, this was not the way an endangered country provided for its fighting men. He wrote a blistering letter to Blair, confirming Washington's complaints, as well as the effects of two years of official indifference. The men, he fumed, were "without arms, clothing or blankets, so that the court house and other houses are full of the sick, and no surgeon to attend them, nor is there one kettle in the whole regiment to make broth for these poor wretches. The only excuse your honor has to account for this neglect is that you are and will remain 200 miles from this place, while the other governors are on their frontiers as their duty to their king and country requires."

However pleasing this rebuke of Blair might have been to Washington, it was largely irrelevant, since Francis Fauquier arrived in Williamsburg on June 5 to begin his education in the arcana of this bizarre war. Washington was, of course, quick to make himself known to Fauquier. "Although but a poor hand at complimenting," he wrote, "but permit me, nevertheless, to offer your honor my congratulations." Fauquier's response carried a whiff of condescension from a man who had been flattered by experts: "Your congratulations and kind wishes do me the greater honor as you profess yourself a gentleman not addicted to compliments."

At a June 12 conference at Conococheague, Washington heard the details of the coming campaign and for the first time met the man who would play the key military role in directing it. This would not be Forbes, as it turned out, who was stricken with dysentery soon after his arrival and was seldom thereafter able to travel enough to keep in touch with his forces. Instead, he would rely on Colonel Henry Bouquet, a thirty-nine-year-old Swiss mercenary with an impressive record. Bouquet's pudgy form and amiable manner masked a keen mind and steely courage, both of which would be amply tested by this campaign.

One of the first issues over which Washington and Bouquet took each other's measure was that of uniforms. The fussy British parade-ground getup of breeches, hose, boots, waistcoat, overcoat, belts, hat, and so forth was manifestly unsuited for wilderness travel, camping, and fighting. Washington knew this, and had seen the superiority of the simple hunting shirt, breechclout, leggings, and moccasins adopted by the traders from their native clients. Clearly the army would be better off to change its method of dressing, but Washington did not want to seem radical. He broached the idea backhandedly. "Were I left to pursue my own inclinations," he told Bouquet in July, "I would not only cause the men to adopt the Indian dress but the officers also, and set the example myself: nothing but the uncertainty of its taking with the General causes me to hesitate a moment." The British officer side of him wanted to let it go at that, but the neophyte Westerner had one more thing to add: "Tis an unbecoming dress I confess for an officer, but convenience rather than show I think should be consulted." He was no doubt more than a little surprised at Bouquet's prompt response that he had recommended the idea to Forbes, who "approved it extremely."

Once again, in June 1758, Washington's history repeated itself with an odd resonance. In May 1755, while rushing to help the Braddock expedition make its ill-fated way to Fort Duquesne, Washington had taken the time for some detailed but abortive political maneuvers, with a view to getting elected to the House of Burgesses. Now, while in the thick of preparing his regiments to march with Forbes's expedition against Duquesne, he did so again. He kept no record of his political correspondences and conferences, as he did of his military affairs, but events showed them to have been considerable.

By the time Washington left Winchester with his men, as he was compelled to do on June 24, 1758, he had announced his candidacy for one of Frederick County's two seats in the assembly and had organized a network of campaign workers. Many of the most active were not from the county. Gabriel Jones, the well-known King's Attorney and burgess from Augusta County, virtually abandoned his own reelection campaign to work for Washington. George Fairfax hopped over from Fairfax County, and John Carlyle of Alexandria campaigned, as did Lieutenant Charles Smith and various other officers of the regiment (motivated to thus flirt with impropriety, no doubt, by the fact that Washington's opponent, Thomas Swearingen, was an officer of the despised militia). Washington did have local support, however, most notably that of James Wood, veteran of Fort Necessity and now generally regarded as the Winchester area's leading citizen.

On election day, set for July 24, the landowners of the county would come to town, visit the receptions hosted by the candidates, talk with each other, and at length stand before the registrar and declare their vote. As long as Washington was a visible, protective presence in Winchester, his election seemed certain. But as voting day approached, he was not in Winchester, and the people of the county were not feeling particularly well protected. On his departure with the regiment, Washington had ordered the ranger units that had been posted among the frontier settlements to move into Fort Loudoun and remain there in garrison during the expedition. Some of the county's leading landowners and most influential voters, such as Joist Hite and Robert Rutherford, were making no secret of their displeasure at the change. Washington's campaign managers told him flatly that if he wanted to win, he must fix the ranger problem and get back to Winchester to campaign on or before election day.

For three weeks, Washington seriously considered the request, and even asked for Colonel Bouquet's permission to return. But after Bouquet reluctantly approved, on July 19, Washington decided not to go. Adam Stephen, with a detachment of the regiment at Bouquet's Raystown, Pennsylvania, headquarters, had let Washington know that Bouquet had been troubled by the request for leave. Bouquet found himself, according to Stephen, "in a great dilemma betwixt his great inclination to serve you, and the attachment he has to regularity, duty and discipline." Washington decided to leave the election campaign to his friends.

Washington's confidence was not misplaced. In the poll taken on July 24, Washington led all the candidates with 309 votes, while Lord Fairfax's nephew Thomas Bryan Martin was also elected with 240 votes. Besides some anxiety, it had cost Washington nearly £40 for 46 3/4 gallons of beer, 35 gallons of wine, 2 gallons of cider, 3 1/2 pints of brandy, and about three barrels of rum punch.

In the throes of one career, Washington had successfully embarked on another, one that had taken considerable forethought and that had profound implications for the future, more so than anything he had done since his campaign for the adjutancy. With his election he had achieved a large measure of the status and public visibility he had craved. Yet the entire matter, and what he may have thought of it, is virtually invisible in his writings.

Washington spent election day embroiled in an unrelated issue, one that had first engaged his attention at least three years earlier (at the same time that he first thought seriously about getting into politics, a coincidence that may or may not have been merely coincidental). In June of 1755, he had protested bitterly to William Fairfax about General Braddock's agreement to build a road into western Pennsylvania—a colony that was providing the army with more supplies and wagons than any other. Such a road, Washington had fumed at the time, would "give all manner of encouragement to a people who ought rather to be chastised for their insensibility of their own danger, and disobedience of their sovereign's expectation. They are to be the Chosen people, because they have furnished what their absolute interest alone induced them to do."

Washington had written of a similar concern in April of 1758, shortly after returning to the frontier, when he asked John Stanwix where the forces involved in the Duquesne expedition were going to rendezvous. He was worried that it might be in Maryland instead of Virginia. A week later he stressed the same point to John St. Clair: "I fear the rendezvous of troops at the mouth of the Conococheague will give them [the Cherokee allies] some disgust; because, from long use, this place [and by that he meant, of course, Winchester] is become perfectly known and familiar to them: and it is here they repair on every occasion: here also all their scouting parties, which are gone to war, will return: and at this place the earliest intelligence of occurrences on the frontiers will always arrive."

There was more to this than intercolonial rivalry or a sudden sensitivity to the preferences of Cherokee warriors, as Washington's increasing vehemence on the question of the army's westward route would soon demonstrate, to the considerable mystification of his superior officers.

On taking up his duties in North America, General Forbes had soon found, as had Braddock before him, that his worst enemy was not the French, but the country. "My offensive operations are clogged with many difficulties," Forbes complained to William Pitt on June 17, "owing to the great distance and badness of the roads, through an almost impenetrable wood, uninhabited for more than 200 miles." Forbes had to get his men, guns, and supplies from the port of Philadelphia to the objective of Fort Duquesne, a straight-line distance of about 250 miles. There was, of course, no straight line route. Braddock had marched from Alexandria northwestward along the Potomac River to Frederick, where he had been forced to turn southward into Virginia to follow an old wagon road from Winchester to Fort Cumberland. Washington wanted Forbes to follow in Braddock's footsteps, on the stated grounds that Braddock's slow, hard work of clearing and bridge-building should not be left to go to waste while it was duplicated elsewhere.

Forbes, however, persisted in gazing westward from where he was, beginning with Philadelphia. There, in May, he had ordered his men to open a road west from Shippensburg, Pennsylvania, to Raystown, where they were to build Fort Bedford, and from whence they would look for a direct route across the remaining mountain ridges to Fort Duquesne. Shippensburg and Raystown were only a few miles south of the straight-line route to Duquesne, whereas Winchester was seventy miles south of the line, and Fort Cumberland was more than forty. Forbes planned to build "a stockaded camp with a blockhouse and cover for our provisions at every forty miles' distance. By which means, although I advance but gradually, yet I shall go more surely by lessening the number and immoderate long train of provisions, wagons, etc." Instead of Braddock's long, sluggish leaps—from Alexandria to Winchester to Cumberland to Duquesne—Forbes was going to inch his way west.

Forbes did not know, of course, whether the route he wanted would prove feasible, and so he had to maintain alternatives. Washington did not know of Forbes's ultimate intentions, but his mood gradually descended from disappointment that the army was not going to rendezvous at Winchester to despair at the thought that it might not even pass through Fort Cumberland.

By the beginning of July, matters were in considerable confusion. Washington was at Cumberland, arguing strenuously for the army to join him and take Braddock's road from there. Colonel Bouquet was with Forbes's advance at Raystown, thirty miles northeast of Cumberland, looking for a route west from there. Forbes was seventy-five miles to the rear at Carlisle, suffering from what he described as "a most violent and tormenting distemper," too ill to travel, trying to make sense of things. To maintain his alternate routes, he had Captain Dagworthy and a party of Marylanders cutting a road from Fort Frederick to Cumberland on the north side of the Potomac, while Washington worked on a road between Cumberland and Raystown.

Early in July, Adam Stephen reported to Washington with some satisfaction that Bouquet's engineers were having trouble finding a passable route over Laurel Ridge, west of Raystown. And George Mercer wrote that the work parties had progressed only a few miles from Fort Bedford because they were clearing a thirty-foot roadbed to accommodate two wagons abreast, when "a road for one wagon might be cleared as fast as it could drive." When Bouquet suggested strongly that he would like Washington to bring the Virginia regiments from Cumberland to Raystown, Washington resisted, saying such a move would be a mistake "if the army is obliged to take this route, as I am told from all hands it inevitably must."

Bouquet was finding Washington's attitude wearing. "All the letters I receive from Virginia are filled with nothing but the impossibility of finding a passage across Laurel Hill, and the ease of going by Braddock's Road," he wrote Forbes. "This is a matter of politics between one province and another." And yet neither Bouquet nor Forbes could be sure that Washington was not right. Toward the middle of July, Forbes gave up on the Maryland road (from Fort Frederick to Fort Cumberland) and hedged his bet against Braddock's Road. On this point he got some sage advice from James Glen, former governor of South Carolina, who was with the army to try to help deal with the Cherokees from his colony. "Though Washington is a cool, sensible, modest young man," Glen observed, "yet he and all the Virginians espouse Braddock's road with warmth, and should you meet with any difficulties in your march on any other path it will be said, why did you not take the well-known, tried and beaten road."

Thus the hedge: Bouquet told Washington to repair Braddock's road for a distance of ten miles or so from Cumberland, while Forbes continued to assess all options. Washington should be aware, Bouquet wrote with a careful regard for sensibilities, that before making a final decision the general "may send a body of troops by this road, over Laurel Hill." In that case, "I would be glad to know before hand (between us) if it would be agreeable to you to march that way or wait until the General is able to determine fully about the roads." This was Bouquet's delicate way of asking just how far Washington was prepared to push this issue. Washington responded immediately that he would be happy to march by any route, that he "shall never have a will of my own where a point of duty is required." But, since no final orders had yet been given, and thus no point of duty was yet involved, he requested "one hour's conference" to discuss the matter further.

The meeting was held on July 30, less than a week after his election to the House of Burgesses, and Washington used it to argue as completely and forcefully as he was able that Braddock's road was the only feasible route to the west. Traders and warriors had selected the path of least resistance ages before, he said; Ohio Company workmen and Braddock's engineers had perfected it; there were no difficulties worth mentioning involved in using it. Besides, with just three months of campaigning weather left, and four months until the enlistment of the entire 2nd Virginia Regiment expired, there was not enough time both to build eighty miles of new road and to conduct a successful siege of Duquesne. Washington presented a detailed plan for moving the army via Braddock's road to Duquesne in "34 days, at which time there will be 87 days' provisions on hand." Washington reported to Governor Fauquier that he "said and did everything to avert a measure that seemed to forebode our manifest ruin." And in doing so, he insisted to Bouquet, he "cannot be supposed to have any private interest, or sinister views."

Bouquet maintained his smooth and amicable demeanor, but he was distressed by Washington's relentless advocacy. As he expressed it to Forbes the day after the meeting, "We are in a cruel situation." If the army took Braddock's road, it would find forage for the horses in only three places between Fort Cumberland and Gist's plantation, a little more than halfway to Duquesne, and that forage would be useless after the October frosts killed the grass. "I had an interview with Colonel Washington to find out how he imagines these difficulties can be overcome. I learned nothing satisfactory. Most of these gentlemen do not know the difference between a party and an army, and find everything easy which agrees with their ideas, jumping over all the difficulties."

For his part, Washington was in agony as he awaited the result of his pleading. He wrote an intemperate appeal to Francis Halkett, whom he knew from the Braddock expedition and who served on Forbes's staff: "If Colonel Bouquet succeeds in this point with the General all is lost! All is lost by Heavens! Our enterprise ruined, and we stopped at the Laurel Hill for this winter."

Washington's strident dissent was not impressing his audience. John St. Clair, James Glen of South Carolina, Colonel Bouquet, and General Forbes had all come to the same conclusion after considering Washington's arguments along with the other information available to them. They all agreed that the direct route west from Raystown was shorter, more secure, and better supplied with water and forage than was Braddock's road. On August 3, Bouquet wrote Washington that it was all over, that Forbes had sent "express orders to begin to open the road from this place," that is, westward from Raystown. Bouquet reported that his men had found a gap, some fine springs, and several sources of good forage, and summed up pointedly by saying that he "cannot therefore entertain the least doubt that we shall all now go on hand in hand."

But Washington's conduct in the matter of the road had been, and continued to be, uncharacteristic. Never before had he pressed his contrary views so bluntly with his superior officers. He had felt strongly, for example, about permitting his men to adopt the hunting shirt and leggings, yet had been dismissive to a fault in proposing it, until he found out what Bouquet and Forbes thought of the idea. His worst and most frustrating disagreements with Dinwiddie had been conducted, for the most part, with measured and reasonable language scrubbed clean of any hint of reproach. In this case, however, he had shown himself willing to alienate not only his immediate superior, Bouquet, but the commander of the expedition. "By a very unguarded letter of Colonel Washington that accidentally fell into my hands," General Forbes told Bouquet in mid-August, "I am now at the bottom of their scheme against this new road, a scheme that I think was a shame for any officer to be concerned in."

Forbes did not elaborate about the letter he had seen, or what it said about Washington's deeper motives in this case. But it was clear to Forbes and Bouquet that the discussion was not merely about the best way to reach and conquer Fort Duquesne. Washington had good arguments on that score, but so did the officers who disagreed with him. The choice was not as clear-cut as Washington tried to make it seem. Yet he insisted on advancing his opinion to the point of damaging his military standing.

Nor can the matter be fully explained in terms of colonial rivalry. Competitive feelings were rampant among the traders and the border-dwellers, but Washington had spent years among them without expressing or demonstrating any particular passion for Virginia's advancement over the other colonies. But he was intensely interested in his own economic advancement. And he, along with everyone else remotely connected with the western trade and lands, understood that Forbes's choice of a route west would affect the fortunes of a generation.

It had been the vision of the Ohio Company, shared with quiet passion by Robert Dinwiddie, that it would open the gates to the west, and then collect tolls from all who came later. The Company had already selected its main route and the locations for its first settlements when it had been overrun by world war. Braddock had used and improved the Company's infrastructure, but he had been defeated, leaving behind a road to no-man's land. If Forbes now succeeded, then the wagons of the fortune-seekers would roll by the thousands in his wake.

From this point of view, Washington's stake in the argument can be seen as having intense personal and political dimensions. Although he was not a partner in the Ohio Company, his financial ambitions were inspired by it, and entwined with it. The only land that he owned outright, that he had selected and bought by and for himself—his Bullskin plantation—lay directly on Braddock's road.

Furthermore, he was now an elected representative of the area that would become one of the major way stations on the road west—provided that road was Braddock's. For all his protestations that he "cannot be supposed to have any private interest," Washington's intemperance in expressing his views was consistent with a frank definition of his motives that he expressed in a slightly different context.

In making a passionate argument to John Robinson the previous October about the need for an expedition against Duquesne, Washington had specified that he was speaking "not only as an officer, but as a friend, *who has property in the country and is unwilling to lose it*" (emphasis added). He then went on to explain that his motivation as a landowner transcended the merely military: "This it is, also, which makes me anxious for doing more than barely represent; which is all that is expected of an officer commanding."

Thus Washington's own words help explain why he threw military etiquette to the wind in contesting the road issue, and why he continued to carp about it even after Forbes had pronounced a final decision and issued explicit orders. Not surprisingly, Virginians serving with Bouquet's road-builders shared Washington's preference for a Virginia route and reported what he expected to hear—that the new road, as Washington's old friend and neighbor William Ramsay put it, "is steep, stony and of very difficult access." Bouquet saw things differently, writing to Forbes a few days after the date of Ramsay's letter, "I went yesterday to reconnoiter that terrible mountain and found a road where a six-horse carriage could be taken without difficulty."

To Bouquet, Washington was for the most part polite but unyielding: "I am glad the new road turns out so much to your liking." But when Bouquet exulted on August 26 that "the first division of the artillery is over the Allegheny and had no stop or difficulty to go over the gap," Washington's acknowledgment was anything but gracious. "We might have been in full possession of the Ohio by now," he snapped, "if rather than running ourselves into the difficulties and expense of cutting an entire new road, Braddock's had been adopted." It suited him and his colleagues to return to his theme of 1755, that scurrilous Pennsylvanians had somehow defrauded their virtuous neighbor. Washington liked the way his secretary, John Kirkpatrick, put it, and adopted the words as his own:

"It has long been the luckless fate of poor Virginia to fall a victim to the views of her crafty neighbors."

On into September Washington ranted, stating and restating his case to all his correspondents. He reported to John Robinson that the latest scouting reports estimated the maximum strength of French forces at Duquesne at eight hundred men. "See therefore how our time has been misspent, behold the golden opportunity lost." Someone should go to the King, Washington suggested, "let him know how grossly his honor and the public money have been prostituted. I wish I was sent immediately home with some other on this errand." With Governor Fauquier he was more circumspect: "The General I dare say, from his good character, can account fully for these delays that surprise all that judge from appearances only, but I really cannot."

The distrust was mutual. On a question of tactics that came up early in September, General Forbes advised Bouquet to "consult Colonel Washington, although perhaps not follow his advice, as his behavior about the roads was no ways like a soldier." His sour view of the controversy and Washington's role in it no doubt contributed to Forbes's pungent opinion that the whole lot of provincial officers was nothing more than "an extreme bad collection of broken innkeepers, horse-jockeys and Indian traders."

The main body of the army had begun its next inchworm movement west during the last week of August. With a camp and depot secure at Raystown, a detachment marched about forty miles to set up the next base at Loyalhanna, beyond Laurel Hill and forty miles from Fort Duquesne. By this time Forbes, still weakened by his illness, had struggled from Carlisle to Shippensburg to Raystown, but was in no condition to travel when, on September 7, Bouquet and most of the remaining troops departed Raystown for Loyalhanna. Meanwhile Washington, still at Cumberland, fumed over the report of a scouting party back from Fort Duquesne that had counted there only three hundred French troops and fifty or so Shawnees. He no doubt took satisfaction from Adam Stephen's first missive from Loyalhanna: "You have no reason to alter your opinion of the route of the army."

Washington, feeling low, took time to write a long letter to Sally Fairfax. In her few communications to him she adopted a relentlessly mocking, teasing tone that seemed to stimulate his adoration. In this way she had needled him about being in a hurry to complete the conquest of Fort Duquesne so he could rush home to the arms of his fiancée, and he responded as always with heavy sentiment, avowing that his true love was not Martha, but Sally: "Misconstrue not my meaning; doubt it not, nor expose it. The world has no business to know the object of my love, declared in this manner to you, when I want to conceal it. But adieu to this till happier times, if I ever shall see them."

CHAPTER 14

Ashes of Victory

"I expect we shall give the expedition over, and retire to the inhabitants, condemned by the world and derided by our friends."

SEPTEMBER 25, 1758

While Washington pined at Cumberland, Bouquet's men at Loyalhanna were harassed constantly by snipers and raiders. In order to stop the continual loss of a man wounded here, another snatched into captivity there, Bouquet planned to send out small parties to find and engage the raiders. But Major James Grant of the 77th Regiment of Royal Americans had what he thought was a better plan. Grant was highly regarded by his superiors for being a well-trained regular officer, with the usual contempt for provincial officers and irregular warfare. Neither he nor Bouquet had ever conducted operations in these circumstances.

Grant argued long and hard for command of a large detachment, of about five hundred men, with which to reconnoitre the very walls of Fort Duquesne. Bouquet may not have known, as he listened to Grant's fervent arguments, that Forbes had already received and firmly rejected similar requests from Grant. Major Andrew Lewis, the senior Virginia officer and probably the most experienced frontier fighter present with the advance, had no confidence whatsoever in the ability of a large, unwieldy force of British regulars to accomplish anything deft while stumbling about in the forest. Over his strenuous opposition, Bouquet approved Grant's ambitious plan, changing it only to make it safer, by enlarging it to eight hundred men.

Neither Major Grant nor Colonel Bouquet defined the mission of this operation—it was cobbled together using elements of what each man wanted. Bouquet wanted the Mingos discouraged from harassing his men, and apparently thought that an attack on their camps near Duquesne would make them withdraw their raiding parties. What those parties would then do to his attacking force did not appear to have been a concern. What Grant wanted, later events were to indicate, was to be turned loose on his own. Bouquet assented, ordering Grant to scout the route to Fort Duquesne, count the enemy forces there, and attack any Mingos camped nearby if he thought such an attack would be advantageous. No attack on Fort Duquesne was mentioned, nor was any distinction made between an attack on the fort and an attack on those camped immediately outside it. Grant had what he wanted, and on September 9 he marched with a will, west from Loyalhanna.

Whatever Major Grant knew of the fate of Braddock's expedition, he had learned nothing from it. He carried in his mind a picture of what he was going to do and how his enemy would respond. It was a simple picture, based on neither knowledge nor experience, that contained few variables and no alternatives. He would sting the enemy, when he found them, with a sudden attack by a small force that would then retreat, leading the enemy into a prepared ambush. There was no question in his mind that his enemy would react by bunching up and running pell-mell into the slaughter. Nor did he question the scouting reports that assured him he outnumbered all his foes.

At dawn on September 13, Grant thought he was about ten miles from Duquesne when in fact he was more than fifteen. His Catawba, Tuscarora, and Nottaway scouts had little knowledge of this terrain and even less enthusiasm for this operation. Grant sent Major Lewis forward with two hundred men, to march halfway to the fort and set an ambush for any opposing force sent out to meet them. Meanwhile, to make sure such a force came out, a detachment of fifteen men under Lieutenant Colesby Chew was to proceed to the fort, shoot a few defenders, and draw the rest to their doom in the ambush. Lieutenant Chew's detachment had little more than got under way when the native guides deserted him, leaving him unable to find the fort, and barely able to find his way back to the main force by sundown that evening.

At midafternoon, Grant moved forward with the main force to see how his plan was working. It was not. Major Lewis had gone four miles, set an ambush, and for the rest of the day had enjoyed peace and quiet. Chew was nowhere to be found. Grant, thinking he had seven miles to go to the fort, pushed on. When he had gone ten miles, he parked his baggage train, assigned fifty Virginians under Captain Thomas Bullett to guard it, and pushed on. Finally, at about 11:00 P.M., in total darkness, Grant reached the top of a rise overlooking Fort Duquesne.

The fort, a few hundred yards northwest of Grant's position, was dark. To Grant's left the Monongahela and to his right the Allegheny ran toward their confluence beyond the fort. Below him to the left front were the fort's garden and cemetery, to his right front an area of storehouses and barracks, although he could not see these features. All he could see was two or three campfires burning just outside the fort walls. Whether that meant there were only a few warriors camped there or only a few awake, Grant had no way of knowing.

Nor did he care. He ordered Major Lewis to take four hundred men (dressed in white shirts so they could distinguish each other from the enemy, at least at close range), advance to the campfires, fire a volley at whomever was near, and then run. Grant would align his remaining 350 men on the top of the hill. There they would beat their drums and the Highlanders would play their pipes to guide Lewis's men back to safety.

This was a truly extraordinary plan of attack. It was to be launched in the dead of night, on unfamiliar ground, against an uncounted enemy that had reinforcements of unknown number available inside the fort. Not surprisingly, Grant became increasingly nervous as time went by with no shots fired. He was beginning to fret seriously when Lewis stepped out of the gloom to tell him that the advance was impossible. The men were not only losing formation and communication, but their way, among the dark trees. To open fire in these conditions was unthinkable; they would do more harm to each other than to any enemy.

Grant, no doubt in considerable heat as he saw his imagined triumph slipping away from him, came up with an alternative plan as outlandish as the first. He sent Lewis with 250 men two miles to the rear to join the baggage guard and, once again, to set up an ambush. Then Grant picked another fifty men and insisted they go forward and shoot somebody. They attacked a barn, set it afire, and came back to the lines.

By now it was dawn, and Grant did perhaps the oddest thing of all: he stayed put. Within rifle shot of the fort, with his small force divided in two, the parts separated by a gulf of two miles, with neither detachment knowing what the other was doing or what it was supposed to do, he simply fiddled with his formations. And in this bizarre scenario, perhaps the most peculiar fact of all was that the French and their warrior allies, after six hours or more of this marching, countermarching, and blundering within a stone's throw of their camps, remained unaware of the presence of several hundred enemy soldiers. Only now, after sunup, did someone stumble into the left of Grant's line and raise the alarm. Grant's response was typically unrealistic. In order, he explained later, "to put on a good countenance and to convince our men that they had no reason to be afraid," he ordered every drummer in his command to beat reveille.

Instantly, the farce turned ugly. The gate of Fort Duquesne swung open and, to Grant's horror, disgorged eight hundred French troops who moved confidently to the attack with another three hundred or so Mingos and Shawnees. Instead of bunching up and running into an ambush, they did exactly as they had done four years before when Braddock had appeared a few miles to the south: they spread out in skirmishing parties, moving from cover to cover, expertly picking off the British soldiers standing dumbly in their formations. The effect on Grant's detachment was exactly what it had been on Braddock's army: confusion followed by terror and dissolution.

Two miles to the rear, Lewis and the Virginians heard the firing and knew exactly what was happening. Lewis was inclined, as he had been throughout this misbegotten exercise, to attempt only what he was told to do, but he soon yielded to the pleas of his officers to move forward to the rescue. As he advanced toward the fighting by one path through the trees, Grant and his men fled to the rear along another. When Lewis arrived at the fight he had no one to support, or to support him; when Grant reached the baggage he had no reserve formation on which to rally. Only Bullett's fifty Virginians were there, fighting as if they were a regiment of demons, and as the rest of the force fled, only Bullett's detachment preserved its organization and conducted an effective fighting retreat.

Grant was no tactician, but neither was he a coward; he and Lewis stayed with their men and in the fight too long for safety, and were taken prisoner. Years later, they would make their way back home from long detention in Canada. But about three hundred of their men, nearly 40 percent of the detachment, lay dead on the field.

Washington was matter-of-fact in reporting this appalling new defeat to Governor Fauquier and other correspondents. He expressed his satisfaction that the Virginians involved "have acquired very great applause for their gallant behavior during the action. I had the honor to be publicly complimented yesterday by the General on the occasion." Other than that, he was merely disdainful: "What may be the consequence of this affair, I will not take upon me to decide, but our affairs in general appear with a greater gloom than ever."

Washington's gloom was deepened by a rare conference with General Forbes at Raystown, held a few days after Grant's disaster. The news of the defeat weighed less on Washington's mind than the orders from Forbes to bring his regiments to Raystown and advance with the main body. It was clear now that this army would not even touch Braddock's road. "So miserably has this expedition been managed," Washington wrote Sally Fairfax on September 25, "that I expect, after a month's further trial and the loss of many more men by the sword, cold and perhaps famine, we shall give the expedition over as impracticable this season, and retire to the inhabitants, condemned by the world and derided by our friends."

This was not the view of either Forbes or Bouquet, who were happy to delay the final battle for Duquesne as long as possible. For one thing, they believed that every passing day made the defense of the fort more difficult for the French, who had to contend with a long and fragile line of supply that was incapable of sustaining a large force through the winter, while the English advance was as relentless and secure as it was slow. No doubt shaken by Grant's defeat, they nevertheless saw it for what it was—the misfiring of a personal ploy for fame, not a military disaster. Nor were Forbes and Bouquet especially dismayed when, on October 12, the French attacked the road-builders and the unfinished works at Loyalhanna with a relatively large raiding party. After a four-hour engagement the English had lost sixty casualties and a little time, but nothing more.

What Washington feared for the future had already happened: Pennsylvania had replaced Virginia as the primary agency of British power in North America, simply because Forbes was in Pennsylvania. His needs, and those of his army, had to be fulfilled in Pennsylvania, people had to come to Pennsylvania to see him. Washington and the Virginians, even now that they were belatedly in Pennsylvania and at work on the hated road west, were out of the play. This was one factor contributing to Washington's ignorance of the most important reason Forbes was convinced that time was on the side of the British. Momentous events were afoot, and had been all summer, about which Washington apparently knew nothing.

Back in March, even before Forbes's arrival in Philadelphia, a diplomat delivered there a fateful message. Teedyuscung was the principal sachem of a confederation of Delawares and other tribes living in the Wyoming Valley along the Susquehanna. He also acted in some sense as an emissary, or at least under the instructions, of the Iroquois League. His message was that the Ohio tribes were now reconsidering their alliance with the French, and could be won back to the English. He could accomplish this, Teedyuscung assured Pennsylvania authorities, but not if the Cherokees and Catawbas misbehaved in any way. The Iroquois, along with the rest of the northern tribes, were very nervous about the presence in their territory of seven hundred of their traditional enemies from the south.

Forbes, who had been immersed without preparation or help in a morass of intertribal, intercolonial, and interpersonal politics, did not fail to grasp the military significance of Teedyuscung's approach. As obvious as that importance would seem in retrospect, Braddock would not have seen it, nor did most of Forbes's subordinates. In fact, his principal consultant in these matters, William Johnson, tried to discredit Teedyuscung; apparently Johnson preferred having his familiar Iroquois at the center of all negotiations, and resented the intrusion of the Delawares. But Forbes, despite his lack of experience with or knowledge of the tribes, saw at once that he had an opportunity here, and that the established, responsible officials were not going to do anything to help him grasp it. Accordingly, he identified and recruited the people who could help him—the Quakers and Moravians who all along had been struggling to establish a lasting peace between the white and red races. His insight undercut the personal ambitions of both William Johnson and Teedyuscung.

In accordance with Forbes's wishes, over the strenuous objections of Pennsylvania's civil authorities, two unlikely ambassadors began in June 1758 a series of trips to the Ohio country bearing the good wishes of the English crown. They were the Quaker businessman and pacifist Israel Pemberton and the Moravian missionary Frederick Post. Post, especially, spent an exceedingly dangerous summer visiting the villages of French tribal allies, often under the very walls of Fort Duquesne, to present the arguments of the British and an invitation to a peace conference. All the time he was followed, watched, and overheard by French agents eager for a chance to kidnap or assassinate him. But thanks to Teedyuscung, Post traveled under the alert and effective protection of the Delawares. This protection, guaranteed by Teedyuscung's eastern Delawares, was somewhat reluctantly afforded by the Ohio Delawares under the warlike Shingas and his brother Tamaqui. But even they listened closely to what Post had to say.

While the Ohio tribes were thinking abut deserting the French, five hundred of the seven hundred southern warriors accompanying Forbes's army deserted him and returned home in disgust. These shifting alliances were incomprehensible to most Englishmen, who, like Washington, did not trouble themselves to inquire into the causes. The Cherokees, Washington wrote to Forbes in reporting their defection, "naturally are of a discontented temper." But the reaction of the Cherokees and Catawbas was straightforward: they were not being rewarded properly for their sacrifice in leaving their families and their tribal affairs. The only thing that could compensate the southern warriors for the stinginess of the English would have been the plunder of a successful battle, but the English army was not doing anything except lumbering through the woods a few miles a day, day after day. The warriors saw no reason to stay.

The case of the Mingos was similarly clear. French supplies for their warriors had always been scanty, but the Mingos had accepted the lack of bounty as long as the French seemed powerful and the English, timid. But by the fall of 1758, supplies were even harder for the French in the Ohio country to come by, because the English had severed their supply line by destroying their Great Lakes navy and its base at Fort Frontenac. Moreover, a large English army was plodding implacably toward Fort Duquesne. Obviously it was time to reexamine Mingo alliances.

In October, a fateful peace conference was convened at Easton, Pennsylvania. For nearly three weeks the representatives of the Onandaga (eastern) and western Iroquois tribes, of the eastern and western Delawares, the northern and southern Shawnees, of virtually every tribe and clan involved in the war thus far, wrangled with representatives of the various white clans—the Pennsylvania government, proprietorship, Quakers, and military, along with the English government and military. Out of this, in the last week of October, emerged a new treaty.

Although it encompassed a great deal of maneuvering and jostling by the various tribes and confederations, the terms of the treaty were straightforward and dramatic: the Ohio tribes would abandon the French cause, in return for which the English would guarantee to the tribes eternal posession of all land west of the Allegheny Mountains. What remained unclear after the conclusion of the conference was whether either side would be willing, or able, to observe the treaty terms. Wearily, Frederick Post set out once again for the Ohio country to tell the tribes there what had been agreed to in their name, and find out whether they would accept the terms.

But by the time Post stopped at Loyalhanna on November 7, to inform Forbes of the successful outcome of the treaty, Forbes was deep in despair. He had run out of time, and faced the knowledge that Washington may have been right all along. Once again it was not the military enemy but the country that had dealt him the worst blow. It was the rain.

Washington, now in charge of road construction, had advanced to Loyalhanna on November 2 (with Forbes along, languishing in a litter), when a steady, drenching rain put an end to all further road-building efforts. Half the army had not yet made it over Laurel Hill from Fort Bedford, and there were still miles to go—no one knew for certain how many miles—to Fort Duquesne. In one more month the enlistment of the entire 2nd Virginia Regiment would expire, and the men of the First had been promised they would return to the colony on that date. Other colonial forces had also been provided only until the 1st of December. As one day of leaden skies and dripping branches blended into another, Forbes prepared to admit total failure to William Pitt.

Matters deteriorated even further on November 12, when scouts reported an enemy force once again approaching Loyalhanna. Washington took five hundred men and advanced to meet the attack, leading troops into action for the first time since Fort Necessity. Behind him, with orders to help cut off and destroy the raiding force, came George Mercer with another five hundred men. Late in the afternoon, three miles from his fortifications, Washington caught the French party around a campfire and attacked. The little skirmish with the enemy was over by the time Mercer arrived on the scene—Washington's force had managed to kill a French soldier and take three prisoners. But in the gloom of the advancing November night, Washington and his men mistook Mercer's Virginians for enemy reinforcements and opened fire. Seeing the mistake, Washington desperately rode between the firing lines of men, knocking up muzzles and shouting orders to cease fire. But by the time he regained control, fourteen Virginians had been killed and twenty-six wounded by friendly fire.

Understandably, Washington had little to say about this tragedy for years to come. His first armed engagement (the ambush of Jumonville) had been called murder; his second and third had been bloody and humiliating defeats; now his fourth had been fratricidal. There was, however, an unexpected payoff. One of the three prisoners Washington had taken turned out to be an Englishman, a prisoner of the French for many years, who had just come from Fort Duquesne, and who now revealed to his countrymen what the situation was at the enemy fort.

As Forbes had expected, the long delay had taken a fearful toll on the French, who had become desperately short of food. The victory over Grant had convinced the French allies from the northern tribes that their work was done, and since food was scarce anyway they had departed for more congenial camps. Only a few Shawnees, Delawares, and Mingos remained near Fort Duquesne, and they were working on a new treaty with the English at Easton. The hard rains had convinced the rapidly weakening French that campaigning weather had ended before the English force could get within striking distance, and with great relief they had dispatched to winter quarters on the faroff Great Lakes all but a little garrison force of two hundred men.

Forbes saw his chance. The key French installation in the heart of the American continent was virtually undefended, and the rains had stopped. On the other hand, little more than two weeks remained before the enlistments of the colonial forces would begin to expire. And no one knew for sure how far it was to Fort Duquesne. Still, Forbes had to try.

He put together three brigades, each made up of about eight hundred of his healthiest men (although he could not fully regain his own health). These brigades were to be commanded by Colonel Bouquet, Lieutenant Colonel Archibald Montgomery, and George Washington, who would enjoy the temporary, informal rank of brigadier and who would take the lead. Once again, the problem was the road. Now the task was not to build a road, but merely to clear a way for foot soldiers and a few wagons and guns. Even so, Washington was able to make only six to eight miles per day, and that only by working his men hard and long. Time continued to run out.

On November 16, with fourteen days left before the 2nd Virginia Regiment and others would disband, with his men hacking at trees and brush and struggling forward, Washington got in one last argument about the long-since-abandoned Braddock's road. He had tried to get Forbes to get on it at Winchester, and had failed; had tried to get him to take it west from Cumberland, and had failed; now, with the tenacity that was becoming his hallmark, Washington tried one more idea: perhaps the army could take it on the way back: "The keeping of Fort Duquesne (if we should be fortunate enough to take it) in its present situation, will be attended with great advantages to the middle colonies; and I do not know so effectual a way of doing it, as by the communication of Fort Cumberland and General

Braddock's road; which is in the first place, good, and in the next, fresh, affording good food if the weather keeps open, which is more than a road can do as much used as this has been."

There was, of course, no response to this sally, and Washington's men labored on through the forest, working constantly "from daybreak till night," short of axes, short of food, unsure how far they had to go, expecting attack at any moment. Doggedly, they kept on, many of the men counting down the days until they could walk away from this hell toward home.

On the night of November 22, the army camped along Turtle Creek, about ten miles upstream from its confluence with the Monongahela and the site of Braddock's defeat of 1755. Now, three years later, the English force approaching Duquesne was twice as large as Braddock's had been, but was equally blind. Like Braddock, Forbes had virtually no native scouts left to help him, and he had only a vague idea of where he was. George Croghan had come into camp two days before with fifteen Iroquois warriors, a disappointingly small result of the favorable conclusion of the Easton treaty.

With muskets kept at hand, pickets out, and noise forbidden, the army marched all day on the 23rd, then made a miserable camp—without tents in the penetrating November cold. Scouts debated whether the force was twelve or fifteen miles from the fort. All day on the 24th was spent in final preparations for the attack. Forbes, sicker than ever, urged his officers to maintain order and keep the men calm when the fighting started, "as our honor, interest, and *in fine* our all, depends on the happy issue of the service we are just going on." He had always been better at organization than oratory.

Early on the evening of the 24th, a scout came into camp to report a large column of smoke in the direction of Fort Duquesne. A second scout reported shortly thereafter that the French had abandoned the fort and had set it afire. Forbes dispatched his light horse, or cavalry, that night and his infantry the next morning, and the reports were soon confirmed. The French and their Mingo allies were gone. The fort, its outbuildings, and a second, incomplete fortification had been reduced to burning embers. Yet the outline of what had been there was enough to make Forbes, after an inspection, fervently grateful that he had not been required to lay siege to such works as these.

In one of the great anticlimaxes of history, Forbes had stepped from humiliating failure to decisive victory. Without fighting a battle, he found himself in possession of the key to a continent, and to the heart of his first minister (and Forbes lost no time in setting that hook by gracing the smoldering ruins he had conquered with the name Fort Pitt, soon to be Pittsburgh). If it was not a heroic victory, neither was it an accidental one, as Colonel Bouquet pungently pointed out. "After God, the success of this expedition is entirely due to the General," Bouquet wrote, going on to define three grounds for his opinion. First, Forbes had not only brought about the Treaty of Easton, and thus "struck the blow which knocked the French in the head," but had given the blow time to land, by "temporizing wisely to expect the effects of that treaty." The delays that had so frustrated Washington had been, Bouquet argued, strategic. If the army had rushed to Fort Dusquesne and attacked it while all the French forces and all the French allies of the summer had been still present, the outcome could hardly have been the same.

Second, said Bouquet, Forbes had all along demonstrated his competence, reassured his men, and impressed his foes "in securing all his posts, and giving nothing to chance." Third—and on this point Bouquet placed heavy emphasis—Forbes had been entirely right in "not yielding to the urging instances for taking Braddock's Road, which would have been our destruction." Forbes was given little time to enjoy being right. He made it back to Philadelphia, but he was too far sunk into illness and exhaustion, and there, early in the new year, he died.

To Washington, the victory clearly tasted of ashes, although he was too good a soldier to say so. He reported to Governor Fauquier in dutiful tones the occupation of Fort Duquesne, "or rather the ground on which it stood." Unlike Bouquet, he was only vaguely aware of the causes of the outcome. "The possession of this fort has been a matter of great surprise to the whole army, and we cannot attribute it to more probable causes than those of weakness, want of provisions, and desertion of their Indians." He obviously knew nothing of the import of the Easton Treaty, and he did not care. Britain had all but won its war; Washington had lost his.

* * *

Dispirited and ill once again, George Washington made his way back to Winchester with the regiment, and then, alone, to Belvoir and by the end of December to Williamsburg. There he resigned from the military forces of Virginia and, as far as he was concerned, from military life forever. On January 6, he married Martha and took up residence at her home until the renovation of Mount Vernon could be completed. On February 22, which with the adoption of the Gregorian calendar in 1752 had become the date of his twenty-seventh birthday, he took his seat in the House of Burgesses.

It was an emotional day. He had come through the hardest trials a man could endure, and it would be a long time before their memory released him. He had spent five years in pursuit of military success and a King's commission, had achieved neither, and had turned his back on both. Now he was born again to the strange new life of a planter, politician, husband, and stepfather. But before going forward, on this February day, there was a long looking back. Seated among the people with whom he had for so long contested for money and for recognition, Washington listened to his friend John Robinson, as Speaker of the House of Burgesses, deliver that body's valediction to Washington's military life.

Here at last was vindication. Here was the fulsome praise of his peers and his social betters that Washington had longed to have. And yet, while Robinson talked of the triumph and the victory, Washington must have been thinking of the failures and the mistakes. The young men he had left in the mud of Fort Necessity, on the banks of the Monongahela, in the forest near Loyalhanna. All the powerful men whose esteem and favor he had sought in vain: Dinwiddie, Braddock, Loudoun, Forbes. The stubborn British regulars at the Monongahela, the reluctant Virginia recruits and the elusive deserters, paymasters, and suppliers, the proud and enigmatic Iroquois and Cherokees.

Yet here he was, despite them all, receiving the gratitude of the leading men of his colony. Here he was, alive, despite all the bullets that had not quite found their mark. If he had not met the extravagant expectations of the self-centered youth he had been ten years before, yet he had endured, had made a name, had come through to a safe harbor. Most importantly, for him and for the subsequent history of his country, he had won time for reflection on the tempestuous events of a decade of strife. He had not yet been transformed by his experiences, but that transformation would come, as he worked over, again and again, the causes and the effects, the lessons and the truth. The grain had been threshed, and now only time and gentle breezes were required to dispose of the chaff. Hard kernels of new ideas—about the worth of a human being, the requirements of justice, and the rights of citizens—had survived the flail.

It was unfortunate, for him and for his country, that these ideas did not embrace people of differing colors or cultures. The ways and the worth of red people and black would remain virtually invisible to him for the rest of his life (although he would be troubled somewhat by slavery). It was unfortunate, too, that the lessons were underlain by a lust for land that would see him contest with his former subordinates, to the limits of legality, to snatch some of the contested western lands that had been promised as a bounty to recruits of the Virginia Regiment (land claimed by the Ohio Company, then certified forever to the western tribes).

It was George Washington, a man who had just completed a lonely and a difficult initiation, not a marble monument to immaculate virtue, who sat and listened, and thought, and was deeply moved. It was a man, flawed and struggling, who stood on the floor of the historic House of Burgesses to acknowledge the praise, to utter the words that would begin his new life and set his new course. It was a man who could not speak. He stammered. Moments went by, and he stuttered again. When everyone's embarrassment had become acute, Speaker Robinson gave a gentle order: "Sit down, Mr. Washington, your modesty equals your valor, and that surpasses the power of any language that I possess."

In the early evening of January 1, 1760, George Washington sat down at his desk in the newly expanded mansion of his newly enlarged estate, dipped quill to ink, and resumed the keeping of a personal journal, a practice he had abandoned five eventful years before.

Much had happened in the year since he had left the Regiment. Quebec had fallen to the English after a climactic battle on the Plains of Abraham. Washington had got himself into debt by improvident expansion of his land holdings. Christopher Gist had died of smallpox on the road to Winchester, while his old friend and rival George Croghan managed to put himself in charge of the massive fur trade being conducted out of Pittsburgh, thus resuming the preeminence he had enjoyed on that site ten years earlier, before the schemers of the Ohio Company had tried to jostle him aside. Croghan's brother-in-law William Trent, formerly chief agent for the Ohio Company, shared in his new prosperity as his chief assistant.

Washington had just passed the first day of a year that would see the surrender of the last French bastion in Canada, and the ascension to the English throne of George III. But such events were not his concerns. "Visited my plantations," he recorded, "and received an instance of Mr. French's great love of money in disappointing me of some pork, because the price had risen to 22 shillings and sixpence after he had engaged to let me have it at 20 shillings. Called at Mr. Possey's in my way home and desired him to engage me 100 barrels of corn upon the best terms he could in Maryland. And found Mrs. Washington upon my arrival broke out with the measles."

Bibliography

Abbot, W.W., ed. *The Papers of George Washington.* Colonial Series, vols. I-V. Charlottesville, Va.: University Press of Virginia, 1983.

Alberts, Robert C. *A Charming Field for an Encounter: The Story of George Washington's Fort Necessity.* Washington, D.C.: Office of Publications, National Park Service, U.S. Department of the Interior, 1975.

———. *The Most Extraordinary Adventures of Major Robert Stobo.* Boston: Houghton Mifflin, 1965.

Alden, John R. *Robert Dinwiddie, Servant of the Crown.* Williamsburg, Va.: Colonial Williamsburg Foundation, 1973.

Ambler, Charles H. *George Washington and the West.* Reprint. New York: Russell and Russell, 1971.

Anderson, Fred. *People's Army: Massachusetts Soldiers & Society in the Seven Years' War.* Institute of Early American History and Culture Series. Chapel Hill: University of North Carolina Press, 1984.

Anderson, F. W. "Why Did Colonial New Englanders Make Bad Soldiers? Contractual Principles and Military Conduct During the Seven Years' War." *William and Mary Quarterly* 38(3) (1981): 395–417.

Anderson, Niles."New Light on the 1758 Forbes Campaign." *Western Pennsylvania History Magazine* 50(2) (1967): 89–105.

Aquila, Richard. *The Iroquois Restoration: Iroquois Diplomacy on the Colonial Frontier, 1701—1754.* Detroit: Wayne State University Press, 1983.

———. "The Iroquois as 'Geographic' Middlemen: A Research Note." *Indiana Mag. of Hist. 80(1)* (1984): 51–60.

Axtell, James, and William C. Sturtevant. "The Unkindest Cut, or Who Invented Scalping?" *William and Mary Quarterly 37(3)* (1980): 451–472.

Bailey, Kenneth P. *Christopher Gist: Colonial Frontiersman, Explorer, and Indian Agent.* Hamden, Conn: Shoe String Press, 1976.

Baker-Crothers, Hayes. *Virginia and the French and Indian War.* Chicago: University of Chicago Press, 1928.

Bell, Whitfield J., Jr., and Leonard W. Larabee. "Franklin and the Wagon Affair." *Proceedings American Philosophical Society* 101 (1957): 551–58.

Billings, Warren M. *Colonial Virginia: A History.* White Plains, N.Y.: KTO Press, 1986.

Bird, Harrison. *Battle for a Continent.* New York: Oxford University Press, 1965.

Brown, Stuart E., Jr. *Virginia Baron: The Story of Thomas 6th Lord Fairfax.* Berryville, Va.: Chesapeake Book Company, 1965.

Campbell, Charles. *History of the Colony and Ancient Dominion of Virginia.* Philadelphia: J.B. Lippincott and Co., 1860; Reprinted 1965 by the Reprint Company, Spartanburg, S.C.

Champion, Walter T., Jr. "Christian Frederick Post and the Winning of the West." *Pennsylvania Magazine of History and Biography* 104(3) (July 1980): 308–25.

———. "The Road to Destruction: The Effect of the French and Indian War on the Six Nations." *Indian Hist.* 10(3) (1977): 20–22, 62.

Cleland, Hugh. *George Washington in the Ohio Valley.* Pittsburgh: University of Pittsburgh Press, 1955.

Colden, Cadwallader. *The History of the Five Indian Nations Depending on the Province of New York in America.* Ithaca, N.Y.: Cornell University Press, 1988.

Craven, Wesley Frank. "Indian Policy in Early Virginia." *William and Mary Quarterly,* Third Series, 1(1): 65–76.

Darlington, Mary C., ed. *History of Colonel Henry Bouquet and the Western Frontiers of Pennsylvania.* Reprint. Arno Press, 1971.

Darlington, William M. *Christopher Gist's Journals: With Historical, Geographical and Ethnological Notes.* Pittsburgh: J.R. Weldin & Co., 1893.

Downes, Randolph C. *Council Fires on the Upper Ohio: A Narrative of*

Indian Affairs in the Upper Ohio Valley until 1795. Pittsburgh: University of Pittsburgh Press, 1969.

Every, Dale Van. *Forth to the Wilderness: The First American Frontier 1754–1774.* New York: Mentor Books, 1962.

Ferling, John. "Soldiers for Virginia: Who Served in the French and Indian War?" *Virginia Magazine of History and Biography* 94(3) (1986): 307–328.

Fisher, Lewis F., ed. *The Family of John Lewis, Pioneer.* San Antonio, Tex.: Fisher Publications, Inc., 1985.

Fitzpatrick, John C., ed. *The Writings of George Washington.* Washington, D.C.: United States Government Printing Office, 1931.

———. *The Diaries of George Washington 1748–1799.* Vol. I. New York: Houghton Mifflin, 1925.

Flexner, James T. *George Washington.* 4 vols. Boston: Little, Brown, 1965–72.

———. *Lord of the Mohawks: A Biography of Sir William Johnson.* Rev. ed. Boston: Little, Brown, 1979.

Ford, Henry Jones. *The Scotch-Irish in America.* Princeton, N.J.: Princeton University Press, 1915.

Franklin, Benjamin. *The Autobiography and Other Writings.* New York: Viking Penguin, 1986.

Freeman, Douglas Southall. *George Washington: A Biography.* Vols. 1–2. New York: Charles Scribner's Sons, 1948.

Gipson, Lawrence Henry. *The British Empire Before the American Revolution.* Vol. 4. New York: Alfred A. Knopf, 1939.

Gist, Christopher. *Christopher Gist's Journals.* Edited by William Darlington. Cleveland: Arthur H. Clark & Co., 1893.

Graymont, Barbara. *The Iroquois in the American Revolution.* Syracuse, N.Y.: Syracuse University Press, 1972.

Greiert, Steven G. "The Board of Trade and Defense of the Ohio Valley, 1748–1753." *Western Pennsylvania History Magazine* 64(1) (1981): 1–32.

Gwathmey, John H. *Twelve Virginia Counties: Where the Western Migration Began.* Baltimore: Genealogical Publishing Co., 1981.

Hamilton, Charles, ed. *Braddock's Defeat.* Norman: University of Oklahoma Press, 1959.

Hanna, Charles A. *The Wilderness Trail: Or, the Ventures and Adventures of the Pennsylvania Traders on the Allegheny Path, etc.* 2 vols. New York: G. P. Putnam's Sons, 1911.

Heckewelder, John. *Thirty Thousand Miles with John Heckewelder.* Edited by Paul A. W. Wallace. Pittsburgh: University of Pittsburgh Press, 1958.

Henderson, Archibald. *The Conquest of the Old Southwest.* New York: The Century Company, 1920. Reprinted 1974 by the Reprint Company, Spartanburg, S.C.

Hofstra, Warren. " 'A Parcel of Barbarians and an Uncooth Set of People': Settlers and Settlements of the Shenandoah Valley." Winchester, Va., 1989.

Hough, Walter F. *Braddock's Road Through the Virginia Colony.* Winchester, Va.: Winchester-Frederick County Historical Society, 1970.

Howard, James H. *Shawnee!: The Ceremonialism of a Native Indian Tribe and Its Cultural Background.* Athens: Ohio University Press, 1981.

Jackson, Donald, ed. *The Diaries of George Washington.* Vol. 1. Charlottesville: The University Press of Virginia, 1976.

Jacobs, Wilbur R., ed. *The Appalachian Indian Frontier: The Edmond Atkin Report and Plan of 1755.* Lincoln: University of Nebraska Press, 1967.

James, Alfred Proctor. *The Ohio Company: Its Inner History.* Pittsburgh: University of Pittsburgh Press, 1959.

Jennings, Francis. *Empire of Fortune: Crowns, Colonies, & Tribes in the Seven Years War in America.* New York: Norton, 1988.

———, et al., eds. *The History and Culture of Iroquois Diplomacy: An Interdisciplinary Guide to the Treaties of the Six Nations and Their League.* Syracuse, N.Y.: Syracuse University Press, 1983.

Kemper, Charles E., ed. "The Early Westward Movement of Virginia, 1722–1734." *Virginia Magazine of History and Biography,* 9(2)(1905): 113–174.

Kent, Donald H. *The French Invasion of Western Pennsylvania.* Harrisburg: Pennsylvania Historical and Museum Commission, 1954.

Kercheval, Samuel. *A History of the Valley of Virginia.* Harrisonburg, Va.: C. J. Carrier Company, 1981.

Knollenberg, Bernhard. *George Washington: The Virginia Period, 1732–1775.* Durham, N.C.: Duke University Press, 1964.

Koontz, Louis Knott. *Robert Dinwiddie: His Career in American Colo-*

nial Government and Westward Expansion. Glendale, Ca.: The Arthur H. Clark Company, 1941.

Kopperman, Paul E. "An Assessment of the Cholmley's Batman and British A Journals of Braddock's Campaign." *Western Pennsylvania History Magazine* 62(3) (1979): 197–220.

———, and Michael J.Freiling. "A British Officer's Journal of the Braddock Expedition—Et Cetera." *Western Pennsylvania History Magazine* 64(3) (1981): 269–287.

———, and Russell S. Nelson. *Braddock at the Monongahela.* Pittsburgh: University of Pittsburgh Press, 1977.

Lewis, Virgil A. *Soldiery of West Virginia in the French & Indian War . . . to the War with Mexico.* Reprint of 1911 edition. Baltimore: Genealogical Publishing Co., 1978.

Lowdermilk, Will H. *History of Cumberland, Md.* Reprint of 1878 edition. Baltimore: Regional Publishing Co., 1971.

McCardell, Lee. *Ill-Starred General: Braddock of the Coldstream Guards.* Reprint of 1958 edition. Pittsburgh: University of Pittsburgh Press, 1986.

Morgan, Gwenda. "Virginia and the French and Indian War: A Case Study of the War's Effect on Imperial Relations." *Virginia Magazine of History and Biography* 81(1) (1973): 23–48.

Mulkearn, Lois, ed. *George Mercer Papers Relating to the Ohio Company of Virginia.* Pittsburgh: University of Pittsburgh Press, 1954.

Neill, Edward D. *The Fairfaxes in England and America etc.* Albany, N.Y.: Joel Munsell, 1868.

Nordham, George W. *George Washington's Women: Mary, Martha, Sally and 146 Others.* Philadelphia: Dorrance & Company, 1977.

Pargellis, Stanley, ed. *Military Affairs in North America 1748–1765.* Reprint of 1936 edition. Hamden, Conn.: Archon Books, 1969.

Parker, Arthur C. *Parker on the Iroquois.* Edited by W. N. Fenton. Syracuse, N.Y.: Syracuse University Press, 1968.

———. *The Constitution of the Five Nations.* Reprint. Ohsweken, Ontario: Iroqrafts Ltd., 1984.

Richter, Daniel K. "War and Culture: The Iroquois Experience." *William and Mary Quarterly 40(4)* (1983): 528–559.

Rogers, Alan. *Empire & Liberty: American Resistance to British Authority, 1755-1763.* Berkeley: University of California Press, 1974.

Russell, Peter E. "Redcoats in the Wilderness: British Officers and Irregular Warfare in Europe and America, 1740 to 1760." *William and Mary Quarterly* 35(4) (1978): 629–652.

Sargent, Winthrop, ed. *The History of an Expedition Against Fort Duquesne, etc.* Philadelphia: Lippincott, 1856.

Sears, Stephen W. "The Lion's-Eye View." *American Heritage* 29(4) (1978): 98–107.

Seaver, James E. *A Narrative of the Life of Mrs. Mary Jemison.* Syracuse, N.Y.: Syracuse University Press, 1990.

Shy, John W. "A New Look at Colonial Militia." *William and Mary Quarterly,* 3d ser., 20 (1963): 175–85.

Sipe, C. Hale. *Indian Wars of Pennsylvania.* Reprint of 1929 edition. Salem, N.H.: Ayer Company, 1971.

Slick, Sewell Elias. *William Trent and the West.* Harrisburg, Pa.: Archives Publishing Co., 1947.

Stetson, Charles. *Washington and His Neighbors.* Richmond, Va.: Garrett and Massie, 1956.

Stokesbury, James L. "John Forbes and His Wilderness Road." *American History Illustrated* 9(3) (1974): 28–40.

Stotz, Charles Morse, and Louis M. Waddell. *Outposts of the War for Empire. The French and English in Western Pennsylvania: Their Armies, Their Forts, Their People, 1749–1764.* Pittsburgh: Historical Society of Western Pennsylvania, 1985.

Timberlake, Henry. *Memoirs of Lieutenant Henry Timberlake.* First American Frontier Series. Reprint of 1927 edition. Salem, N.H.: Ayer Company, 1971.

Titus, James Russell Wade. "Soldiers When They Chose to Be So: Virginians at War, 1754–1763." Ph.D. diss., Rutgers University, 1983.

Todish, Timothy J. *America's First World War: The French and Indian War, 1754—-1763.* Grand Rapids, Mich.: Eagles View, 1987.

Tomlinson, Abraham, ed. *Military Journals of Two Private Soldiers, 1758–1775.* Era of the American Revolution Series. Reprint of 1855 edition. New York: Da Capo Press, 1971.

Trigger, Bruce G., ed. *Northeast.* Vol. 15 of *Handbook of North American Indians,* general editor William C. Sturtevant. Washington, D.C.: Smithsonian Institution, 1978–.

Trimble, David R. "Christopher Gist and the Indian Service in Virgina,

1757–1759." *Virginia Magazine of History and Biography* 64 (1955): 143-165.

Wallace, Anthony F.C. *King of the Delawares: Teedyuscung 1700–1763.* Salem, N.H.: Ayer Company, 1984.

Wallace, Paul A. *Indians in Pennsylvania.* Harrisburg: Pennsylvania Historical and Museum Commission, 1989.

White, Kenneth A. "The Phantom Atrocity." *Western Pennsylvania History Magazine* 66(4) (1983): 383–388.

Woods, Bill M. "The Fort Upper Tract (West) Virginia Massacre April 27, 1758." *Daughters of the American Revolution Magazine* 106(5) (1972): 556–561.

Index

Note: GW = George Washington